CAMBRIDGE LATIN AMERICAN STUDIES

56

PRE-REVOLUTIONARY CARACAS

*For a list of other books in the
Cambridge Latin American Studies series,
please see page 246*

PRE-REVOLUTIONARY CARACAS

POLITICS, ECONOMY, AND SOCIETY 1777–1811

P. MICHAEL McKINLEY

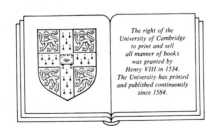

The right of the
University of Cambridge
to print and sell
all manner of books
was granted by
Henry VIII in 1534.
The University has printed
and published continuously
since 1584.

CAMBRIDGE UNIVERSITY PRESS

Cambridge
London   New York   New Rochelle
Melbourne   Sydney

Published by the Press Syndicate of the University of Cambridge
The Pitt Building, Trumpington Street, Cambridge CB2 1RP
32 East 57th Street, New York, NY 10022, USA
10 Stamford Road, Oakleigh, Melbourne 3166, Australia

First published 1985

Printed in Great Britain at the University Press, Cambridge

British Library cataloguing in publication data
McKinley, P. Michael
Pre-revolutionary Caracas: politics, economy
and society 1777–1811 – (Cambridge Latin
American studies; v. 56)
1. Caracas (Venezuela) – History
I. Title
987'.703   F2341.C257

Library of Congress cataloguing in publication data
McKinley, P. Michael
Pre-revolutionary Caracas.
(Cambridge Latin American studies; 56)
Bibliography; p.
Includes index.
1. Caracas (Venezuela) – Politics and government.
2. Venezuela – Politics and government – To 1810.
3. Caracas (Venezuela) – Economic conditions.
4. Social classes – Venezuela – Caracas – History.
I. Title.
II. Series
F2341.C257M37 1985   987'.7   85 13294

ISBN 0 521 30450 4

CE

To my mother

Contents

List of Maps		*page*	viii
List of Tables			viii
Acknowledgements			ix
Measures and Money			x
Glossary			xi

Introduction 1

Part One Society

1 The Caste Society 9

Part Two Economy

2 The export economy 1777–1809 35
3 Agriculture 46
4 Commerce 63

Part Three Politics

5 Elites 77
6 Politics 1777–1808 98
7 The balance overturned 1808–1810 146

Epilogue 169
Appendix A Geographical distribution of haciendas and
 hatos in Caracas 1785–1787 175
Appendix B Consulado membership 176

Notes 178
Bibliography 212
Bibliographical appendix 218
Index 239

Maps

1 The province of Caracas in the Captaincy-General of
  Venezuela   *page* 3
2 Geographical regions of the province of Caracas and titular
  municipalities 1785–1787   8

Tables

1 Population of Caracas by race 1785–1787 and 1800–1809 *page* 10
2 Annual *per-capita* general consumption by class of the
  non-Indian population of Cumaná in 1794, with
  extrapolations for the province of Caracas   27
3a The diversification of exports 1775–1809: changes in
  volume   36
3b The diversification of exports 1775–1809: shifts in value
  among major exports   36
4 The shift in markets for *caraqueño* exports 1784–1809   41
5 Shifts in market demands for individual crops 1797–1800
  and 1809   42
Appendix A Geographical distribution of haciendas and *hatos*
in Caracas 1785–1787   175

Acknowledgements

There are many people whose time, interest and guidance made this work possible. Foremost among them are John Lombardi of Indiana University, Malcolm Deas of the Latin American Centre of Oxford, and Manuel Pérez Vila, director of the Fundación John Boulton of Caracas. The latter institute also provided funds which greatly facilitated my research in Caracas. Special thanks go to Kathy Waldron and Bob Ferry for their encouragement and useful insights on the Caracas of the colonial period. In Seville, Eugene Lyon and Paul Hoffman taught me much of what I needed to know to work in archives. Also in Seville, Carmen Yuste and Gustavo Palma helped me refine my methodological approach to this study. Along the way Simon Collier, David Bushnell, Pedro Grases, Manuel Pinto and Ermila Troconis de Veracoechea made suggestions on how best to proceed with and revise this work. I would also like to acknowledge the aid and service of the personnel at the archives I worked in. Finally, thanks and everything else to Ketti, Peter, Margaret, Brian, Elena, Marjorie and Fatima without whom this would never have seen the light of day, not forgetting the efforts and patience of Elizabeth Wetton, my editor, Jane Hodgart and the staff at C.U.P.

1985   PMM

Measures and money

arroba: 11 kilogrammes or 25 pounds
fanega (weight): 50 kilogrammes or 110 pounds
fanegada (of land): 2 hectares or about 4.9 acres
legua (of land): 3,105.5 hectares or about 12 square miles
peso (of money): 8 reales
quintal (of weight): 45 kilogrammes or 100 pounds
zurron (of weight): 45 kilogrammes or 100 pounds
tonelada: nautical ton (20 quintals)

Glossary

abogado: lawyer
agricultor: planter
aguardiente: cane-based spirits
alcabala de tierra: sales-tax
alcalde: mayor
añil: indigo
arrendamientos: rental contracts between landowners and tenants
Audiencia: Imperial Appellate Court
auditor de guerra: legal adviser to the military
Ayuntamiento: City Council
bienes de difuntos: estates-duties branch of Treasury
bodega: small retail shop
bodeguero: small-scale retailer
Cabildo: Town Council
caña: sugar-cane
canario: native of the Canary Islands
cancelario: chancellor
caraqueño: native of Caracas
castas: all persons of mixed or black descent
caudal de manejo: a merchant's investment capital
caudillo: strong-man, military leader
censos: mortgage on property
cimarrón: runaway slave
cofradia: religious brotherhood
Colegio de Abogados: Lawyers' Guild
comerciante: import–export merchant
composición de tierra: fee or tax paid to the Crown for lands occupied
    without due title
comunidad: community
conde: count

Consulado: Merchant–Planter Guild and its court
contador: auditor
conuco: small plot of land
corregidor de indios: magistrate overseeing Indian affairs
creditos activos: passive assets
cuenta y riesgo: shipment made on one's own financial responsibility
cumbes: communities of fugitive slaves
deudas incobrables: loans or credits which are written off by merchants
diezmo: tithe
diezmeros: tithe collectors
encomienda: a grant of tributary Indians
escribanías: notarial offices
escribano: notary
estanco: monopoly
extremeño: native of Extremadura
ferias: fairs, markets
fiador: guarantor
fianzas: surety
fiscal: attorney
fuero: right to trial by members of same profession
fundador: founder
ganado mayor: cattle, horses and mules
generos, frutos y efectos europeos, consumo de: general consumption
gente de color: free-coloureds
gracia: royal exemption
granadino: native of New Granada
gravamenes: mortgage, debts, charges
gremio: guild
guerra a muerte: war to the death
hacendados: plantation-owners
hatillos: small livestock holdings
hateros: ranchers
hatos: ranches
hijo natural: person of illegitimate birth
indios de tributo: tributary Indians
indígenas: Indians
informe: report
ingenio: sugar-mill
interventor: comptroller
isleño: native of the Canary Islands
jornalero: rural day worker
junta de diezmo: body established to oversee the collection of tithes

juntista: being of a junta
labradores: planters
libranza: promissory note
libre: free
marqués: marquis
mayordomo: overseer
mercader: large-scale retailer
mercería: retail store
mestizo: person of mixed Indian and white descent
moreno: dark-skinned person
negros: blacks
obispo: bishop
pardo: person of mixed African descent
pariente: relative
partido: district
*pedimiento:*petition
peninsular: native of Spain
peón: resident rural worker
plantaciones: holdings
pleito: lawsuit
poblacion volante: floating population
provinciales: countrymen
pueblo: people; village
pulpería: grocery
pulpero: grocer
Real Hacienda: Royal Treasury
reconquista: reconquest
regente visitador: investigative Regent of the Audiencia
regidor: town-councillor
registro: merchant ship
representación: memorial
rochela: community outside legally established boundaries
tablones: sugar-cane plots
tasajo: jerked beef
temporalidades: branch of treasury dealing with ecclesiastical properties
tenientazgo: district under a Justice of the Peace
teniente de justicia: Justice of the Peace
tiendas and *casas-tiendas:* stores and stores doubling as residences
tierras de comunidad: Indian communal property
tonelage: imperial restrictions on the volume of trade to given colonies,
   in force until 1789
tributarios: tributary Indians

trapiche: sugar-mill and, in common usage, sugar plantation
trujillano: native of Trujillo in Venezuela
vago: vagrant
vecino: inhabitant with full civil rights
verdadero comerciante: bona fide merchant
vendible: for sale
vitálico: for life
víveres: foodstuffs, provisions

Introduction

The current historical portrayal of late-colonial Caracas, and by extension of Venezuela, is that of a society transformed and terminally upset by the Bourbon reforms of the late eighteenth century. A dualistic, colonial economy, supporting a fixed and not particularly comfortable caste society within the framework of a detrimental relationship with the mother country, is seen as creating the conditions for an unusually violent struggle for independence after 1811.

This book portrays a quite different colonial society. By the tail-end of the eighteenth century, Caracas was emerging for the first time as a significant member of the Spanish Empire; and in the process it revealed itself to be an unusually well-balanced and harmonious developing colonial society. An economic flowering unparalleled in the region's long history brought Caracas temporarily out of the relative obscurity in which it had lain, and into which it subsequently relapsed after independence. This economic transformation was accomplished within the confines and with the aid of the empire. Spanish legislation and imperial administrations either anticipated or accommodated the needs of the provincial economy; and the changes in the imperial trade system which may have hurt other American colonies only seem to have given Caracas an added incentive to grow. Not even the increasingly difficult years after 1796, when the negative effects of the Napoleonic Wars intensified, entirely obscured the essentially positive economic relation between province and empire.

Economic growth was accompanied by political stability and social calm. The picture we have of a captive creole *hacendado* elite producing cash crops for Spanish export merchants is a distortion of the character of the market economy in the province. As we shall see, Caracas in many ways was atypical rather than representative of a plantation economy; and, most importantly, the production sector was not at the mercy of a Spanish mercantile community. The commercial branch of the economy was too weak and the agricultural interests too strong to allow such an imbalance to develop. In addition, a growing community of interests between the merchants and the creole landed elite was breaking down the traditional separation between the two groups as the colonial period drew to a close. As to the relations between the white caste and the rest of the province's population, economic mobility and a heterogenous occupational structure made for a relatively tranquil social environment. The potential for such a structure to diffuse rather than escalate social and racial tension was considerable, and Caracas was generally more peaceful before 1808 than we have been led to believe.

A similar structural flexibility was apparent in the political sphere. The creole elite of Caracas was most definitely not on the defensive as 1808 approached. Rather, it was experiencing a new assertiveness born of economic success, social pre-eminence and an awareness of political strength. Furthermore, the imperial representatives sent to Caracas from the late 1770s onwards tended to rule and act in the province's interests in consultation with the local elites. The latter consequently felt no compelling need to lay claim to the higher bureaucratic and political posts in the colony, and did not develop the feeling of exclusion from the political process which arose among colonial elites elsewhere in the empire.

The initial reaction of the *caraqueño* ruling groups to the French invasion of Spain in 1808 was therefore genuinely loyal to the cause of the Spanish resistance and of the dethroned Spanish monarch Ferdinand VII: but as the severity of the political vacuum in the empire became more apparent across 1809 and 1810, consensus between unoccupied Spain and the American colonies in general broke down on just how to meet the crisis. At the same time the parallel political revolution set in motion in the mother country from 1808 onwards helped unleash radical ideologies and forces in both Spain and the colonies which questioned the nature of the imperial connection and the ultimate survival of the empire. The struggle for independence across the Americas was the result. That the struggle in Caracas proceeded to become as violent and destructive as it did, is because key individuals, reacting to the political exigencies of the moment, cold-bloodedly chose the use of extreme violence to break the stability of the colonial order which for so many years previously had successfully accommodated disparate political and social elements.

Late-colonial Caracas formed part of the larger Captaincy-General of Venezuela. Caracas had actually been known as the 'Gobernación'

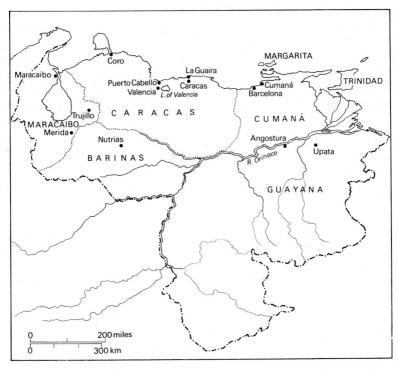

1. The province of Caracas in the Captaincy-General of Venezuela

(Governorship) of Venezuela for much of the colonial period. Imperial decrees in 1776 and 1777 extended 'Venezuela' to incorporate six provinces which until then had been commonly referred to as 'Tierra Firme'.[1] The six were Maracaibo, Cumaná, Margarita, Trinidad, Guayana and Caracas.[2] Before the creation of the Intendancy in 1776 and Captaincy-General in 1777, the provinces had been subject to the control of the Viceroyalty and Captaincy-General of nearby New Granada on political matters and to the Audiencias of Bogotá and Santo Domingo on judicial questions. Only the province of Caracas had enjoyed any measure of autonomy under its own, not fully-empowered governors and captains-general. The new statutes changed the arrangement radically. The economic, political and military administration of Tierra Firme was centralized in the province of Caracas. The creation of the Audiencia of Caracas in 1786 further strengthened the province's hold on the imperial administration of the colony as a whole.[3]

The administrative centralization of 1776–7 was primarily a recognition of Caracas' near-total dominance of the links between Venezuela and the empire. La Guaira, the main port of the province, handled almost 90% of Venezeula's trade with Spain.[4] Caracas' predominance in foreign trade was all the more impressive since the province also led in the production of the major export commodities. Nearly 80% of Venezuela's cacao crop was grown in Caracas, and the two major-growth exports of our period, indigo and coffee, were produced almost exclusively in the province.[5] In addition, Caracas was the natural geographical and population centre of the region, containing over half of the roughly 800,000 inhabitants of Venezuela.[6] Furthermore the province was the institutional centre of the Captaincy-General, although it was late in gaining this distinction. It housed the colony's only university (since 1717), the Audiencia (from 1786) and the Consulado (from 1793), and from 1803 was the seat of the Archbishopric of Venezuela.[7]

By 1777, Caracas was also becoming the most valuable non-mining American colony in the empire. Only Havana, its neighbour in the Caribbean, rivalled it in economic importance. This had not always been the case. At the beginning of the eighteenth century, Caracas had played only a relatively minor role in the imperial structure, providing cacao for the mineral-producing colony of New Spain.[8] The rising popularity of cacao in Spain in the early 1700s changed this. The colony, as the major producer of the commodity, attracted the attention of the mother country and in 1728 the Royal Guipuzcoa Company of Caracas was formed to exploit the province. The Caracas Company, which lasted formally until 1784, was the first, most successful, longest-lived and most thorough application of the corporation colony policy in the Spanish American Empire.[9] In the process of exercising its power, the company redefined Caracas' relation to the empire: by 1750 Spain had overtaken Mexico as Venezuela's major market and by our period cacao had moved into first place in terms of value in the portfolio of Spain's non-mineral imports from the colonies, with Caracas maintaining a virtual monopoly position as supplier.[10] The colony's economic emergence coincided well with its enhanced political role, signalled by the creation of the Intendancy and Captaincy-General of Venezuela. By 1777 Caracas was set to enter its golden age of economic expansion and political maturity within the boundaries of empire.

PART ONE

Society

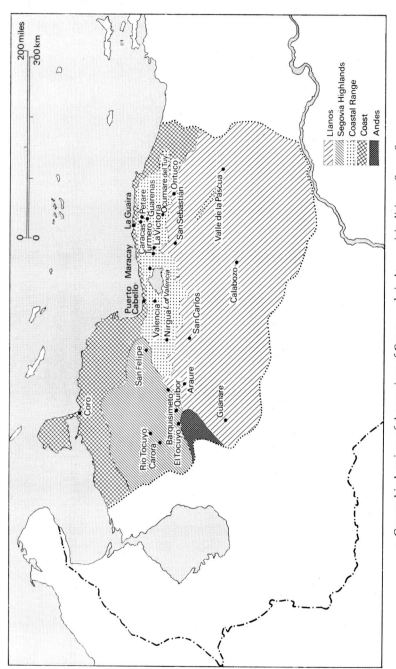

2 Geographical regions of the province of Caracas and titular municipalities 1785–1787.

1

The caste society

The demographics of Caracas

The population of Caracas can be examined with a great degree of accuracy thanks to the extraordinary compilation of data for the colonial Bishopric of Caracas carried out by John Lombardi.[1] By extracting and quantifying the information contained in several hundred parish censuses, he has presented a unique picture of the demographic history of the province in the late eighteenth and early nineteenth centuries using the data available for the decade 1800–9 as the centre-piece of his analysis. Of particular interest are his figures on Caracas' racial composition and the regional, urban and rural distribution of the province's population. If Lombardi's study is compared with the more modest census carried out by José de Castro y Aráoz between 1785 and 1787, some observations can also be made about the growth rate of the population and of specific racial groups in our period.[2]

The province of Caracas had about 455,000 inhabitants in 1810 (Table 1). The racial composition of this population can be broken down into four broad categories: whites, free-coloureds of mixed or black descent (the *castas*), black slaves and Indians. The overwhelming majority of the *castas* in Caracas were mixed free-coloureds of part-African ancestry and were commonly known as *pardos*. The term *pardo* as it was used in Caracas erased the finer legal distinctions between mulattos, *zambos* and the like.[3] The *castas* as a whole were the most numerous racial group in the province, representing just over 45% of the total population. Whites followed with roughly 25% and slaves and Indians with about 15% each.

The population was scattered unevenly over the province, in accordance mainly with the economic potential of the different geographical regions. The racial composition of the inhabitants of different areas also responded in part to economic realities, as will be seen. The province

Table 1 *Population of Caracas by race 1785–1787 and 1800–1809*

Race	1785–7	%[a]	1800–9[b]	%
castas	147,564	44	197,740	46
whites	79,232	24	108,920	26
slaves	53,055	16	64,462	15
Indians	53,154	16	56,083[c]	13
	333,359	100	427,205	100

[a] The percentages are rounded.

[b] The municipality of Coro is not covered by the 1800–9 figures although it did form part of the province. If Coro is included on the basis of its population in 1785–7 it brings the number of people in Caracas up to the 455,000 mentioned in the text.

[c] The discrepancy in the growth of the Indian population is statistical, not demographic. If Coro's 1785–7 Indians are included, the *indio* total comes much closer to equalling the slave total in 1800–9, even after Coro's 1785–7 slaves are added: 63,994 Indians *vs* 67,733 slaves.

Sources: for 1785–7 see *Estado General de 1787*. For 1800–9 see Lombardi, *People and Places*, p. 132.

has been broken down into four major regions by Lombardi: the Coast, the Coastal Range, the Llanos and the Segovia Highlands.[4]

Two regions were closely linked by geographical, economic and social ties: the Coast and the Coastal Range. The Coast borders the Caribbean in the north, and is a strip of land, usually backed inland by mountains, with a hot and generally humid climate. In late-colonial times cacao and coffee were grown among the foot-hills of the mountains, and two ports, Puerto Cabello and La Guaira, provided the major outlets for the province's exports. Inland from the central area of the Coast is the Coastal Range. This is a relatively narrow stretch of mountains and hill-chains, valleys, lakes and rivers extending from far east of the capital of Caracas to just east of the town of San Felipe. It has a milder, though still tropical, climate, and in the colonial period contained the richest agricultural lands of the province. These were concentrated in the Aragua valleys to the west of the city of Caracas and in the Tuy valleys east and south of the city. The bulk of the province's cacao, coffee, indigo and tobacco were produced in this region.[5] Together, the Coastal Range and the Coast formed the production and commercial axis on which the wheels of the export economy turned.

It comes as no surprise that the Coastal Range with its fertile valleys, economic primacy and agreeable climate held 166,000 or nearly 40% of the total population of the province, although it represented only about one-tenth of the land area. It was consequently the most densely populated region of Caracas. A developed network of towns, separated often only by farmland, extended from Nirgua and Valencia in the west to Guarenas, Guatire and Ocumare del Tuy east and south of the capital. Almost half of the province's white population lived in the Coastal Range but whites made up only 30% of the region's inhabitants. Free-coloureds, as elsewhere in the province, were the most numerous racial group, representing 40% of the Coastal Range's population. One notable feature of the region was the high proportion of slaves among its inhabitants: they represented over 20% of the total compared with a provincial average of 15%. Over half of the province's slaves lived in the Coastal Range, where they were needed to work the heavy concentration of plantation agriculture in the area. Indians were least numerous and made up less than 10% of the population.

The urban network of the Coastal Range spread into the Coast, and La Guaira and Puerto Cabello were large towns. Outside the ports, however, the agricultural activity of the Coast was too minor to attract a large population. The region held 67,000 or about 15% of the province's total. Over 20% of its inhabitants were slaves, less than 15% were whites. Plantation agriculture was sufficiently widespread to require a proportionally large number of slaves but not important enough to entice whites to settle in the inhospitable climate. Free-coloureds made up half of the population and Indians about 15%.

South of the Coastal Range the mountains and hills give way to a vast expanse of plains, the Llanos of the interior. Most of the surface area is grassland crossed with rivers and subject to an uncomfortable climate, with annual variations ranging from droughts to floods. The Llanos covered over half of the area of the province of Caracas. Just under a third or 134,000 of the population of the province lived here, and of these half formed part of the *castas*. Nearly a third of the region's population were whites, less than a tenth were slaves and just over a tenth were Indians. The population of the Llanos lived scattered over the region with a number of market towns such as San Sebastián and San Carlos acting as focal points for an economy based on the *hatos* or live-stock ranches. As meat was the major foodstuff of the province, the live-stock industry gave the region an importance in the internal market which made up for its negligible role in the export economy.[6] The impact of the *hatos* on the demography is most noticeable among the slave segment of the population. The wide, open ranches depended mostly on free labour to work them, so slaves were a much smaller proportion of the population than nearer the coastal areas. An economy based on far-flung ranches also prevented the urbanization present in the Coastal Range.

The Segovia Highlands made up the fourth region of the historical province of Caracas. Its terrain fans out inland from the north-west coast around Coro and is characterized by a broken topography of low mountains, high plains, valleys and semi-desert. Important towns such as Barquisimeto, Carora, and El Tocuyo provided the network for an active economy revolving around cacao, sugar-cane production for the internal market and the commercial handling of livestock from the Llanos.[7] Only 71,000 or 15% of the province's inhabitants lived here. Almost 60% of its inhabitants were free-coloureds, a proportional superiority unequalled elsewhere. Whites were less than a fifth of the population and slaves only one-tenth. Indians were almost as numerous as whites, representing over 15% of the total.

The urban–rural distribution of the population of the province in some ways followed the patterns laid down by the regional distribution. There were many more large towns in the densely populated Coastal Range than in the sparsely populated Coast and the Llanos. Lombardi provides data on the distribution of the population among urban centres of different sizes. Perhaps his most interesting discovery is that 170,000 or 40% of the population lived in towns containing 4,000 people or more.[8] The Coastal Range and the Segovia Highlands had a particularly high level of urbanization. The Coastal Range valleys were dotted with large towns and cities: Valencia, Maracay, La Victoria and Turmero to the west of the city of Caracas had between 7,000 and 8,000 inhabitants each, while Caracas itself had over 31,000. The Highlands population was even more concentrated in large communities than in the Coastal Range. Quíbor, Carora, El Tocuyo and Barquisimeto all contained over 8,000 inhabitants. The Llanos, as might be expected, had fewer large towns, although there were towns on the plains' trade routes which had outsize populations. Guanare in the south-west and San Carlos in the northern Llanos each had around 11,000 people. Curiously enough, the ports of the coast had much smaller populations: Puerto Cabello had around 6,500, including military personnel stationed there. La Guaira, with 4,500, had even fewer inhabitants, though it dominated the export trade.

The population was growing rapidly in the decades leading up to 1810. The trend had been established earlier in the eighteenth century, and it is clear that Caracas was sharing the demographic boom which affected much of Europe and colonial America in the same period.

Between 1785 and 1810 the population of the province probably increased by over a third in size. Such a rapid rise in the number of inhabitants can be expected to have had an impact on the environment of colonial Caracas. Surprisingly perhaps, the increase did not markedly alter the racial balance in the colony. The proportion of whites and *castas* may have increased a percentage or two but not at each other's expense. Their shares of the population remained at roughly a quarter and just under half of the total respectively. Slaves and Indians suffered relative declines but continued to grow in numbers.

The impact of the increase can most clearly be seen in the shifting patterns of settlement in the province throughout the eighteenth century. New towns and villages sprang up to the south and east of the Coastal Range region, especially after the mid-century. The Llanos region was the main beneficiary of the changes. The number of new settlements in the Llanos after 1760 is striking and includes towns such as San Carlos and San Fernando de Apure, which quickly became population centres in the area.[9] The reasons for the population shift are unclear. It can well be conjectured that the Coastal Range and the Segovia Highlands, which were among the earliest areas settled, became comparatively overcrowded; and demographic pressure as well as the lure of the frontier and the labour needs of the ranch economy drew people inland. This would be especially true of free-coloureds seeking to escape the legal and social restrictions imposed on them in areas more heavily populated by whites.

Whites

Caste distinctions derived primarily from racial differences formed the basis of the established social hierarchy in colonial Caracas. In this order the whites dominated provincial society, and the combination of their privileged legal status with their relatively small numbers ensured at least a basic community of interest *vis-à-vis* the other castes of the province. This did not prevent the whites from being stratified among themselves.

The most easily identifiable divisions inside the white caste were those resulting from the ethnic differences among them. They were subdivided into three broad categories: mainland Spaniards or *peninsulares*, Canary Island immigrants or *isleños* and *canarios*, and creole or Venezuelan-born whites. The proportional and numerical distribution of ethnic groups is difficult to establish with certainty. The only information available is provided by A. von Humboldt, and none too specifically at that. His rough estimates for about 1800 indicate that *peninsulares* and *canarios* together represented only 6.6% of all Venezuelan whites.[10] Assuming that the concentration of Europeans would be greater in the province of Caracas than elsewhere in Venezuela, they can be estimated to have numbered at least 7,000–8,000 out of a provincial white population of about 110,000. The creoles therefore made up over 90% of the white caste. The often-stated observation that many of the creoles were not pure-blooded Caucasians is worth repeating. This was particularly true of poorer whites. A captain-general in 1801 observed that 'the whites of the common estate [are] . . . rarely free of any connection to the blood of the inferior [coloured] classes . . .'[11]

The small component of foreign-born whites in the population was added-to in the late eighteenth century by a considerable influx of new, white immigrants into Caracas. The *peninsular* contribution to the immigrant total was probably small. Depons at the turn of the century estimated that an average of perhaps 100 Spaniards a year were arriving in Venezuela as a whole.[12] An incomplete listing of licenses for travel from Spain to Caracas granted between 1790 and 1810 suggests that most of those who did come were connected to *caraqueño* merchants or were administrative officials and clergy sent to take up new posts.[13] What Caracas does seem to have attracted is a sizeable and illegal emigration from the Canary Islands. In separate studies of the problem spanning over a decade, the Captain-General of Caracas and a high-level Tenerife bureaucrat tried to find ways to stem the departures which were threatening to depopulate the Canarias.[14] Three ships from the Canarias deposited respectively 120, 187 and 143 immigrants between 1787 and 1802. It may not be too far-fetched to speak of a Canario influx numbering thousands between the years 1780 and 1810.[15]

Immigrants were also coming from other places nearer *caraqueño* shores, thanks to the turbulence affecting much of the Caribbean in the 1790s and 1800s. By far the largest single identifiable number came from the Spanish half of the island of Hispaniola. Once Toussaint L'Ouverture's revolution spilled over into Santo Domingo, the whites fled in large numbers, taking their families and slaves with them. Over 1,500 refugees arrived in 1801 alone and there is every indication that they came to stay.[16] In addition, French refugees from the black revolutions in Haiti and Martinique also settled in Caracas. In one shipment in 1793, 122 arrived via Trinidad; in 1797 another 100 entered the province directly at La Guaira.[17]

The composition of the white population between 1780 and 1801 was, therefore, being affected by a varied immigration. Its impact on the ethnic composition of the white caste is unclear, however. In view of the rapid, natural increase of the native white population in our period, it is possible that the proportion of Europeans was dropping in spite of the new influx. What may be beyond question is the rapid absorption of the Europeans into the creole ranks through inter-marriage. A study of the wills deposited in the notarial records of the city of Caracas between 1781 and 1820 makes it possible to begin to measure the rate. In a sample of European wills, 41 or 48% of 85 *peninsulares*, and 69 or 58% of 119 *canarios* married creoles.[18] Inter-marriage was thus blurring ethnic differences in the province even as immigration was accentuating them; and, as will be seen more clearly when I examine the elites of *caraqueño* society, integration was probably winning out.

Whites in Caracas, as whites everywhere in the empire, dominated a whole spectrum of occupations and activities to the disadvantage of the other races in the province. Imperial administrators, local government bureaucrats and lawyers were invariably white. So were most wholesale and retail merchants, most middle-sized shopowners and most of the province's well-to-do landowners. It is therefore surprising to note that privileged status and access did not prevent many whites from descending to the most abject poverty. The occupational activities of whites in fact included almost all those present in colonial society.

Outside of agriculture, the numbers involved in the various occupations were not particularly large. The officials who provided the frame-work for the local colonial administration numbered at most a few hundred.[19] In the legal profession there were perhaps 600 persons employed of which only 60 were actually practising lawyers.[20] Small numbers also characterized the clergy. There were only 500 or so priests, monks, nuns and higher clergy in the province in 1810.[21] Commerce, in all its facets, offered at most a few thousand whites their livelihood. There may have been no more than 1,500 commercial establishments throughout the province, in addition to the concerns run by the 100 or so import–export traders.[22] Most economically active whites, therefore, worked the land.

In keeping with Spanish colonial tradition, the highest-placed imperial officials and administrators of the province were almost inva-riably natives of the mother country. The most important positions such as the Captain-General, the Intendant, the Regent of the Audien-cia, the director of the tobacco monopoly and the regular army's com-mandant, were usually held by *peninsulares*. The immediate subord-

inates of the preceding including the auditor de guerra, the lawyers of
the Audiencia and the chief administrators of the four regional treasury
branches in the provinces, were also likely to have been *peninsulares*,
although creoles and *isleños* were on occasion appointed to these positions.[23]

The control which *peninsulares* held over the upper strata of imperial
administration did not necessarily result in the emergence of a separate
caste. The reason may have been that the Bourbon system of regularly
rotating imperial officials from colony to colony broke down in our
province. Most officials serving in Caracas in the late-colonial period
had spent decades in the colony, working their way up the promotional
ladder inside the province's bureaucratic structure.[24] Only the Captain-
General and the Intendant seem to have regularly come from outside
the official pool inside Venezuela. The Spaniard José de Limonta, who
in 1810 was the chief auditor of the Caracas Treasury, began his provincial service as Protector de Indios in 1782.[25] Domingo de Garate, in
1809 chief auditor of the tobacco monopoly, began as a minor assistant
in 1770.[26] Like them, there were many others among the small group
of senior adminstrative bureaucrats.[27] Even among the intendants there
were the cases of Esteban Fernández de León (1791–1802), who began
as a middle-level official in the 1770s, and of Dionisio Franco
(1812–15), who was first the director of the tobacco monopoly
(1802–10) and who married locally, leaving a son who also became a
royal official.[28] Royal bureaucrats who arrived to serve in Caracas in
their youth, therefore, generally came to stay. Correspondingly, their
economic and personal interests became identified with the life of the
province. As we shall see when we consider the politics of our region,
the lack of ethnic rivalry over bureaucratic appointments is striking,
and the reasons for this peaceful state of affairs must have had much to
do with the willingness of government officials to identify with their
environment.

As was the case with the imperial administration, the upper level of
the merchant community was *peninsular* in origin, and if it is combined
with *canario* involvement in the commercial network, the European
contingent was dominant indeed. In the 1790s and 1800s probably
well over 80% of the major import–export traders of the province were
European. In the city of Caracas less than 10% of the resident large-
scale retailers were creoles.[29] It would seem that this European predominance also extended down to the level of shopkeepers. Nonetheless
the monolithic ethnic character of the mercantile community was not
what it appeared to be. As we shall see, many of the largest merchants

were also inextricably linked to the creole agricultural sector, not by holding planters in debt or by controlling the buying and selling of commodities, but by owning the land itself and through intermarriage with creole, planter families.[30] Conversely, enough creole *hacendados* participated in commerce to suggest a growing communion of interests.[31]

Outside the commercial and governmental occupational sectors, the links between ethnicity and occupation disappeared. The clergy, for example, seem to have included an overwhelming majority of creoles, with Europeans only proportionately represented. Of fifty-seven wills of secular clerics located in the notarial archives of the city of Caracas, 88% were of creole origin.[32] Furthermore, the top positions in the Church were not necessarily reserved for *peninsulares*. One of the bishops appointed between Bishop Mariano Martí and Archbishop Coll y Prat was a member of a leading creole *caraqueño* family, *Obispo* Francisco Ibarra.[33] Likewise, among lawyers, it would seem that there were no ethnic links to trace. Outside the four to five lawyers of the Audiencia, who were almost invariably from Spain or other parts of the empire, most of the fifty to sixty practising lawyers in Caracas would seem to have been native-born creoles.[34]

In agriculture the connection between ethnicity and occupation was also as insignificant, and probably as non-existent, as that in the professions. Although the upper stratum of landowners was overwhelmingly creole in composition, this predominance was less a factor of creole inclination for agriculture than of their crushing numerical superiority. As we shall see, the small European component of the population was well represented in proportional terms in the *hacendado* elite. It is in fact possible to suggest that the majority of Europeans, like the majority of creoles, earned their living from agriculture. A *representación* by the *teniente de justicia* for some of the province's richest agricultural lands presented the following picture of Maracay, the major centre of indigo production in Caracas: the majority of whites 'are European and among them are a large number of Basques because the initiator of indigo farming in the province was one of them, and so attracted his fellow countrymen'.[35] If even an unspecified number of Basques, the most commerce-oriented of the European whites, was engaged in agriculture, it is fair to assume that the same was true of the majority of Spaniards and *canarios* throughout the province.

Poverty also cut across ethnic lines. Poor whites are always overlooked in discussions of *caraqueño* colonial society: yet there is no question that a large number of whites did not 'make it' even at the lower end of the occupational ladder, as petty officials, soldiers, shopowners, tenant farmers, small landowners, overseers, or as artisans. From all that is known about white colonial attitudes towards race and occupations, these unsuccessful whites were unlikely to have turned to manual labour to ward off unemployment. So, what happened to them? One royal official observed that many of the *canario* immigrants who came seeking their fortune 'became entirely useless because they only dedicate themselves to earning their living by noxious means ... the poverty which in these cases then afflicts their women and families, almost reduced to begging, the breakup of marriages and the resulting illegitimacy ... can have dire results'.[36] It is not unreasonable to assume that an unquantifiable but significant percentage of the majority creole element of the white caste found themselves living in similarly straitened circumstances.

Pardos

The free-coloureds, or *castas* and *pardos* as they were often known, were the single largest racial group in the province, and very nearly formed a majority of the population.[37] As it was, they represented nearly 60% of the free population and it is important to place them in their social context, however imperfectly. That context was not as clear-cut as might be supposed because, in spite of the heavy legal discrimination against them, the caste still had a degree of economic mobility and freedom from social restraint. Yet even if we acknowledge that their lot may have fallen short of naked repression, there was a potential for fierce racial conflict were the social equilibrium to be disturbed.

The general lot of the *castas* was undeniably a hard one. Statutes restricted all aspects of their lives, both social and personal.[38] Discriminatory dress codes forbade their wearing apparel which might connote equal status with whites. Racial intermarriage was to all intents and purposes forbidden. *Pardos* were excluded from the possibility of entering the Church, the university and, thus, the legal profession. The avenues of employment and advancement open to *pardos* were correspondingly limited. They tended to be artisans in the towns, plantation overseers, rural day-labourers in the countryside on either haciendas or *hatos*, and soldiers and lower-rank officers in the militias of the province. Many of them probably lived at a subsistence level with no fixed occupation. Nevertheless the general image of any social group should never be accepted without a closer look, and in the case of the *pardos* the complexities hidden by the broad strokes are numerous.

The occupational composition of *pardos* is best approached through the divisions of the economy. Agriculture, as was the case with all racial groups, provided the majority of *pardos* with the means of earning their living. Of those dedicated to agriculture, chances were that the largest and predominant segment were part of the free rural labour force, divided into *jornaleros* and *peónes libres*. Of the two, day-workers who hired their labour out to plantations and ranches were far more numerous than the resident labourers, who lived on the haciendas they worked for. It must be stressed that this latter component was almost insignificant, and that indebted servitude was rare in the *caraqueño* agricultural structure. Evidence can be offered as to the reality of the dearth of peonage in the province. Most, if not all of it, comes from the regular attempts by white agriculturalists to tie down as resident labour what they saw as a wandering, indolent coloured population.

The following extracts are graphic in their description of the nature of free rural labour. A 1796 official report on the state of the province speaks of the 'hoodlums and improperly employed [read 'coloured'] [who] are a grievous weight on the state . . . if even ten thousand of these could be forced to dedicate themselves to agriculture the results would prove more beneficial than the importation of forty thousand blacks'.[39] A petition from the same year, by the worthies of the Caracas Cabildo, who were all white, protesting against a royal measure permitting elements of the *castas* to buy dispensation from their colour, was even more explicit: 'the presence of *pardos* in the cities and in the militias leads them to disdain the cultivation of the countryside, abandoning agriculture to the whites and black slaves'.[40] Another petition, in 1788, spoke of 'the grievous harm *hacendados* experience each day finding themselves without hands to work their land or harvests'.[41] A 1794 *representación* by some Tuy valley *hacendados* went so far as actually to outline a pass system: 'to avoid doubts and confusion all coloured people, in order to prove their freeman status, should carry their baptism certificate upon leaving their area . . . When a *jornalero* leaves an hacienda he should take a document from the owner or *mayordomo* as to his not being a delinquent or in debt on pain of imprisonment'. The same would apply to *peónes libres* living and working on the haciendas.[42]

The white-sponsored petitions clearly point to the difficulty of tying down the rural labouring population onto the plantations. The reason for the unusual independence of the *caraqueño* labourer may have been due to a real labour scarcity; but it was more likely the result of large numbers of free-coloureds working their own land plots, either as squatters or as owners. The survey of Caracas province carried out between 1785 and 1787 pointed to the existence of an incalculable number of '*hatillos* [and] ... infinity of plots of wheat, maize, rice, coffee, cotton ... of small consideration and of people of limited means'.[43] These *conucos* allowed rural workers to scratch out an existence and at least partially divorced them from having to contract their labour to haciendas.

The existence of a large landholding peasant class, which occupied and worked land for itself, therefore had a significant impact on the character of the free labour force in the countryside. Indebted peonage did not make many inroads in Caracas, and the rural labourer retained a marked sense of independence *vis-à-vis* the plantation and ranch owners, especially when he is compared to his counterparts in other colonies.

The rural *pardo* population also included *hacendados*, although their number was likely to have been small. Two surveys of the plantations of Caracas carried out in 1721 and 1745 named at least a few dozen in specific terms.[44] Individual wills of *castas*, however, provide witness to the continued existence of *pardo hacendados* in the late colonial period.[45] Ten of the wills in the sample refer to agrarian holdings, for a total of seven cacao haciendas, two sugar-cane plantations, one coffee hacienda, two *hatos* and assorted properties in the Llanos.[46] Seven of the owners had slaves working their possessions, which, as will become clear when I discuss agriculture, suggests that the holdings were of at least moderate size. Two individuals of the sample stand out: One is Gervasio de Ponte, the illegitimate son of a scion of an old Caracas family, who owned 10 square leguas of land in the Llanos, in addition to 2 haciendas of cacao and 1 of sugar-cane.[47] Less spectacular but more representative was the case of Juan Tomás del Valle, a captain in the *pardo* militias. He owned an apparently large sugar plantation as well as a middle-sized coffee hacienda.[48]

If free-coloureds in the countryside offered a different profile than might be expected, their counterparts in the city could be equally mobile, to judge from the same sample of wills. The two Bejarano representatives owned thirty-one houses between them, eighteen designated as *tiendas* or stores.[49] One other, with marriage links to the Bejaranos, owned another twelve houses in the city at the time he left his will.[50] A number of other *pardos* had more modest holdings which they worked themselves, including Jose Ramon Piñango who owned two *casas-tiendas*.[51] Others such as María Apolonia Bolívar and Petronila de la Madrid owned *casas-tiendas* and rented out slaves as day labour.[52]

Information on the activities of urban *pardos* is not confined to wills, or to our general knowledge, which places them in the role of artisans, the poor, or a *Lumpenproletariat*. An 1816 list of *pulperías*, or groceries, for the city of Caracas suggests that there were 20 *pardos* among the 132 individuals who ran 134 *pulperías* across that year.[53] Twenty cannot be called anything but a visible minority, but their presence is notable in an occupation which in Caracas City would seem to have been a white preserve. The proportion was likely to have been higher in a number of towns in the interior where *pardos* were much more numerous than whites. A measure is provided by the sales-tax books of provincial towns, which listed *pulpero* and *bodeguero* owners together with the taxes they paid on sales. The use or lack of the title 'don' is the only indication as to the social standing of the people involved, but the information is still of interest. Thus for the city of Barquisimeto, a heavily coloured town, only five of sixteen *pulperos* are listed as 'dons'.[54] On the other hand, in a town like La Victoria, where whites were numerous, comparatively speaking, of seventeen *pulperos* listed, only two were without the title 'don'.[55]

The tax books also provide an impressive glimpse of the network of internal trade in which many petty traders, muleteers, and errand-men for the large *hacendados* took part. Again the only evidence of lower social standing is the use or lack of the title 'don', and the data are too erratic to use in any concrete form. Nevertheless one interesting *pardo* will allows the hypothesis that some of the above were coloured. One Juan Jose Mexías acted as an agent for a Caracas-based merchant, Francisco Echenique, buying cacao from the *hacendados* of the valley of Curiepe. Hundreds of pesos passed between them.[56] The degree of trust implied in such a transaction, as in the presence of *pardo* and even slave *mayordomos* on the haciendas of whites, suggests a degree of social stability unimaginable if racial conflict was boiling continuously below the surface, as some historians have implied.[57]

This section must end on a traditional note: regardless of the economic advances of elements of the *pardos* and the very real freedom the rural labourer and plot-holder had to pursue his own economic well-being divorced from the plantation system, life was difficult for *pardos* as a caste. The vast majority of them – a far greater proportion in all probability than the equivalent white one – lived at or barely above the subsistence level. The social restrictions were burdensome and affected many aspects of daily life. The lack of a stable family structure must have wreaked havoc on personal lives. And the fact remains that the majority of urban dwellers were *pardos* who had a much harder go of it than their *compadres* who stayed in the countryside. The urban poor were a constant presence in and pressure on the city of Caracas. In 1801 the acting Prior of the Real Consulado spoke of 10,000 people, or one-third of the population of the city of Caracas, 'who live without exercising an occupation capable of providing their daily substance, whilst the public beggars gather . . . 1,200 {strong} in front of the bishop's place every Saturday'.[58] That he was speaking of the free-coloured masses can be ascertained from the incorporation of the above information in yet another proposal to develop a tied rural labour force, this time by transferring urban inhabitants to the countryside.

Slaves

Black slaves were an important component of the province's export economy, which revolved around commodities produced on plantations. Yet the fascinating aspect about the province's slavery was that it was so much less a part of the plantation structure than might be expected of an agricultural economy. As will be demonstrated, slaves fulfilled a number of functions which had little to do with the economics of plantation life, and the planter class showed a marked disinclination to increase slave labour on their holdings at precisely a period when production was increasing and when, to judge from the example of Havana, slaves could have been imported wholesale with government aid.[59]

Although the majority of slaves in Caracas worked on plantations, a large minority did not. Before elaborating on this observation it is worth keeping in mind the following. Over 70% of the province's slave population of 60,000 was concentrated in the small Coastal Range and narrow coast where the bulk of the province's plantation agriculture was centred. The Coastal Range was also the most densely populated area of Caracas. The resulting concentration of demographic and productive resources had important but differing implications for the institution of slavery. Agriculture made great demands on it, but so did urban conglomerations where domestic servants, household artisans and the like were required for the households of the wealthy and the not so well-off.

The evidence as to the non-agricultural occupations of slaves is actually quite strong. It is easy enough to look at censuses and uncover the presence of large numbers in the cities but these figures in themselves are not proof enough. After all many haciendas were on the borders of towns, and slaves and workers could be shifted daily to and from the plantations without trouble. But two documents would seem to put beyond doubt the heavy presence of slaves as urban residents divorced from agricultural pursuits. A 1796 review of the state of affairs in the province spoke of the entire slave population of the city of Caracas – 8,000 strong in 1785 – in terms of domestic servants.[60] Moving from the Coastal Range region to the Segovia Highlands and the district of Tocuyo, a similar picture emerges. The population of the city itself was divided into urban and rural residents *within* city limits for the years 1787–8. Out of a total population of 8,829, some 1,454 were slaves. Of these 604 or 41% were classified as domestic servants.[61] The rest were distributed mostly on haciendas in the environs of the city. If similar percentages were to hold for all the major cities and towns of the province, a large portion of the slave force would have to be considered non-agricultural. For example, if the 1796 figures on Caracas City seem exaggerated and the lower Tocuyo percentages were applied to compare rural and urban proportions, there would still be over 3,000 slaves taken out of agriculture by the needs of the city of Caracas alone.

The information contained in the notarial records of the city of Caracas offers some interesting insights into another aspect of slave society: the incidence of manumission or the voluntary freeing of slaves by their masters in return for services rendered and the like. At least one author suggests that this process, especially from the mid-1750s onwards, represented a conscious and popular attempt by *hacendados* to create a tied labour force by freeing slaves on condition they developed fallow parts of haciendas or worked directly on the plantations. The advantage for the *hacendado*, so the argument goes, would be to lessen the costs of maintaining a large slave force, the latter being exchanged for free labourers who would have to fend for themselves.[62] The suggestion sounds plausible but the data in the wills do not bear it out.

Roughly 6,300 slaves appear in a sample of 231 wills from the notarial archives of Caracas. Only 280 slaves out of the total were manumitted or freed, or less than 5%.[63] Of those who can be clearly identified as being either in rural or urban occupations, 74 were from agricultural holdings and 104 from households in the city. A further 101 were drawn from both categories but without any clear distinction as to their activities. More revealing, is the number of owners involved in the rural and urban manumissions. Thirteen owners were involved in freeing the rural slaves, and thirty-four in the liberation of the urban contingent. Eight of the latter held both rural and urban slaves, but only two of them saw fit to free any from their agricultural holdings. Their benevolence was limited to household servants. What the preceding information reveals is that on the evidence of wills which refer to 5,300 agricultural slaves, landowners were very unlikely to free this category of worker. Furthermore, the numbers involved in manumissions from plantations were too small for any hard theories to be formulated as to whether the process at this stage (pre-abolition pressures) was used to develop debt peonage.

It is well known that slave imports into Caracas, and Venezuela at large, began to diminish in the 1780s.[64] Paradoxically, the slow-down, as will become apparent, came at a time of economic expansion, when trade laws had been altered to allow Venezuelans to import as many slaves as they needed and when the colonial government was willing to subsidize the imports. The reasons for the decline in slave imports are extremely difficult to fix with any certainty. After all, there are scattered complaints by planters and royal officials alike as to the scarcity of labour in the province and the need to import more slaves or tie down the rural free population.[65] It is possible that the Haitian revolution, and the minor but morale-shaking slave revolt in Coro in 1795 discouraged the white elite from increasing the size of the coloured population, whether free or bonded.[66] A further limiting factor may have been Spain's continuous wars with Britain in the 1790s and the 1800s when Britain was still the major source of slaves for the Caribbean. The largest slave contracts carried out or planned between 1780 and 1810 were all with British traders, or at least traders operating from British possessions.[67]

Planters in any case were much less interested in slave imports than they appeared to be, and the scarcity, if it existed, was more apparent than real. If the *caraqueño* agricultural infrastructure had needed or could have responded to the stimulus of an intake of more slaves, doubtless a flow of imports would have occurred as in the case of Havana, in spite of the wars with Britain.[68] Inside Caracas, the high proportion of slaves employed in urban pursuits and the unwillingness of *hacendados* to divert these chattels to their plantations, imply a basic lack of interest in increasing the size of the agricultural slave population. In the end, as we shall see, the majority of haciendas were too small to warrant large numbers of slaves, and got by in good times with the assistance of free labour. Certainly no complaints about labour needs ever surfaced in periods of economic upswing.

Indians

Information on the Indian population of the province of Caracas is singularly lacking. Actually it might be better to say it has not been collected and analysed. The archives in Seville, for example, contain an imposing amount of data on the Indian population in the post-1750 decades but, unfortunately, the limits of this study prevent the incorporation of this information. The following brief discussion is therefore limited to a few, very general, observations on the *indígenas* in the late-colonial period.

The 1785–7 survey of the province of Caracas divided the Indian population of 53,154 into tributary Indians (*indios de tributo*) and free Indians (*indios libres*).[69] The two categories were roughly equal in size: the tributary Indians numbered 27,764 and the free Indians 25,390. It is nearly impossible to establish what relationship the *libres* had to organized society but something can be said about the *tributarios*. They were concentrated in two main areas: the valleys immediately surrounding the city of Caracas, which contained 19.3% of them; and the Segovia Highlands, where 54.7% of them resided. They lived in *pueblos* or villages built around the working of communal lands, the *tierras de comunidad*.[70]

The community lands, and therefore their means of an independent livelihood, were under constant threat from white *hacendados* throughout the eighteenth century. One historian speaks of the disappearance of whole *pueblos* before the 1780s, and there is no reason to think that the process of encroachment stopped in the late-colonial period.[71] The Indians found themselves fighting lawsuits to protect territorial boundaries which had suddenly become part of neighbouring haciendas. It does not take much imagination to guess who was winning the battle. In addition, the Crown, which through its agent the Protector de Indios was supposed to look after Indian interests, was doing a poor job. The appointment of a new commissioner in 1777 led to an official acknowledgement of the *abandono* the Indians found themselves in.[72] Another report in covering a case of fraud in an Indian *comunidad*, referred in passing to the general ill effects of alcohol on the 'temporal and spiritual health' of the Indians.[73] Even within the confines of so sketchy an outline, it is clear that the lot of the Indians was both unenviable and marginal to the rest of society.

General social characteristics

It should be apparent from our look at the individual castes that a more fluid social structure existed in Caracas than might be surmised from taking into account solely the legal aspects of racial distinctions. Economic mobility and occupational interchangeability to some extent tempered the rigidity of the hierarchical caste divisions and, among the white caste, lessened the impact of ethnic differences.

Economic mobility does not necessarily result in a more graduated class structure, but in Caracas' case the evidence is that it did. There was a relatively narrow spread between rich and poor in the province. In 1783 Intendant Saavedra stated that '[there] are few men in the capital or in the province who are truly wealthy'.[74] Whether he was measuring wealth by income or by assets he was correct in his judgement. Although the richest men in the late-colonial period, the third Marqués del Toro, the Conde de Tovar and the Marqués de Casa León, were estimated to have the comparatively high incomes of between 25,000 to 50,000 pesos a year, the fall-off from that figure was steep.[75] The Conde de la Granja, who was probably one of the twenty wealthiest men in the province in the 1790s and 1800s, estimated his annual income as a relatively modest 13,000 pesos.[76] The implication of these estimates is that virtually all of Caracas' population, including most of the elite, had an income of less than 10,000 pesos a year.

The stark contrast between wealth and poverty so easily discernible in a place like New Spain was therefore absent in Caracas. It can of course be argued that to a *pardo* living on a subsistence plot with no calculable income whatsoever, or to a *jornalero* earning 9 pesos in a good month, the rich in the province seemed very wealthy indeed.[77] If all of the population besides the wealthy had been in equally modest circumstances there would indeed have been only differences of degree between the class structures of New Spain and Caracas. This was not the case. A 'middle class' of whites and free-coloureds existed in our province which may have been numerous enough to act as a buffer between elites and masses.

The best data currently available on the breakdown of colonial society by class, and correspondingly the best proof that a large middle social ground existed, are provided by a survey of the neighbouring province of Cumaná done in 1793.[78] In that year an official calculated the *per capita* consumption of *géneros, frutos, y efectos Europeos* of the non-Indian population by *clase* (class). His calculations on consumption are less interesting than his description and quantification of each *clase* of consumer. Significantly the categories are not based on race, nor should they have been. In a society with economic mobility, levels of individual consumption were bound to have only a partial relation to colour bars. The survey reveals, as might be expected, a tiny class at the top

Table 2 *Annual 'per-capita' general consumption by class of the non-Indian population of Cumaná in 1794, with extrapolations for the province of Caracas*

Category[a]	p/c Consumption	Cumaná	Caracas	%[b]
1. *caballeros y señoras principales*	102ps. ¾ rl.	615	3,923	1.4
2. *hombres, mugeres etc. en qualquier gerarquía y color con lo necesario para mantenerse en decencia*	57ps. 5½ rls.	3,659	23,537	8.4
3. *gentes libres: soldado, labrador de propria mano, oficiales etc.*	39ps. 5 rls.	8,054	51,838	18.5
4. *peónes libres pobres, esclavos y las personas que se le comparan en el servicio civil*	8ps. 2⅛ rls.	15,985	103,115	36.8
5. *gente pobre, niños pobres, pobres de solemnidad* (beggars)	6 rls.	15,155	97,792	34.9
Total		43,468	280,205	100

[a] See text for translations.
[b] The percentages are rounded.

composed of just over 1% of the non-Indian population. Under it, however, is a sizeable middle group roughly equidistant in its level of consumption from both the top and bottom categories. This middle is made up of the second and third *clases*, which together represented 27% of the population tallied. They are described as those of 'whatever . . . colour [who have] the necessary to keep themselves *en decencia*' and as 'official people in all the professions and [those of] comparative class . . . [such as] soldiers, [small-scale] farmers, etc.'. Below them are the two remaining *clases* which composed 71% of the population. Yet, even among them there is a clear differentiation between 'free *peónes*', and 'the poor', and the desperately impoverished.

Cumaná was a much less populated province compared to Caracas, and it was also in an earlier phase of development. Nevertheless, it is the Venezuelan region most similar in economic diversity and growth to Caracas and most likely to have had the variety of occupation we saw exhibited by the social structure of our province.[79] It is therefore possible to speculate at least that the *clase* divisions in Caracas were comparable to the ones laid down for Cumaná. Table 2 summarises the

Cumaná findings and presents extrapolations for Caracas' 1787 population, excluding Indians.

The unusual character of the agricultural structure of Caracas further
supports the parallels with Cumaná. In addition to the unmeasurable
but large class of plot-holders in the countryside, a much more numerous and therefore more varied *hacendado* class existed than has been
thought. In 1787 there were at least 2,695 agricultural holdings within
the province's boundaries large enough to be denominated 'haciendas'
or *hatos*.[80] Ownership was not particularly concentrated: the sample of
808 wills in the Bibliographical Appendix contains reference to 559
haciendas and *hatos* distributed among 289 individuals representing
212 separate family groups.[81] As these families include the wealthiest
and most extensive land-holders of the time, it can very plausibly be
suggested that the 2,000 or so other holdings were far more widely
distributed than the ones in the sample. Whatever the final tally of
hacendados in Caracas, it is clear that their number was several times
greater than the 160 suggested by one historian.[82] Correspondingly a
large class of middle-sized plantation and ranch owners was probably in
existence.

As a corollary to the above, it is possible to suggest that economic
distinctions between many whites and many free-coloureds were not
that pronounced, which tends to support our earlier observations on the
poverty of some whites and the economic success of some *pardos*. It does
not follow that this greater economic balance between the two castes
was likely to increase mutual understanding. Indeed, in a highly race-
conscious environment the opposite would be more likely to happen.
Nonetheless, the broader coexistence of castes was probably made easier
by the small and scattered character of *caraqueño* settlement, which
worked against the build-up of tensions that characterized areas of
greater population density such as the Bajío in New Spain. More importantly, in Caracas, as we have seen and will continue to see, the
economic system was open enough, administrative rule was lenient
enough and food plentiful enough to prevent a social crisis from developing on the scale of the Tupac Amaru rebellion in Peru, the famines in
New Spain and the Comunero revolt of New Granada.

The role of social institutions[83]

Institutions in Caracas reflected the small-scale and far-flung pattern of
settlement, as well as the relative normality of day-to-day affairs. They
played a supportive rather than guiding or leading role in society. The

comparative newness and the structural weaknesses of many of the institutions further contributed to making their presence less imposing.

The long-established town councils or cabildos may have had the greatest contact with the population. This did not necessarily result in any major exercise of influence over political life. The quotidian activities of the ayuntamientos were of a routine, administrative nature, ranging over such parochially important, but hardly earth-shaking, issues as supervising market-days, the sale of urban properties and controlling city water-supplies.[84] The matters considered do not seem to have been weighty enough to ensure the regular attendance of council members, and interest in purchasing these posts seems to have been declining as the eighteenth century drew to a close.[85]

Other institutions were hardly more prominent, except in name. The Imperial Appellate Court, the Audiencia, set up in the province in 1786, did not develop into a major political influence as its counterparts in other colonies did. Instead it spent its time on litigation over water-rights and criminal cases.[86] The Consulado, the Merchant and Planter Guild established in 1793 to foment economic co-operation between the elites of the two groups and to stimulate the provincial economy, instead functioned primarily as a *fuero* tribunal for commercial disputes between individuals.[87] In the wider economic sphere it achieved little of concrete value, partly perhaps because its meetings were so poorly attended by the very persons who should have been interested in seeing the institution succeed.[88] The same lack of interest seems to have afflicted the disorganised local militias, which appear to have served primarily as prestige props for the provincial elites.[89]

The Church in Caracas also had its share of problems as an institution. The number of clergy in the province, both secular and regular, was small and probably declining in our period. Worse, the distribution of the available clerics was disproportionately concentrated in the city of Caracas, which with less than a tenth of the population held half of the province's clergy.[90] In contrast, large towns in the Llanos like El Pao, San Fernando de Apure, El Bául and Araure, all with populations in 1805 of between 1,500 and 6,000 inhabitants, got by with the services of one priest or none.[91] Province-wide, dozens of towns and villages did without a resident clergyman altogether. Nor was the Church's tenuous representation at the parish level reinforced by the presence of flourishing missions, as was the case in the neighbouring provinces of Cumaná and Guayana. The need for missions to subdue and 'civilize' Indians and to protect boundaries had long since vanished in Caracas, and Depons, visiting the province in the early

1800s, remarked there were far fewer friars than there had been earlier in the century.[92]

The Bishopric of Caracas was not only lacking in human resources. Its economic base was less than formidable and in the process of being undermined, as religious donations in the province dropped in the late eighteenth century.[93] Paradoxically, the provincial Church's annual income from tithes compared favourably with other colonial bishoprics: in 1795 Caracas ranked fourteenth out of a total of forty-four.[94] Tithes-intake however is only one measure of ecclesiastical wealth and a misleading one at that: in Caracas most of the tithe income was used to cover operating expenses.[95] More indicative of the Church's wealth were the worth of ecclesiastically-held agricultural and urban properties, the size of private bequests and the value of Church-held mortgages on the province's haciendas. Unfortunately for the Church, these sources of income were also flawed. As an institution it possessed comparatively few properties, and of those it did own few were likely to have been very profitable. In 1801 the Vicarage of Puerto Cabello earned just 144 pesos a month on 20 houses it rented out, and the cacao hacienda it owned was described as producing very little, with a sick and ageing slave labour force.[96] A *cofradía* in a parish in the city of Caracas was led to consider selling its cacao plantation, which did not produce even enough to feed the slaves on it.[97] Many individual priests did of course own profitable haciendas, but we would be mistaken if we counted these holdings as an extension of the Church's wealth. The latter plantations were owned as private properties and disposed of as such. In terms of their impact on the institution, they probably only served to accentuate the differences between well-off and poor members of the clergy.

The other economic pillars of the Church were hardly in better condition. As noted before, religious donations seem to have been falling off in a population never renowned for its spiritual fervour. Perhaps the greatest weakness of the *caraqueño* Church's economic foundations, however, was the probable low level of Church-mortgaged haciendas in the province. Unlike the case in New Spain, where as much as half of agrarian property was in Church hands in one form or another, the *caraqueño* hacienda structure retained a marked independence from the Church as a financial institution. To be sure, the Church was used as a credit facility in the province in much the same way as elsewhere in the empire, but the vast majority of *hacendados* seem to have carried their Church mortgages with ease. Their total level of indebtedness was in fact surprisingly low and even insignificant, as we will see later.[98] In any event the amount the Church held in *censos* in our period was small in absolute terms, probably not even reaching 2,500,000 pesos in the early 1800s.[99] Church wealth in general was probably much less imposing than has been supposed and, when this is taken in combination with the institution's weak organizational network in the province, it can be concluded it did not represent the powerful institution it was elsewhere in the empire.

If the preceding has sounded like the deliberate down-playing of the importance of institutions in Caracas, it is because their presence alone has too often been considered a sign of their importance. Their role was fairly limited, so that giving prominence to institutions in a society where the dynamics were not institutional can be very misleading, suggesting a structural organization and cohesion which simply were not present in late-colonial Caracas. Not even the institutions connected with the political administration of the province were totally free of the relative feebleness which characterized the bodies discussed above, as we will discover when we examine the politics of our area.

PART TWO

Economy

2

The export economy 1777–1810

The diversification of production

The activities which supported the society of Caracas were those of a plantation–ranch economy producing primarily for export. The diversification of the production base of this economy is the most striking characteristic of its evolution between 1777 and 1810. The fact that it did occur remains a major unexplained enigma of the colony's development. It would seem that by the beginning of our period structural distortions had so taken over the economy that no radical departure from a dependence on cacao could take place.

Monoculture is the best word to describe the export economy in existence when the Intendency came into full operation in 1777.[1] The *caraqueño* economy had always been oriented primarily towards export production; its population base had been too small and its agricultural resources were too limited to support a large internal market. But it had not always been a virtual monoculture: in the seventeenth century wheat, cotton, livestock and tobacco had been produced and exported in quantity along with cacao. With the ascendancy of cacao in the middle of the seventeenth century Caracas was swept down the path towards one-crop domination. Under the rule of the Caracas Company (1730–84) the process was carried out to its fullest extent. By the 1770s the volume of cacao production had almost doubled since the 1720s, implying the spread of production at the cost of other crops.[2] Furthermore, cacao represented, by the later years, over 85% of the colony's exports.[3]

The province's dependency on cacao was not abolished in the period under study but it was substantially reduced, so that by 1809, on the eve of the independence struggle, the crop accounted for less than 50% of export earnings. The question, of course, is why the transformation took place at all.

Table 3a *The diversification of exports 1775–1809: changes in volume*

Product	1775[a]	1783–5[a] (avg./yr)	1786–90[b] (avg./yr)	1791–5[b] (avg./yr)	1809[a]
cacao	58,923 fas.	78,964 fas.	86,257 fas.	75,421 fas.	94,779 fas.
indigo	8,710 lbs.	163,221 fas.	294,023 lbs.	718,074 lbs.	697,451 lbs.
coffee	400 lbs.		18,677 lbs.	218,102 lbs.	6,574,555 lbs.
hides	37,058	66,865			80,981
tobacco	112,592 lbs.		73,022 lbs.	286,506 lbs.	
cotton			67,440 lbs.	340,902 lbs.	823,200 lbs.
sugar	150 lbs.		441 lbs.	58,318 lbs.	486,523 lbs.
copper			319 lbs.	24,778 lbs.	79,484 lbs.
currency (value)		255,744 ps.[c]	217,050 ps.	131,387 ps.	

[a] Totals for the province and to all markets.
[b] Exports from La Guaira to Spain and the Canaries.
[c] For 1785 only.

Sources: For 1775 see Arcila Farías, *Economía Colonial*, I, 335–6. For 1783–5 see A.G.I., Caracas 482, tables of foreign trade, Saavedra, 11 June 1786. For 1786–95 see A.G.I., Caracas 513, accompanying table to memorial by syndic of Consulado, 20 February 1796. For 1809 see *Semanario de Caracas*, 9 December 1810, in *Semanario de Caracas*, (Caracas, 1959), pp. 47–8.

Table 3b *The diversification of exports 1775–1809: shifts in value among major exports (percentages)*

Product	1775[a]	1784–5[a]	1791–5[b]	1809[a]
cacao	85–90	65	55	45–50
indigo	1	15	40	30
coffee			1	20
other	10–15	20	5	1–5

[a] Based on total exports from the province.
[b] Based on the La Guaira–Spain trade only, but at a time when Spain was taking 95% of the province's exports and when La Guaira was the outlet for 95% of provincial exports. See Table 4.

Note: The above percentages are all estimates made from what we know about the prices of individual commodities, the composition and volume of exports across time, and the total value of exports for the given years. The volume exports of individual products have been given in the first table in this series and the value of exports will be given in the next. It remains to disclose the prices used per unit:

Table 3b *(cont.)*

	1775	1783–6	1793–6	1808–9
cacao/fa.	16 ps.		18–20 ps.	17 ps.
indigo/lb.		11–13 rls.	12–14 rls.	12 rls.
coffee/quintal			12 ps.	11–12 ps.

Sources: for 1775 price see Arcila Farías, *Economía Colonial*, p. 335. For 1783–6 see A.G.I., Caracas 501, despatch by Saavedra, 23 November 1786. For 1795–6 see A.G.I., Caracas 180, syndic of Caracas Cabildo to Leon, 6 October 1800, and Humberto Tandrón, *El Real Consulado de Caracas y el Comercio Exterior de Venezuela* (Caracas, 1976), p. 160. For 1808–9 see Miguel Izard, 'La Agricultura Venezolana en una Época de Transición: 1777–1830', *Boletín Histórico*, XXVIII (1972), 143.

The diversification of the colony's economic base can first be approached through an examination of export statistics. The most complete are for the years 1784 to 1795, which happen to be the years when the foundations for the transformation of the composition of exports were laid. The first date was actually the symbolic starting-point of the final phase of Caracas' development, a period when the province was unrestricted by the exigencies of corporation rule. It was also the first year of normal trade activity after five years of interruptions caused by Spain's war with Britain (1779–83). The last possible date in which trade can be said to have been unaffected by the advent of the Napoleonic Wars was 1795. Although growth and diversification did continue after that year, they did so in a less uniform fashion, constantly disrupted by new wars.

Table 3 quantifies the transformation. By 1784–5, when cacao exports were surpassing their pre-war levels, cacao accounted for 65% of total exports, down from 85–90% in the mid-1770s. Indigo in the interim had come into the picture and took up some 15% of the total value, with currency transfers bringing up the rear. In the 10 years after 1785, cacao's share dropped to 55% in an expanding economy, whilst indigo's increased to around 40%. Coffee and cotton made their first major incursions into the export lists. As can be seen, the volume increases in the periods 1786–90 and 1791–5 are remarkable even when taking into account the small take-off base from which the boom in secondary crops sprung. Their monetary value remained small, however, and the total value of exports rose less than 50% in the same time period.[4] The increase in value was even less marked if exports of hard currency and tobacco are subtracted from the totals. Both ceased to be exported in any quantities after 1795.[5] By 1809, the next year for when comparable trade figures are available, it is clear that a major transformation had taken place.[6] Official trade figures for the year reveal that cacao accounted for less than half the total, with indigo and coffee a respectable second and third.

It would be easy to pick out almost at random reasons accounting for the diversification and growth revealed by Table 3, perhaps deceptively easy. It is true that the move away from cacao began within the production sector of the economy in the 1770s and early 1780s, when new commercial crops started to be produced in quantities.[7] Their development was of course aided by the end of Spain's participation in the American War of Independence in 1783, the collapse and dissolution of the Caracas Company (1779–84) and changing imperial trade policy, which ushered in a period of peace and economic liberalization, allowing nascent forces in the economy to acquire strength.[8] The destruction of the giant agricultural colony of Haiti in the 1790s certainly provided a stimulus to Caracas' secondary crops, especially coffee.[9] Moreover, cacao was in trouble; it faced competition and a declining demand in New Spain, its major market after the mother country.[10]

   The preceding list is a useful index and a familiar one, but only partially accounts for the long-term influence affecting the process of diversification. The reasons given above do not adequately clarify the fundamental issues: the development of markets for the new crops and the reaction to the new demand inside the province. Peace, for example, is always an inducement to experimentation, especially in a period of general economic expansion; and the end of corporate rule removed an onerous, even formidable obstacle to diversification, if contemporaries are to be believed.[11] But these factors by themselves did not create new demands for new commodities. More significantly, Caracas was not included in the liberalization of imperial trade until 1789, and could not thus have benefited from the measures in the period of greatest diversification of its production base. In any case the demand for *caraqueño* goods from the rest of Spanish America was limited. Furthermore, the Haitian economy, with its dominance of world coffee and sugar production, was not disrupted until the early 1790s, so no stimulation could have been forthcoming from that development during the years the decisions were made to produce new crops. Cacao's decline in any case was only relative. Its prosperity was indeed hit by the entry of cacao from Guayaquil into the New Spain markets, but prices of cacao remained high in the 1780s and early 1790s and in fact rose to their highest point in the mid-1790s.[12] Interestingly, the volume of cacao's exports held remarkably constant throughout the late-colonial period.[13] It was cacao's share of the increase in the total export trade which proved negligible. Its relative decline did not provide enough of an inducement to diversify.

Of greater importance was the impact of shifting international demands for commodities produced in Caracas and imperial intervention in the direction of the provincial economy. It was Spanish interest and markets which led to the first noticeable shift away from cacao by sparking the boom in indigo production. Caracas rivalled the imperial leader, Guatemala, as an indigo producer only because royal policy and officials had fostered, protected and subsidized the development of a crop in great demand in Spain.[14] Internally, the creation of a state tobacco monopoly resulted in a profitable enterprise which provided funds for other economic activities in the province.[15] But perhaps the most important legacy of imperial policy was a 1777 measure affecting existing but as yet relatively untapped markets in the neighbouring non-Spanish territories of the Caribbean.

The role of changing markets

The question of markets, trade statutes and their interrelated roles in the process of diversification bears closer inspection. Going into the 1770s, two legal markets existed for Caracas' exports: Spain and the Canary Islands (jointly 'La Metrópoli') and New Spain. Exchange by contraband was fuelled by a third market, the non-Spanish colonies of the Caribbean.[16] It was this trade which the 1777 measure affected. The character of inter-imperial trade is well known and requires little further exposition below.[17] The same cannot be said of the third commercial outlet, yet understanding its role is essential to understanding the commerce of the province in the late-colonial period. If Spanish demand was responsible for the first burst of growth and diversification, the foreign colonies were the reason why the process was sustained after the mid-1790s.

The royal decree of 13 June 1777 may or may not have formalized a system of exchange which was already *de facto* in existence.[18] But it is clear that the legalizing of trade with foreign colonies for the express purpose of bringing badly-needed hard currency and slaves into the colony opened the channel through which a third legal market for *caraqueño* goods developed across the following thirty years. That market consisted of the French and Dutch Caribbean possessions at first, but in the years after 1783 widened to include the British possessions, the Danish island of St Thomas and the nascent United States of America. [19]

The 1777 statute was far from being a *carte blanche* allowing the province to trade at will with foreign colonies. Traders were only allowed to bring back slaves and cash for whatever they sold, thus maintaining Spain's monopoly on supplying the province with the most essential imports. Furthermore, not all *caraqueño* produce could be traded: cacao, which represented at this stage over 85% of Caracas' exports, was explicitly excluded from the list of goods which might be exchanged. It would seem that the liberalizing character of the imperial decree would have little effect in practice.

The new regulation, however, had an importance which far exceeded any immediate impact it may have had. It was never really rescinded across the next three decades, even though its specific restrictions were occasionally modified. And its central tenet survived intact: any crop other than cacao could be exchanged for slaves and hard currency in the Antilles. Royal decrees in 1789, 1791 and 1804 reinforced the original principles, although there was a short period between 1803 and 1805 when the concession was suspended. [20] The potential impact of legal access to foreign markets and different demands must have been noticed by the colony's producers.

The commercial leeway allowed Caracas after 1777 was greatly increased by the very real open trade forced on the empire by the wars of the late-colonial period. Spain's inability to supply or buy regularly from its possessions in times of war led the mother country to open its colonies temporarily to unrestricted trade with the merchants of neutral or friendly nations and their colonies. Venezuela as a whole may have been more continuously affected by this liberalization than any other colony. Four times between 1780 and 1810 (1780–4, 1797–9, 1800–1 and 1806–10) the colony was free to trade with all but enemies for the duration of the several wars. There were no major restrictions on what could be traded, and so even cacao found its way to foreign markets. The combination of the free-trade periods with the specific regulations governing the province from 1777 onwards probably gave Caracas a unique position in the empire, a *de facto* freedom to trade regularly with markets outside the empire. [21]

The foreign Antilles connection only gradually acquired importance across ensuing decades. When the transformation did come however, it was profound. It is possible to chart the changing structure of external demand in terms both of the shifting importance of the three markets and of the kinds of commodities involved in the different exchanges.

Table 4 *The shift in markets for caraqueño exports 1784–1809*
(value in pesos)

Year	Spain–Canaries	Spanish America	Foreign Caribbean	Total
1784	838,320	180,697	339,988	1,359,005
1785	1,641,453	222,371	327,551	2,191,375
1795	2,650,135	139,314[a]	99,014	2,888,465
1797–1800[b]	1,382,321		3,100,000	4,482,321
1809	2,042,723	255,795	1,207,779	3,506,297

[a] This total includes 9,399 pesos in 'exports' to other provinces of the Captaincy-General of Venezuela.

[b] These are exact statistics for Spain–Canaries and for all but half a year (August–December 1799) of the exchange with the foreign colonies. Volume figures available for 1799 allow a reasonable estimate of value to be made for the missing months. As is the case for all figures on this period, the above only carry over partially into 1800: in the case of Spain–Canaries until October and in the case of the foreign Caribbean until the end of May. For an analysis of the same years by volume of traffic see Tandrón, *Real Consulado*, p. 160.

Sources: for 1784–5 see A.G.I., Caracas 482, tables of foreign trade, Saavedra, 11 June 1786. For 1795 see A.G.I., Caracas 513, accompanying table to memorial by syndic of Consulado, 20 February 1796. For 1797–1800 see A.G.I., Caracas 117, tables in despatch on issue of free trade, Quintana and León, 10 February 1800. See also A.G.I., Caracas 180, memorial by syndic of Caracas Cabildo, 6 October 1800. For 1809 see A.G.I., Caracas 491, tables of commerce for 1809, Basadre to Saavedra, 27 March 1810.

Trade figures for given years between 1784 and 1809 tell the story (Table 4).

The first revelation of the statistics is that Spain, and not the foreign colonies, provided the primary impulse to growth and diversification until the mid-1790s. In 1783 an Intendant's report weighed the value of the imperial markets as being far higher than that of the incipient Caribbean market.[22] The Spain–Canaries link was worth 1,000,000 pesos of the annual trade, New Spain 500,000 pesos and the foreign colonies well under that sum. This picture did not really change for many years. With the demise of the New Spain trade by the early 1790s and with no appreciable increase in exports to the foreign colonies, Spain's share grew both in volume and at the expense of the other markets. By 1795 La Metrópoli was taking over 2.6 million pesos worth of provincial exports, or 95% of the total.

The gradual swing upwards in the share of the foreign colonies began

Table 5 *Shifts in market demands for individual crops 1797–1800 and 1809 (percentages)*

	1797–1800		1809[a]	
	Spain– Canaries	Foreign Caribbean	Spain– Canaries	Foreign Caribbean
cacao	44.7	55.3	90–5	2–3
indigo	19.1	80.9	65	35
coffee	4.4	95.6	20–5	70–5

[a] The 1809 export figures include exports to Spanish America which took some cacao, perhaps as much as 3–4% of the total.

Sources: the percentages for 1797–1800 are done on the basis of volume calculations contained in Tandrón, *Real Consulado*, p. 161. Those for 1809 are estimates made from what we know about prices for commodities in that year and about the composition and volume of exports for 1809; as well as from the breakdown on the value of exports to individual markets contained in A.G.I., Caracas 491, tables of commerce for 1809, Basadre to Saavedra, 27 March 1810.

with the 1797–1801 period, when war interrupted commerce with Spain and very few products of any nature reached that country. The colonies and the United States stepped in to pick up some of the slack, although, curiously enough, only a small part of it. Under abnormal conditions, when the total volume of trade declined by half, over 65% of provincial exports may have been going on to the foreign Antilles. The foothold once gained was not lost. Although detailed statistics on trade are unavailable for the 1800s until 1809, the figures for that year, when volume was high in spite of a new war, point to the importance of the foreign colonies as a market. Of a total volume of 3.4 million pesos, Spain's share had fallen to under 60% and the foreign Antilles had risen to over a third, leaving less than 10% for the once-flourishing trade with New Spain.

Over the long term there was a strong connection between the survival of the new export commodities and the growth of the market in the foreign Caribbean. The link developed only gradually (Table 5). In the late 1770s, when cacao represented virtually all of Caracas' legal exports, Spain was taking around 80% of the total and New Spain about 15%.[23] The preponderance of Spain as the determining factor in external demand increased across the 1780s, as indigo, cotton and coffee were produced to meet a diversifying and widening Spanish market. New Spain disappeared as an influence as its consumption of cacao slowed to a trickle. The foreign colonies failed to develop as a major market, only taking the small livestock exports and insignificant quantities of the new crops. The wars of the late 1790s began to change the export patterns. During the period 1797 to 1799, when cacao was available for export to the foreign colonies, the latter chose to ignore the temporary access to the province's premier crop. Instead they purchased proportionately larger quantities of coffee, indigo and cotton. The predilection for the newer crops did not vanish with the end of the war in 1802. By 1809, the next year for which full figures are available on the destination of exports, the non-Spanish Caribbean was taking roughly 35% of the value of indigo exports and an overwhelming 70–75% of coffee exports.

The pivotal role increasingly played by the foreign colonies in the fate of *caraqueño* exports and the structure of local production was clearly not just a result of their powers of consumption. Spain, after all, supplied the stimulus to growth and diversification through the 1780s and 1790s, both as a market and as a promoter of the production of new crops. The mother country, however, was unable to hold onto its controlling position. The reasons are unclear but some conjectures can be made. The Spanish economy, never very strong, was capable of generating demand in a boom period such as the late 1780s and early 1790s, but unable to sustain it once less favourable conditions set in. The small quantities produced of the new crops were easily absorbed by a growing market in Spain. The one new commodity produced in bulk volume, indigo, was likewise stimulated by the Península's expanding textile production.

War and the economics of production, however, upset the balance between the colony and the Spanish market. If the war of 1796–1802 did not break the back of Spain's growing economy, it certainly destroyed her grip on the province's new crops.[24] The near-cessation of trade between Spain and Caracas during those years occurred at precisely the time when the scale of production of new crops was increasing. New markets were needed, and the foreign Antilles, so long dormant as consumers, turned to Caracas as an alternative commodity-supplier once Haiti was ravaged. The base developed by Spanish demand was thereby exploited, and coffee in particular benefited. The non-Spanish purchase of commodities other than cacao, legalized by the aforementioned trade measures, grew across the 1800s to become, as we have seen, central to the health of the province's export economy by 1809.

The preceding pages open the way for a different perspective on the issue of contraband. Was contraband in fact as big a factor in the trade of the province as has been supposed by generations of historians? I would argue that at least in the post-1777 decades it was not. The colony had the right to trade most of its produce legally with the foreign Caribbean. The one major exception, cacao, could not in any case have been sold in great quantities to a market uninterested in the commodity, as was graphically demonstrated in the free-trade period of 1797–9. Even taking into account the fact that taxes on exports outside the empire were substantially higher than those on inter-imperial trade, producers and local merchants were unlikely to run the risks inherent in contraband for a few dollars more when legal outlets were available. After all, facilities existed at La Guaira and Puerto Cabello to handle the trade. They were sufficiently accessible to the production areas and were a convenient gathering-point for all involved in the province's commerce. But the best evidence as to the low level of contraband is provided not by circumstantial observations but by the trade figures. As we have seen, the foreign Antilles showed little interest in *caraqueño* goods for decades. When they did, they were able to exploit the supplier legally. It is perfectly reasonable to assume that the Consulado official Linares was not far off the mark when he said that contraband by 1796 was close to extinction.[25] Significantly, the instance when contraband was a problem in our period, 1803–5, was when the liberal trade decrees governing the province were suspended.[26]

Contraband in any case was likely to have been more of a problem with imports than with illegal exports. Spain had long been unable to supply its colonies from its own industrial–agricultural base, and much of what Caracas imported from Spain was actually European merchandise first passing through the hands of companies based in Cadiz and other ports. Up to half of *caraqueño* imports of flour, textiles, wines and the like were non-Spanish.[27] The foreign colonies and later the United States provided an alternative and more direct supply of manufactured goods and other commodities. Under the guise of bringing back slaves and hard currency, locally-based concerns could import Caracas' needed goods from the Caribbean and more directly from the producers. The closing of trade with the foreign colonies between 1803 and 1805 may have been largely an attempt to stamp out the import smuggling.[28]

Several aspects of Caracas' export economy should be obvious at this stage. First and perhaps foremost is the diversification of the agricultural base which took place between 1777 and 1810. With the possible exception of Havana, no other Spanish American colony underwent the transformation which characterized Caracas' move away from total dependence on cacao. The significant addition of coffee and indigo, and to a lesser extent other crops, gave the province a variety of income-earners which was truly remarkable for such a small primary producer.

A second important characteristic of the province's trade structure was its curious and possibly unique status inside the empire. In addition to its traditional markets of Spain and New Spain, whose demands centred around cacao, the province was able to develop a third, broad market for its other commodities: the foreign colonies of the Caribbean and later the United States. This evolution was not achieved, as is often thought, through contraband, but within the structure of a liberal set of regulations governing the colony's trade. From 1777 onwards, and with only a brief suspension between 1803 and 1805, Caracas was legally permitted to trade its non-cacao products with foreign markets in return for slaves and currency. As the production of the new crops expanded, so, albeit more slowly, did trade with the foreign Antilles.

Caracas' unusual trade status did not mean that its links to Spain were loosened. It can safely be said that a relatively complementary relationship existed between the two, thanks largely to Spain's continuing importance as the province's major market and, as will be seen, to the imperial government's willingness to promote the province's development.

3

Agriculture

Introduction

The plantation and the large-scale ranch were the basic units of agricultural production in the province, and slaves provided the foundation of the labour supply which worked them. That said, it must be pointed out that these truisms reach the limits of their usefulness almost as soon as they are stated. The different patterns of land tenure, the alternative sources of the labour supply and the different production requirements of the individual crops led to an extremely varied and complex agricultural structure.

What was an hacienda in late-colonial Caracas? 'Hacienda' or plantation conjure up images of acceptably large land-holdings worked by at least a number of slaves growing some cash crop or other. According to the unspecified qualifications used for the survey of the province between 1785 and 1787, there were 1,751 land-plots large enough to be denominated cash-crop haciendas, growing cacao, sugar-cane and indigo.[1] A number of these haciendas no doubt handsomely conformed to the prototype. The majority of land-holdings listed as haciendas, however, departed to a lesser or greater degree from the ideal.

Two of the characteristics most assocated with haciendas are personal ownership and sizeable land-plots. It might reasonably be assumed that *hacendados* owned the land their haciendas were founded on. This was not necessarily the case. There are numerous instances of haciendas being leased, or founded and worked on rented lands. In the case of sugar-cane haciendas, as we shall see, there are prominent examples of rentals whereby large and productive units were placed in the hands of enterprising, rich merchants for nine years at a time. Perhaps the most widespread examples of rental are to be found among indigo growers, who provided the second most important export of the colony after cacao. It may well be that a majority of them grew their crop on land rented from large haciendas in the Aragua valleys. A *representación* by indigo planters in 1809 stated openly that all indigo farmers except a handful produced their crop on rented, previously fallow land.[2]

If landownership and *hacendados* were not necessarily synonymous, neither were size and haciendas. As measured by the land they occupied, even the middle-sized plantations of Caracas were remarkably small. In the case of 61 cash-crop haciendas for which information on land-size is available, only 7 were over 200 hectares or 500 acres in size, including fallow land.[3] This selection includes the haciendas of many of the wealthiest agriculturalists of the province, so it is more indicative of the upper levels of plantation size than the small number of the sample would suggest. The reduced scale of the holdings correspondingly shrank the possibilities for large-scale production. Depons may not have been far off when he stated that not more than 20 plantations in the province earned their owners over 4,000–5,000 pesos per annum.[4] As will become apparent when the individual crops are considered, hacienda productivity in the province was both comparatively and absolutely small-scale. Only the *hato* or livestock ranch exhibited all the traditional characteristics expected of Spanish-colonial agrarian units. As will be seen, the future of latifundia in nineteenth-century Venezuela was mapped out by the existence of huge, if nebulously defined, holdings in the Llanos of the colonial province.

Small holdings inferior in size and potential to haciendas supplemented the plantation structure. Reference has been made to the 1785–7 survey which spoke of 'an infinity of plots ... which are not ... formally haciendas'. It is impossible to calculate their number or to what extent these holdings were owned by their occupiers or merely represented squatter possession or tenant-farmer status. In the 1780s a leading individual of the all-powerful Tovar clan expelled 200 families from lands he claimed in the Llanos, which he had left undeveloped.[5] In contrast, the individual who claimed the title of *fundador* of the Guapo valley, Nicolá Cristóbal de León, granted plots of land to poor people who had the right to buy the land from him.[6] At least one traveller, Humboldt, noticed the widespread presence of small freeholders in the productive Aragua valleys to the west of Caracas.[7] Perhaps the most unusual example of small holdings is provided by the structure of the tobacco monopoly. As we shall presently see, hundreds of what were probably subsistence-level farmers produced the crop on public lands.

The labour system on the haciendas and *hatos* was a two-tier structure employing both slave and free labour, with the *jornalero* every bit as important for production as the chattel. While there is little doubt that the large haciendas growing sugar-cane, coffee and the cacao relied rather heavily on slaves, the same cannot be said about haciendas which were modest in size and productivity or about holdings producing other major commodities of the province. Two of the most important crops grown in the province, tobacco and indigo, were primarily though not exclusively worked by freemen. The planters of tobacco, of which there were anywhere from 600 to 1,000 in a given year, were described in one report as poor and growing the crop on their own land ('those who do own any'), or on public or rented lands.[8] Another report was greatly concerned with finding out 'the number of *peónes* or *jornaleros* who are daily used by each planter . . . and what salary they are paid'.[9] In the case of indigo, Humboldt estimated that 4,000 to 5,000 free workers were needed for two months a year to harvest the crop around Maracay, the centre of production in the province.[10] During the crisis of overproduction of 1787 a deputation of indigo planters stated 'most haciendas, if not all run themselves with *jornaleros*'.[11] A 1790 review of the populatin of Maracay spoke of 'half [being] *jornaleros libres* of all *castas*'.[12] A rather negative indication of the extensive use of *jornaleros* and *peónes* on the cattle ranches of the interior is offered by the concern over crime in the Llanos periodically voiced by large-scale *hato* owners. A 1788 report said that 'the same *peónes* of the *hatos* as well as [the *hatos*'] tenants, ironsmiths, drivers and overseers helped to encourage the robbery and ruin of said haciendas'.[13]

The most innovative use made of free labour was exhibited on some of the large cash-crop plantations least dependent on *jornaleros*. Not all the land occupied by larger haciendas was cultivated: indeed the fallow land often exceeded the cultivated in size. It was in the working of this portion that freemen were to be seen most conspicuously on the big haciendas. The tenant farmer, not the *peón*, was the basis of the relationship between employer and employee, as shown in seventeen examples of explicit contracts between landowner and tenant.[14] *Hacendados* would rent out small plots of fallow land, usually a few fanegadas in size but sometimes well over 10 fanegadas, for a finite period of time, usually nine years. The rent paid was not related to productivity but to the amount of land leased, and so the sums involved tended to be small, around 10 pesos/fanegada/year. As often as not no crop specification was made, and the basic foodstuffs of the province, such as maize, beans and yuca, were produced.

As we observed earlier, indebted peonage was rare in colonial Caracas. *Jornaleros*, therefore, were the most numerous component of the rural labour force, apart perhaps from slaves. In some *hacendados'* eyes, these day-workers had such bargaining power that wages for their services were far higher than the prospective employers considered fair. The wages of *jornaleros* give us little indication of how much they earned or cost per year, since, although the going rate was 3 reales a day plus food or 8 to 9 pesos a month, there is no way to determine how many days or months they worked a year.[15] As was the case whenever the scarcity of slaves became an issue, the question of an overpaid labour force only surfaced when prices for cash crops dropped.

Cacao

The diversification of agricultural production did not rob cacao of its primacy in the *caraqueño* economy: through 1810 it remained the single most important component of exports and a larger number of haciendas in the province were dedicated to its production than to that of any other crop. The 1787 survey of the cacao haciendas in Caracas reveals that the centres of production in the late-colonial period were concentrated in the Coastal Range region and the adjacent Coast.[16] Of 1,144 plantations listed, 779 or 68% were in these regions, with perhaps half the provincial total located in an 80-kilometre (50-mile) radius around the city of Caracas. Within the geographical regions two areas stood out: the jurisdiction of La Guaira with 218 haciendas; and the Guarenas–Sabana de Ocumare districts in the Tuy valleys with 313 plantations.

The majority of plantations in Caracas were either modest or small in size. This in fact was the historical pattern of production in the province and it showed few signs of changing in our period. A census of the cacao haciendas in Caracas in 1720–1 revealed that over 55% of the 769 plantations had less than 5,000 trees. A further 33% had between 5,000 and 14,999. Only 19 haciendas held more than 30,000 trees apiece.[17] A 1745 survey covering only the richest agricultural lands in the Aragua and Tuy valleys and along the coast conveys a similar impression. Over 30% of the 556 haciendas had less than 5,000 trees and over 50% between 5,000 and 14,999. Only 17 had more than 30,000 trees.[18] The slightly larger size of haciendas in the second census can be attributed both to the partiality of the data and to a process of gradual aggrandizement of haciendas in the province.

No equivalent survey has been uncovered for the late eighteenth century; the 1787 survey does little more than list the number of haciendas by jurisdiction. Nevertheless it is not difficult to prove that the same size distribution existed in our period. We know that there were 1,144 haciendas in the province in 1787 and that annual production in the 1780s and 1790s was *circa* 130,000 fanegas. We also know that the average provincial yield in 1721 was 14.8 fanegas/1,000 trees, and that contemporary calculations for *circa* 1800 worked with a figure of about 12 fanegas/1,000.[19] It is possible to apply the latter yield-estimate to 1787. To produce 130,000 fanegas at least 10,833,300 trees would have been needed. This works out to an average of 9,470 trees for each of the 1,144 haciendas. The equivalent ratios for 1721 and 1745 are respectively 5,912 and 9,232. Projecting one step further, it can be estimated that an average plantation in 1787 could expect to produce 110–115 fanegas a year at a gross value of about 2,000 pesos, at a price of 17 pesos/fanega.

The value of the infrastructure of cacao plantations and the economics of cacao production can be examined in some detail thanks to a sample of 199 haciendas collected from documentation of the late-colonial period.[20] The information varies considerably, depending on the thoroughness with which an individual chose to disclose the extent or nature of his holdings in notarial documents. Taken together, however, the data provide an excellent opportunity to investigate both structural and production aspects of the cacao economy. The sample includes the largest plantations in the province; thus the average size for 143 haciendas for which tree-size is given, is an impressive 20,154.

The three basic factors of production on cacao haciendas were trees, land and labour. On any given hacienda there was a mix of tree-types variegated by age and productivity and therefore value. Cacao trees took six to eight years to bear full fruit after first being planted but then had a productive life of twenty years or more before their yield went into a cycle of decline for another twenty years.

According to Codazzi, just over 1,000 trees of all ages fitted into 1 fanegada of land.[21] Thus an hacienda with 10,000 trees would have had to cultivate 9–10 fanegadas. Three separate appraisals calculated that one worker could care for about 1,000 trees.[22] On any hacienda larger than 1,000–2,000 trees it was more than likely that the worker would be a slave. This observation is borne out by a sample of 110 haciendas for which both tree-size and slave numbers are available. Even the haciendas holding less than 5,000 trees each all used slave labour.

The relative value of the different factors of production within the framework of an hacienda can be gauged with a certain degree of accuracy thanks to a sample of 26 haciendas for which reasonably complete inventories are available.[23] Trees almost invariably represented the single most valuable component of the cacao haciendas of the sample. On 23 haciendas they represented over half the total value of the plantation even when variables unconnected to production, such as fallow land and the master's residence, are taken into account. On the other hand, the proportional worth of slaves in the infrastructure of haciendas was lower than might have been expected. Their value was more often than not one third to one half that of the cacao trees. On 14 haciendas of the sample, their value represented 20-30% of an hacienda's worth. Once the value of trees and slaves was discounted, not much was left in the way of appraisable capital in the rest of an hacienda's structure. The value of property was proportionately low: on 22 haciendas of the sample, land represented 16% or less of total worth. This calculation includes the value of both cultivated and fallow soil. If only the planted fanegadas are considered, the true production cost of land was even lower. By extension, the investment in tools, animals for labour and processing equipment was minimal both absolutely and in comparison to other crops. It never represented more than one or two percentage points of an hacienda's value, and usually a good deal less.

The profitability of cacao production in our period was probably lower than that of other crops, but may still have been high enough to offer a reasonable return on both the costs of production and the total value of a plantation. Complete accounts of three haciendas give an idea of the costs of production and the rate of return.[24] On two of the plantations belonging to José Hernández Sanabria, even after including expenses such as the salary of an overseer and the costs of repairs to the hacienda, of cleaning out irrigation channels, of transporting the crop to market, of paying the sales-taxes, of the travel expenses of the owners for visits to and from the plantations and of curing, feeding and clothing slaves, the total cost of production was only about 26% of the value of the cacao produced. In the case of the Sanz family hacienda, expenditures across almost six years amounted to only 30% of the value of the cacao produced. The net return on the total assets of the three haciendas was 5% across three years on the two Sanabria plantations and just under 5% across six years on the Sanz property.[25]

Indigo

Indigo was the second most important commodity produced for export in the late-colonial period. The distribution of indigo haciendas in the province was remarkably concentrated. Of 220 tallied in the 1785–7 survey of Caracas, over half were in the jurisdiction of La Victoria (including the production centre of Maracay), in the Aragua valleys. The other, much smaller, concentration of haciendas was in the Tuy valleys east of the city of Caracas.[26]

As we have seen, the haciendas of the Aragua valleys used a predominantly free labour force. The reasons for the dependence on free labour are not entirely clear but the following hypothesis can be offered. Indigo was rather late in becoming a significant part of *caraqueño* agriculture and grew rapidly when it did. Slaves were unlikely to have been available in large enough surplus amounts to be put to work in the burgeoning indigo fields, especially when it is considered that the major centre of production, the La Victoria–Maracay area, had an insignificant slave population. Free labour filled the gap. In the midst of a crisis of overproduction in 1787, planters warned that 20,000 men would be thrown out of work if the indigo plantations in the province collapsed.[27]

The majority of the Aragua indigo plantations were founded on rented land. The implication of the presence of so many renter *hacendados* is that a majority were likely to have been of modest means. The reaction to the crisis of 1787 highlighted the weak economic footing of most planters: one planter estimate was that only 20 out of 100 producers would survive unless the government intervened with price supports.[28] In any case, the continuous complaints about rent levels hardly reflect the concerns of an elite class, nor does the overwhelming use of free labour in the Aragua valleys.[29]

As was the case with other crops, the wealthy individuals associated with growing indigo usually owned their haciendas and had slaves working their holdings. A sample of twelve plantations growing indigo, taken from the notarial archives, confirms this observation.[30] All but one are privately owned. Interestingly, four of the twelve only grew indigo as a sideline or in conjunction with other crops. Slaves were used not only on the mixed haciendas, but also on a number of the plantations exclusively growing indigo. Felipe de Francia had at least fifty slaves on his holding in 1784; Matías Ovalle twenty-three on his in 1793; and the Bolívar family fourteen on their plantation in Suata in 1792.[31]

The comparable possibilities for profit of the two basic types of hacienda which governed indigo production were probably very uneven. The renter *hacendado* was at a distinct disadvantage to his owner counterpart. A 1787 *representación* by the planters of Maracay calculated that:

'Most of the haciendas here, if not all, use *jornaleros*, paying them each six to seven pesos a month apart from food which . . . adds another two pesos [to costs]; if we add, as we should, the land rentals at ten pesos and even more for each fanega per year, and the salaries of overseers, and the costs of machinery it is not adventurous to suggest that each pound of indigo today costs 9½–10 rls to produce.'[32]

Prices in that year were down to 7 and 8 reales a pound, so their plight was temporarily exaggerated. Nevertheless prices were rarely over 10 to 12 reales even in good times, so the potential for profit remained low. The same cannot be said of the minority of indigo *hacendados* who owned their land and who worked their holdings with slaves. Two major costs, those of rental and salaries, were eliminated, and so the possibilities for making money even in periods of low prices may have been high.

Coffee

Coffee was the last major addition to colonial Caracas' diversifying export economy before the independence struggle broke out in 1810. Coffee exports rose from an insignificant few hundred quintales a year in the 1780s to over 60,000 quintales by 1809, with a corresponding rise in coffee's share of the total value of export from less than 1% to about 20%.[33] By 1830 coffee was the dominant export crop of all Venezuela.[34]

At least until 1810, the growth of coffee did not imply a corresponding decline in the importance of cacao. Rather, an enterprising minority in the province saw the possibilities of profit in coffee and began to found new haciendas dedicated to its production. As far as can be determined, the pioneers belonged to established and wealthy families of Caracas. Few new fortunes were made in this phase of coffee's rise, old ones were merely augmented. The owners of the new coffee haciendas include the wealthiest agriculturalists of the province: Martín de Tovar Ponte, Isidoro López Méndez, the Conde de San Xavier, the Conde de la Granja, the Morenos, the Machillandas, José María Toro, Dr Tomás Hernández Sanabria, and members of the Blanco, Palacios and Ribas clans.[35]

The preponderance of wealth among early coffee growers may have had much to do with the level of investment necessary to start a coffee hacienda. Coffee was not a cheap commodity to begin to produce. The planted tree requires anywhere from five to eight years to enter full production. Labour was needed to care for the trees in their transitional phase from seedling to fruit-bearing *arbores*. Irrigation was an added cost in lands of uneven rainfall. And, unlike cacao, the berries needed husking or at least drying out before being marketed. Terraces or *patios y oficina de beneficio* had to be constructed for these purposes. The *isleño* Juan Hernández Quintero, in company with his brother, in 1805 began a plantation with 70,000 trees on land in Petare worth 511 pesos (including a house), with 8 slaves and 8 mules.[36] The total investment was 5,624 pesos, which, as should be apparent by now, was no small sum in the context of *caraqueño* society. Coffee did have one immediate advantage over cacao: more of its trees could be compressed into a smaller area. Over 5,000 fit into a fanegada versus an average for cacao of little over 1,000 trees.[37] Much less labour was needed as a result. One worker could care for 3,000–4,000 coffee trees *vs* about 1,000 of cacao.[38]

The comparative size of the early coffee haciendas can be measured to some extent through a sample of 33 plantations in production by 1820 growing coffee full-time or in conjunction with other crops.[39] Only 2 held less than 10,000 trees. The distribution of the rest by tree-size is as follows: 10 between 10,000 and 19,999 trees; 7 between 20,000 and 49,999 trees; and 14 over 50,000 trees.

Several of the larger coffee haciendas employed deceptively few slaves: the Conde de San Xavier used 47 for his 174,000 trees; Andrés Moreno and Guillermo Alzuru allocated only 8 and 12 slaves respectively to haciendas of at least 60,000 trees each.[40] As we have seen, this was largely a reflection of the needs of production. Slaves, in whatever numbers, may well have been indispensable to the early years of coffee. The cost of paying free workers to care for trees in their growing years could have been prohibitive. Isidoro López Méndez, probably the largest producer of coffee in the province before 1810, stated specifically in his will that no *peónes* were used on two of his haciendas.[41]

The profitability of coffee production was likely to have been high in the late-colonial period. For a start, the value of a new hacienda increased greatly at no additional maintenance cost as soon as the trees matured. The price per tree rose from ¼ real to 4 and 6 reales over 4 or 5 years, a remarkable appreciation. Once the coffee trees enter their full productive cycle they can bear ½ kilogram (just over 1 pound) of berries a year of first-grade coffee for about 10 years before quality begins to drop. In so far as many, if not most, coffee plantations in Caracas were in, or about to enter, their full productive life, most of the coffee was more than likely of high-priced, first-grade quality. By way of a specific example there is the case of the Conde de La Granja, who in 1796 estimated that a modest coffee plantation of 18,000 trees which he had recently founded would, within a couple of years, earn him 2,000 pesos a year after operating expenses.[42] As for the giant haciendas owned by Isidoro López Méndez and the Conde de San Xavier, with 130,000 and 174,000 trees respectively, the profit margin may have been immense. Both haciendas seem to have been in full production before 1810, and an optimistic calculation of their joint production would give these two men control of 5% of the province's coffee exports in 1809.[43] In addition, López Méndez partly owned two other plantations producing at least another 1,500 quintales across 1808 and 1809.[44] Whatever the actual rate of return, coffee by 1810 was posed to become the wave of the future.

Sugar-cane

Sugar-cane production is always underestimated as a major component in surveys of the colonial economy. It is true that it hardly figured in export lists, but, as was the case with livestock production, its primary function lay in supplying the needs of the domestic market. In a Caribbean world where first Haiti and later Jamaica and Havana were more favourably placed to cultivate sugar-cane in abundance, there was never really any question of late-eighteenth-century Caracas producing for export. That said, *caña* production carried considerable weight within the structure of the internal economy of the province. The crop was an important foodstuff and the basic ingredient for the manufacture of local spirits. In 1775 the annual production of sugar-cane was estimated to be 195,000 arrobas for a total value of over 650,000 pesos.[45] Sugar-cane was marketed in three basic forms: as sugar, as raw canesticks or *papelón* and as the finished by-product *aguardiente*, a cane-based spirits.[46]

The cultivation of sugar-cane in the province already had a long history coming into the late eighteenth century, and showed no signs of having exhausted its potential for expansion. Two surveys dated about twelve years apart indicate that the number of haciendas dedicated to growing sugar-cane was still gradually increasing.[47] Around 1770 there were 348 sugar plantations in the province; by 1787 there were 436.[48] Two regions held the overwhelming majority of the haciendas: the Segovia Highlands and the Coastal Range region. Within the latter, the Aragua and Tuy valleys near the city of Caracas predominated.

Sugar planters had to make comparatively large investments in machinery, slave labour and beasts of burden. The heavy infrastructure of many sugar plantations was primarily a reflection of the complexity of commercializing the crop. The turning of cane into white sugar, *papelón*, brown sugar, alcohol and cane-juice or *melados* required a large labour force as well as different pieces of machinery, which were often driven by animal power. Even modest sugar plantations were likely to have the basic extracting- and grinding-mill (*trapiche* or sometimes *ingenio*), and any planter interested in refining his cane into marketable products also needed boiler units, settling-tanks, ovens and distiller machinery.

Sugar plantations invariably contained slaves, and probably in higher numbers than the haciendas growing other crops. In a group of 61 plantations exclusively growing sugar-cane for which slave numbers per hacienda are available, the distribution is the following: 24% held between 1 and 19 slaves; 45% between 20 and 39; and 31% over 40.[49] One factor may largely explain the sugar plantations' heavy reliance on slaves. Sugar-cane production was a year-round affair; and its needs included not only caring for planted fields and harvesting the crop but also manufacturing cane by-products on a regular basis.

The relative weight of the different factors of production in the total worth of an hacienda can at least be guessed at from a sample of 11 large haciendas for which full inventories are available.[50] Their monetary value did of course account for residential houses, fallow land and the like, which had little or no bearing on the production of sugar-cane, and whose worth could vary considerably from hacienda to hacienda. All the same, the information on the basic factors of production is proportional enough to allow some observations. Slaves would appear to have been the most valuable part of the infrastructure of a sugar plantation. On 9 of the 11 haciendas, slaves represented between 35% and 50% of the total value, and on the remaining two 26% to 27%. The value of sugar-cane plots or *tablones* ranged between 5% to 15% of the total value of the plantations of the sample. The variations in the value of machinery tended to be in direct proportion to the size of the plantation. Two haciendas in the sample worth 21,346 pesos and 21,353 pesos, got by with the basic mill and boiler installations at costs of about 1,600 pesos and 2,200 pesos respectively. Three others, worth 38,723, 40,216 and about 115,000 pesos contained all the possible components at values of 8,000–9,000 pesos each.

What of the profitability of sugar-cane production? The 1775 survey indicates that the average production figure for sugar haciendas was 1,886 pesos. Gross production figures of course say little about net gains. These were likely to have been remarkable on the larger haciendas even after allowing for the probably comparatively high production costs. Around 1800, 'Mocundo', probably the largest plantation in the province, registered a minimum net profit of 15,000 pesos or 13% of the total value of the plantation.[51] When it is considered that the portion of the hacienda dedicated to the production of sugar-cane was less than 60% of its total worth, and that the hacienda had probably long before recovered its initial investment, the profit margin for its owner, the Marqués del Toro, begins to look enormous.

The phenomena of hacienda rentals also attests to the profitability of the crop. Alone among the province's plantations, sugar haciendas were rented out on seven- and nine-year contracts at over 1,000 pesos/year. It was not a case of owners leasing to disguised tenant farmers or care-takers to free the real proprietors of the burdens of running their hacien-das. In two examples the haciendas rented out were turned over to two of the richest merchants of the province.[52] After 1815, when the roya-list government was renting or selling over 200 confiscated properties, only sugar haciendas were taken up with alacrity by eligible renters and buyers.[53] The rentals on three large plantations bear witness to the con-tinued profitability, or at least productivity, of sugar-cane, even in wartime. The Ribas family's 'El Palmar', valued at 30,000 pesos, rented for 2,049 pesos ½ real; Simón Bolívar's 'San Mateo', worth 35,000, went for a lower 1,812 pesos, ½ real; and 'Mocundo' was leased for 9,031 ¼ pesos. It is to be assumed that the value of production was substantially higher than the above figures, if leasing was to be at all viable for the renters.

Tobacco

Little is known about the structure of tobacco cultivation before 1779, the year the state tobacco monopoly was founded.[54] The only estimate of production available for a period before the 1780s is for 1720, a year when 23,200 arrobas were produced throughout Venezuela.[55] Appar-ently most of this crop was exported, legally or via contraband. Some time in the eighteenth century Venezuelans became widely addicted to tobacco if, as seems possible, they had not been before. Certainly the royal intention in creating the monopoly in 1779 was to take advantage of the commercial potential of a local market consuming most of a dom-estically produced crop. In 1779 the number of consumers in the province of Caracas was estimated at 75,000 to 150,000 out of a total population of nearly 300,000 after excluding the poor, children and non-smokers.[56]

The monopoly was virtually an instant success. Production reached a

high of 41,000 arrobas in 1797 in the province of Caracas alone, generating profits of over 50% the cost of production.[57] In quantitative
terms this meant a net income for the monopoly of between 200,000
and 400,000 pesos per year in the 1780s, of over 500,000 pesos in the
mid-1790s and of over 600,000 pesos in the last fifteen years before
1810.[58] The province of Caracas generated two thirds of production and
value.

There were of course difficulties in the first four or five years of the
monopoly's life. Much of it was of a socio-political nature.[59] Hardship
was caused to small planters who lived outside the new designated areas
of production and to the petty retailers who rolled and sold the tobacco
before the *estanco*.[60] Yet the monopoly was able to identify and resolve
these problems. Hundreds of small planters were incorporated into
Guaruto and Orituco, the two main areas allocated for production.
Administrative changes in the early 1780s ensured that cigar rollers and
the like were employed by monopoly factories and retail outlets. The
number of planters in Guaruto and Orituco never dropped below 500
per year between 1791 and 1804 and sometimes rose to over 1,000.[61]
These hundreds of planters employed thousands of day-workers. An
account of the fevers which had decimated the population of the Aragua
valleys between 1806 and 1808 spoke of 7,000 or 8,000 labourers
involved in tobacco.[62]

Tobacco production itself never had an easy time, in spite of the size
of revenue it generated and the relative ease of the institutionalization of
the monopoly. The government must assume some of the blame for the
problems tobacco faced. The low prices it paid planters for the crop
allowed it to make huge profits but they also discouraged and indebted
the small planters who cultivated the crop under monopoly supervision.
Increasingly the monopoly had to bail these individuals out. The
government never claimed its loans, and the subsidies probably permitted a far greater number of small planters to survive than would otherwise have been the case. By 1809 levels of indebtedness among Guaruto
and Orituco planters had reached staggering proportions, possibly over
300,000 pesos.[63]

Among the other obstacles tobacco had to face in the late-colonial
period were the prevailing poor practices in the use of the land. The
impossibility of making a profit must have provided little incentive to
all but the most dogged of individuals to care properly for their crops.
One 1787 report spoke of the 'disorder' in the plantation areas and the
tendency of planters to spend the advances they received on 'gambling
and other vices' rather than for production.[64] An 1804 survey referred

to the 'indolent . . . poor, and vicious' character of most *labradores*.[65] If the planters showed such a lack of dedication to their own welfare, what could be expected of the uninterested, free-labour force which worked the plots? It is not difficult to speculate what cultivation methods in such conditions were like: tobacco is a great waster of soil, and careless cultivating habits must have taken their toll, accounting for the increasingly low yields. The planting of 13 million plants in 1790 produced 34,000 arrobas, or an average of less than 3 arrobas per 1,000 plants. By 1797 some 25 million plants were producing only 41,000 arrobas or less than 2 per 1,000 plants.[66]

It is possible to establish to some extent the size of the hundreds of *plantaciones*, thanks to the thoroughness of the book-keeping by monopoly officials.[67] There is, for example, no question that the size of the holdings declined across the life of the monopoly. In 1785, 192 planters in the Guaruto area, which was by far the largest tobacco-producing enclave in Venezuela, planted 18.2 million plants for an average of 94,661 per planter. By 1797 some 544 planters shared 25.1 million plants for an average 46,250 per planter. By 1804, 627 *labradores* were planting, in an admittedly unusually low crop due to natural disasters, 11.8 million plants for an average of 18,819 per planter. The decline in the average size of holdings must have correspondingly diminished the earnings of most planters. An account book for Guaruto for 1818 gives an indication of the poverty and low earnings of most planters.[68] The picture may be overpessimistic in that by 1818 the monopoly's earnings as a whole were only half what they were in 1809, and many fewer individuals were planting. Still, the figures are of interest. The Guaruto book lists around 650 planters, not all of whom were producing. Of the 321 who were, 65% grossed 200 pesos or less from their crop. A further 26% grossed between 200 and 500 pesos. Only 26 earned beyond that figure. Once costs and advances from the monopoly were deducted, few planters made a profit, and the vast majority of them remained indebted.

Livestock production

The true economic function of livestock production in colonial Caracas has been fundamentally misunderstood. The stress has nearly always been placed on production for export, which generated only a very small part of the industry's income. Animals on hoof were produced essentially for domestic consumption, and together with tobacco and sugar-cane derivatives formed the triumvirate of commodities which dominated the domestic economy of the province.[69]

The province of Caracas held about 800,000 head of *ganado mayor* (cattle, horses and mules) in the late-colonial period.[70] The large herds served a dual function there as elsewhere in Venezuela, providing both food and transport for the population. Perhaps the provision of food should be considered the primary and even paramount use made of the herds. The average consumption per inhabitant in Caracas was over 136 kilograms (300 pounds) a year.[71] The latest year for which information on total consumption in the province is available is 1761. In that year 180,000 inhabitants consumed nearly 140,000 cattle.[72] There was a reason for this comparatively pronounced dependence on meat. Grain production, especially of wheat, had declined in importance since before the end of the seventeenth century, and by the late eighteenth century did not meet the province's requirements. Maize was cultivated mostly on small properties, for commercial purposes to be sure, but probably not in quantities large enough to satisfy demand. That Caracas avoided the famine which plagued New Spain in the 1700s can largely be attributed to the substitution of meat for grain as the basic foodstuffs of the people.

Caracas did not supply all its own needs of livestock produce. It particularly fell short on the question of beef. In order to supply its population in 1787, Caracas would have had to slaughter almost half of its cattle herd. The evidence is that the deficit was made up from the province of Barinas, which had largely been part of Caracas until it became a separate jurisdiction in 1786. It had a population of only 33,000 in 1787 but over 600,000 head of *ganado mayor*, rivalling the size of the Caracas herds.[73] The 504,879 head of cattle listed, produced a surplus of 126,585, far more than the local population could possibly have consumed.

The *hatos* in the late-colonial period were concentrated in the Llanos region. All but 153 or 18% of the 863 ranches of *ganado mayor* listed in the 1787 survey were located in Llanos jurisdiction.[74] The average *hato*, as measured by herd-size in the 1787 survey, had just over 900 head. Gross averages can be misleading, but in this case the calculation opens the way to an important observation. Many if not most *hatos* were smaller than legend would have us believe, and small in absolute terms. A 1789 report actually established what in provincial measures represented large, medium and small *hatos*.[75]

maximum size:	8,000 and over
large:	4,000–8,000
medium:	3,000–6,000
small:	1,000–3,000

A sample from the notarial archives tends to corroborate the above. Of 33 ranches on which herd-size is available only 5 had over 8,000 head, whilst 16 had less than 3,000.[76]

The number of livestock was one measure of size; the amount of land per *hato* was another. A sample of 35 holdings does give some idea of the immense diversity of size: 10 were less than 5 leguas in extent; 7 were between 5 and 10 leguas; 8 were between 10 and 20 leguas; 4 were between 20 and 30 leguas; and 6 were over 50 leguas in size ranging up to the 300 claimed by the Tovar clan.[77] The holdings which immediately attract attention are the largest. They are far greater in area than has been suspected by latifundista theorists and dwarf the size of the *hatos* contained in a list composed by an historian covering the first half of the eighteenth century.[78] It is probable that most of the largest *hatos* of the later period got their start in the earlier decades of the century if not before. It should be pointed out that area totals included much land seemingly not worked in any organized fashion. Thus, Gervasio de Ponte, the illegitimate son of Pedro Domingo de Ponte, sold off portions of his 130 leguas with or without animals, and the 300 leguas owned or claimed by the Tovars included squatters and *hatos* they had nothing to do with. Ultimately, however, perhaps the most surprising aspect of the *hato* economy is not the presence of huge latifundias but the survival of the 863 individual *hatos* listed in the 1787 survey.

It is unlikely that most *hatos* fulfilled their profit potential. For a start, cattle-rustling was a serious and constant problem. Reference has already been made to the apparent complicity of the workers of the *hatos* in such enterprises. The neighbouring province of Cumaná faced a serious meat shortage in 1808 as many *hateros* gave up ranching in the face of widespread rustling.[79] Perhaps even more detrimental to the development of *hatos* was the indiscriminate slaughter of calves and heifers along with cows and bulls, impeding any great increase in herd-sizes.[80] By the early 1800s it was clear that the herds simply were not reproducing fast enough. In 1810 the price of meat was four times what it had been a few years earlier, suggesting a growing scarcity.[81] It is not surprising that when the independence wars began to disrupt production, and wandering armies and marauders killed for food, the herds quickly dwindled to a few hundred thousand head across Venezuela.

The variety of land-tenure patterns, the different economies of production of individual cash crops, the extensive use of free labour, the existence of a middle class of planters and ranchers, the small scale of production and the presence of an independent, salaried labour force clash with the traditional images of *caraqueño* plantation society. But perhaps the most notable characteristic of provincial agriculture in social and political terms was its profitability. The *hacendados* who owned the best of the province's agricultural units were therefore on a strong enough economic footing to deal with their apparent economic rivals, the import–export merchants. The latter, in contrast, worked within a much weaker economic framework as we shall now see.

4

Commerce

The export merchants

The Caracas Company had handled the bulk of the province's commercial activities for over fifty years by the time it was formally abolished in 1784. Only contraband and the New Spain cacao trade had remained in the hands of merchants independent of the company. The relatively sudden demise of the monopoly therefore left a vacuum in the mercantile structure which was only gradually filled during the next decade or so. The distortions caused by the company's departure were real and painful. In 1783 the Intendant, Saavedra, described the deficiencies then current in bleak though not entirely hopeless terms:

'The Country [Caracas] is poor and consumes little . . . and no one [no merchant] can be found who can carry [finance] a [ship] load of 30,000 pesos. As commerce until now has been in one hand there are no runners, agents . . . warehouses, and other conveniences which [however] time will provide. A commerce sub-divided among many hands [traders] will make these provinces flower.'[1]

The development of the competitive commercial structure hoped for by Saavedra was exactly what occurred in the following years. The evolution was a rocky one, and at times it must have seemed to contemporaries that it would never materialize. As late as 1787 there were serious complaints by both royal officials and agriculturalists against the new mercantile establishment which was replacing the Caracas Company. In the first place, the monopoly's ghost lingered on in the form of the Filipinas Company, which exercised a right to carry a high proportion of the province's exports to Spain.[2] Secondly, a manipulative oligopoly seemed to have moved into the space once occupied by the monopoly, if a bitter exposition by indigo planters is to be believed.[3] They acidly remarked that the existing trade structure of Caracas represented anything but freedom of exchange:

Free trade would indeed exist if . . . 'the Province had such a variegated commercial structure that fifty or sixty *registros* a year [coming] from different parts
of Spain and consigned to a like number of merchants . . .' carried the trade,
'. . . because then it would be much more difficult . . . for three or four [mer-
chants] as is the case at present' to collude on prices paid for export goods and
charged for imports. 'But as the number in commerce here is so reduced, the
so-called freedom far from aiding the planter is prejudicial to him. It is a
freedom enjoyed only by the merchant who in his hands has the key to open
and shut the door as he wishes'. Worse, the merchants 'do not have enough
capital to purchase [all] the exportable goods the Province produces.'

To accentuate their point the indigo growers claimed elsewhere that the
Filipinas Company and the two merchant firms of Jose Escorihuela and
the Iriarte brothers controlled the export trade.[4] Only perhaps a half-
dozen other individuals were large enough traders in their own right to
be taken into consideration.

How far this situation had changed by the 1790s, for change it did,
is revealed by the ship registers for trade from La Guaira to Spain
between August 1795 and September 1796.[5] The complete cargo lists
for 41 ships sailing in this period provide an unparalleled opportunity
to quantify both the number of individuals in Caracas involved in the
transatlantic exchange and the size of their transactions. It will be
remembered that the La Guaira–Spain connection represented 90% of
the province's trade by 1795, so we can be confident that the cargo lists
will give as comprehensive an overview of the *caraqueño* export traders as
we are likely to get.

What the figures disclose is that about 250 people were engaged in
sending goods to Spain in the year under consideration. The level of
concentration of the volume of trade was considerably diminished in
comparison to the mid-1780s. In the case of cacao exports (60% of the
total in the mid-1790s) the largest carrier, Segura y Grasi Co., ferried
only 11.5% of the trade.[6] The next largest shipper, the Iriarte brothers,
cornered 7.8% of the market. Another five companies, including the
Filipinas Cia., carried between 2.9% and 6% of the volume.[7] All other
traders had less than a 2.5% share. The distribution was similar in the
case of indigo (30% of total exports). Two merchants, J. E. Echezuría
and J. B. Oruesagasti, each exported about 10% of the crop.[8] The next
four largest firms sent between 3.6% and 5.9% of the volume.[9] It is to
be supposed that with the emergence of a competitive environment the
necessary infrastructure for trade referred to by Saavedra also began to
appear.

It can be argued that the evidence still suggests an abnormally high level of concentration of trade in too few hands. Such a case would represent a prejudiced view, however. The seven biggest cacao traders and the six major indigo exporters controlled only 41.6% and 39% of the export volume of the respective commodities. Furthermore, in the case of both commodities there was a group of 30 or so middle-sized merchants who carried another 23–25% of the trade.[10] As stated, hundreds of others participated in export commerce, albeit at a very modest level. It is misguided to assume that an economy as small as this, and with only one major port, La Guaira, could have supported a more diversified export commercial establishment than that which existed in the 1790s.

The question remains of why the transformation took place. Part of the answer is that it had to. The province was forced to find a commercial structure to replace the Caracas Company's monopoly. That it evolved the way it did is explained by the rapid growth rate of the economy in the 1780s and 1790s and by the application of the 1778 free-trade decree to Caracas in 1789. The pronounced expansion of the economy required the participation of an increased number of traders to traffic in this volume of exports. Already in 1786–7 it was clear that the largest merchant firms in the province did not have the capital or the means to carry all commodities even if they had wanted to. The introduction of the 1778 measure allowing free trade within the boundaries of the empire further speeded the process of transformation. Cumbersome restrictions on the number of toneladas allowed into the province and on possible ports of entry into Spain were removed, destroying the preponderance of the Filipinas Company, which had been based on the *tonelage* statutes. A much wider group of buyers on the Península entered the exchange, employing new purchasing-agents in the *caraqueño* ports. By 1795–6, a minimum of 144 companies and individuals, in centres as far apart as Santander, Barcelona and Cádiz, were receiving goods from our province.[11] The figure is in strong contrast to the situation fifteen years earlier, when one Spanish buyer alone controlled the trade.

Anyone who exported goods abroad for commercial purposes was apparently considered a *comerciante* or merchant, in everyday lexicon in late-colonial Caracas.[12] The generic term covered the occupational distinctions which existed among the group of individuals who trafficked in exports. Wholesalers, large-scale retailers (*mercaderes*), middle-sized and small shopowners (*bodegueros*), transient ship captains and agriculturalists exporting their own produce all participated in the overseas trade.[13] *Comerciante* as a legal term, however, was only applicable to wholesalers engaged in foreign exchange who did not act directly as retailers. Wholesalers did in fact carry the bulk of the import–export trade. Of the 40-odd merchants and firms just analysed in connection with cacao and indigo exports in 1795–6, 26 were represented in the Consulado as wholesalers.[14]

The commercial network structured and run by the merchant community was not complicated. Insofar as exports were concerned, the primary aim was to move the goods from the production areas to the ports and load them onto ships for delivery to import firms abroad. In the case of wholesalers and large retailers, the practice was either to send agents into the countryside to buy direct from producers, or to await the arrival to the ports of commodities bound for export.[15] As the city of Caracas was centrally located between the major producing-areas of the Aragua and Tuy valleys, it too acted as a purchasing-centre for potential exports.[16] From Caracas, merchants then ferried the goods down to La Guaira to be stored in warehouses or placed on ships. In the case of agriculturalists who shipped their own crops, the produce was sent directly to ships, by-passing the middle-men.[17] It seems probable that many producers stopped just short of taking total responsibility for exporting their products by selling instead directly to the captains of individual ships. This hypothesis would help explain the low number of *hacendados* listed in the cargo inventories as well as the high bulk volume of goods consigned to captains who had no direct connection with the province.[18]

The merchants and retailers in their transactions with Spain acted mostly as agents for firms based in Spanish ports. This was recognized by contemporaries and is supported by data in the 1795–6 cargo lists. Comparatively few local shippers took on the risk of the loss of their shipment at sea: more often than not the consignment was a *cuenta y riesgo* of the receiving firm in Spain.[19] The incidence of local ship ownership accordingly seems to have been low. In the case of the Spanish connections local traders seemed to have depended for conduits almost entirely on ships sent from Spain. Of the 41 ships involved in the 1795–6 traffic, only 3 were consigned to locally based merchants.[20] Even this fact did not necessarily connote ownership. A similar dependency on non-*caraqueño* transport was exhibited in the trade with the foreign colonies.[21] Only in the exchange with New Spain was the situation reversed. The ships used in this commerce, as we shall see, were virtually all locally owned. In short the Caracas mercantile community did not really commandeer its own flotilla.

The 1795–6 cargo registers suggest that no merchant or firm in the province invested more than 250,000 pesos a year to send goods to Spain. Indeed only one merchant, Joaquín Segura y Grasi, went over the 200,000-pesos level that year.[22] It is true that 5%-10% of the province's exports in that period were not represented by the La Guaira–Spain exchange; all the same, microeconomic data outside the registers leave little doubt that the latter accurately measured the upper levels of investment by individuals and firms in foreign trade. The participation of even the largest traders in sales to the foreign Caribbean and to New Spain does not seem to have markedly increased their volume of activity. The two largest private (i.e., non-corporate) concerns active in 1787, those of the Iriarte brothers and José Escorihuela, were estimated together to have at most 400,000 pesos to invest in goods.[23] Both these companies traded with Veracruz as well as Spain, and in addition owned their own ships.[24] The fifth largest company in 1795–6 as measured by exports to Spain, Muñoz-Orea, was capitalized in 1785 at 80,000 pesos.[25] In 1808 the Camacho brothers founded a company to be based in Puerto Cabello, capitalized at 142,475 pesos.[26] The latter examples demonstrate, if nothing else, how quick the fall-off was behind the two or three leading exporters. Indeed, the cut-off point which distinguished large merchants from middle-sized and smaller ones seems to have been 50,000 pesos according to contemporary rules of measure.[27] Other scattered cases of the capitalization of export businesses confirm what the 1795–6 inventories revealed: the typical trader in Caracas was of modest economic proportions.[28]

Counted among *caraqueño* traders were major landowners, including the Marqués de Mijares and Martín de Tovar y Ponte. Departing from the image of planters held captive by exploitative, non-native-born merchants, there was in fact a small but powerful group of *hacendados* who also acted as merchants. Their names were most clearly connected with the New Spain trade. Most of the *hacendados* involved in the trade not only exported cacao but also carried it in ships they owned. This display of independence was hardly rivalled by the largest wholesalers engaged in the transatlantic trade. Furthermore their floating transports were not of the schooner variety which plied the coastal trade. The ships were *bona-fide* frigates comparable to the largest ships used in the exchange with Spain. Manuel de Clemente y Francia's ship *San Carlos* was capable of carrying 13,000 fanegas of cacao, or, in other words, the total annual volume of exports to Veracruz in the 1780s.[29] Other ship owning *hacendados* included Manuel Felipe de Tovar, the Marqués del Toro, the Conde de Tovar, José María de Tovar and Diego Moreno.[30]

Hacendado domination of the New Spain exchange was impressive but on its way out, as the trade declined in value through the 1780s and early 1790s. It is difficult to trace in what ways the plantation owners transferred their commercial interests, but transfer them they did. A number may simply have sold off their assets: Manuel Felipe de Tovar gave up his ship to a transient *canario* merchant for 2,000 pesos.[31] More likely, however, was that the *hacendados* moved into the other markets. Manual Clemente y Francia and the Marqués del Toro were well represented in the 1795–6 consignments to Spain, as was another powerhouse of the local economy, the future Marqués de Casa León. Furthermore, other individuals began to move in. Santiago Villalonga of the interior town of Barquisimeto bought a ship in 1801 from a Catalan captain.[32] Joaquín de Ibarra, member of a long-established Caracas family, bought his own boat in 1804.[33] The same Ibarra in 1809 signed a contract with the colonial government to ship 8,000 arrobas of *tasajo*, or dried meat, to Spain.[34] The Marqués de Casa León was involved in a similar contract in 1810.[35] The Marqués del Toro as early as 1782 received permission to export directly to Spain.[36] The Ribas brothers, following in their father's footsteps, became involved in the slave-trade in the early 1800s.[37] Another wealthy *hacendado*, Bernardo Butrageño, received permission to export to Cadiz in 1793.[38]

A separate question affecting all participants in the province's trade was the extent to which they were free to act in their own interests. As has been stated earlier, most traders shipping to Spain were purchasing-agents for parent firms abroad. But what exactly did being a purchasing-agent imply? Whatever else it meant, it did not necessarily tie a local trader down to working for one particular firm in Spain.[39] Nor did being a purchasing-agent preclude engaging in trade for strictly personal profit. Felipe Llaguno in 1789 was not unusual in having deals outstanding in three ports in Spain, in Curacao and in Santo Domingo and Havana.[40] It is probable that the trade with Spain was mostly financed at the receiving end, but this did not necessarily imply that Caracas-based merchants were not capable of financing their other deals themselves.

The financing of commercial transactions, in whatever form it was done, took place in the context of a severe currency shortage in Caracas, which affected not only the circulation of goods and services inside the province but the sale of commodities abroad. Intendant Saavedra in the mid-1780s noted the lagging effect of the lack of currency.[41] The situation may have worsened in the late 1780s. As the economy expanded, treasury revenues increased, generating hard-currency surpluses of up to 300,000 pesos a year in the 1780s and early 1790s.[42] These were regularly shipped to Spain, thus draining the province of much-needed capital even as it was being created.

In 1791 the royal officials of the province, with the co-operation of local merchants and agriculturalists, put into practice a financial scheme which went a long way towards solving the liquidity problem.[43] The government still proposed sending its revenue surplus to Spain, but in such a fashion as not to deplete the local economy. Instead of sending the excess in hard currency, a system was set up whereby the money would be turned over to local traders and planters in exchange for promissory notes payable by the accredited merchant firms in Spain they were written against. The mercantile establishment at both ends of the trade probably gained considerably from the arrangement. For firms in Cadiz, who had previously found it necessary to supply their provincial agents regularly with funds either in cash or in kind to purchase the goods for export, the financial burden was probably markedly lessened. Even for those firms whose agents ran a profitable enough provincial business to pay for operating costs, the new source of credit offered a means of expanding their activities. The borrowing structure also probably allowed local merchants to receive payment in advance on specific shipments to Spain by using the promissory notes as the equivalent of bankers' acceptances.

The creation of a credit source which in lending potential could at times represent 10%-15% of the value of annual trade, was an important and remarkable addition to the financial system. The government in effect had stepped in to fulfill the function of an import–export bank. It did safeguard its interests by limiting participation to major merchants or wealthy *hacendados*. In all, I have located 91 promissory notes with a total value of 1,756,934 pesos issued in 1794–7, 1803–5 and 1809.[44] If further proof were needed that the province's *hacendados* participated in overseas trade, the names of the notes would dispel all doubts: the Mixares, Blanco, Toro, Palacios, Blandín, Tovar, Ibarra, Bolívar, Madriz, Ribas, Fernández de León and Ascanio *hacendado* families all had enough contacts with merchant houses in Spain to issue their own promissory notes.[45]

How profitable was the overseas trading of the province? The question is a difficult one to answer because there were so many different ways of participating in foreign commerce. The profit margins of shipowners, transient merchants, purchasing-agents, independent traders, producer-exporters and retailers were all likely to be different. The same merchant working on commission for a company in Spain probably earned much more exporting independently to New Spain. The prices a merchant could expect for commodities differed, depending on whether his transactions ended in the wharves of La Guaira or in the harbours of Spain, the foreign colonies, or Veracruz. The form of payment also probably varied considerably. It might take the form of imports in the case of an agent exporting to his parent firm in Spain, or it might be hard cash in the case of sales to all three markets. For merchants who had retail activities inside the province, final profit calculations would have to take into account domestic sales.

One case suggests that profits could be substantial. The López Méndez brothers' company, which ran from 1788 to August 1799, yielded a profit of 205,434 pesos 6½ reales, or an average of 17,119½ pesos a year.[46] Unfortunately, even though we can estimate the local market value of the goods it exported to Spain in 1795–6 (70,000 pesos) from the cargo registers for La Guaira, it is really impossible to know the total value of the exports the profits were derived from, or whether the profits were gross or net. Whatever the actual rate of return, it should be pointed out that profits may not have been what they seemed in the commercial branch of the economy. It was common practice for wholesalers and retailers to describe part of their assets in terms of *créditos activos*, that is money owed them by suppliers or consumers who had bought goods on credit. How concrete these assets were, probably varied tremendously from trader to trader but if the common experiences of middle-sized and large merchants approximated the circumstances of Domingo Francisco Zulueta, they were in trouble. A wholesaler, store-owner and *hacendado*, he died in 1831 leaving 109,180 pesos of uncollectable debts dating back to the 1790s.[47]

The internal market

One essential ingredient of the foreign-trade structure has been overlooked in the preceding discussion: the role of imports in merchant activities. They were, after all, fully half of the exchange equation, and it was more than likely that in most transactions they represented payments abroad for the province's exports. All the same, the network of the import trade is more usefully considered in the context of the domestic market which it served. The turnover of this market was composed primarily of the sale of imports such as textiles, flour and wines in addition to the commercialization of locally processed agricultural goods primarily derived from tobacco, livestock and sugar-cane.

Not all the domestic commercial activity in the province was open to the local merchant community. Indeed the evidence suggests it handled a surprisingly small part of it. One of the major indigenous commercial activities was the sale of tobacco products, which was exclusively the preserve of the government monopoly. Merchants were also partially excluded from the meat industry. Ranchers usually drove their own cattle to public, city slaughterhouses.[48] Much of the sugar consumed in the province was probably sold directly to consumers from the plantation. Retailing enterprises in the province were therefore probably limited to the sale of imported products, finished local food products and miscellaneous goods.

Another limiting factor on the retailing establishment was the character of the provincial economy. Outside of production for exports, the *caraqueño* economy lacked sophistication, and the needs it satisfied were basic if not rudimentary. The underdeveloped, underpopulated hinterland of the province prevented the emergence of a sizeable internal demand and the corresponding local production and commercial structures to service it. Only the city of Caracas had anything like enough of a large commercial turnover, and much of its sales activity was export-oriented. The land-sales tax figures give an accurate indication of the concentration of commerce in Caracas City. Although it contained only 9% of the province's population it collected roughly 30% of the *alcabala de tierra*.[49]

The twin effects of so much of commerce passing through untraditional channels and of a small and scattered market, took its toll on the retail traders, most obviously by limiting the size of their operations. Perhaps the only individuals capable of generating a large turnover were the wholesale *comerciantes* and those *mercaderes* who to all intents and purposes doubled as import–export merchants. The purveyors of imported goods had an advantage in being able to act as distributors for imports to all retail outlets removed from the two main ports and the city of Caracas. The inventories of *comerciantes* could be quite large. The López brothers were waiting on a consignment of 32,000 pesos worth of imports at the time of the dissolution of their company.[50]

The wholesalers and large *mercaderes* distributed their goods through a network of muleteers, through agents for the purchasing retailers and through the actual retailers themselves. Agustín Fuentes in Barquisimeto received 1,854 pesos 1½ reales in goods from Caracas for his store in November 1787.[51] José María Arteaga in the city 'imported' 7,543 pesos worth for the same purpose in April 1788.[52] Francisco Camacho in La Victoria in June 1804, instead of buying directly himself, bought 800 pesos of goods from Spain via Caracas through a trader who had first brought them to La Victoria.[53] Those retailers who lived in the city of Caracas of course purchased their inventories themselves. Such was the case of Manuel Franco, a middle-sized *mercader*, who also exported.[54] To supply his stores, he took 'diverse items . . . and effects on credit as is the custom' from the warehouses of city wholesalers.

The average sales volume generated by the retail stores below the level of the wholesalers was generally low. The approximate number of retail outlets throughout the province can actually be calculated because of information available on commercial establishments in fifteen villages, towns and cities holding one fifth of the population of Caracas.[55] The urban units include important regional centres such as Barquisimeto, Valencia, Maracay, La Victoria, Ocumare del Tuy and Calabozo as well as the port of La Guaira and the capital, Caracas. The sample is therefore quite representative. Projecting from the data on the above it can be estimated that the 2 million or so pesos worth of imports were scattered among 1,500-odd outlets. This works out to an annual average turnover of well under 2,000 pesos/year/store. When it is considered that the *mercerías* had a greater size than *bodegas*, which had a larger retail activity than the numerous *pulperías*, the sales potential of most stores begins to look decidedly meagre, even taking into account their undeniable traffic in goods other than imports.

The size of retailers can be established quite concretely through the sales-tax books of various towns. Extrapolating from 1797 figures on collections in Caracas City for one third of the year, the following statistics emerge: 62 *tiendas de mercería* had an average turnover of 1,010 pesos that year; 91 *pulperías* a turnover of 578½ pesos; and 83 *bodegas* a turnover of 420 pesos.[56] The situation was comparable for smaller towns and cities. The data for Valencia, an important population centre in the Aragua valleys, is particularly detailed for the year November 1787 – October 1788.[57] Included are not only the tax-collection figures but the sales volume they were levied on. Twenty *pulperos* reported turnovers in the region of 500-600 pesos for a year. Eleven *mercaderes* displayed more of a range, from a low of 320 pesos to a high of 2,785 pesos. The size of retail commercial establishments can also be measured by another yardstick: the capitalization levels of 78 individual stores.[58] The investments ranged from a few hundred pesos in the case of most *pulperías* and some *bodegas* to over 20,000 pesos in the case of some *mercerías*. Some 19 of the stores were capitalized at over 10,000 pesos each. A further 22 stood between 5,000 and 9,999 pesos, 31 between 1,000 and 4,999 pesos and 6 at less than 1,000 pesos.

If the preceding examples are at all indicative of the state of retailing in the province, it might well be asked why stores were so small. The answer may lie in a simple but viable conjecture. Although profit margins may have been high on sales, the market was finite, or at least expanding very slowly, so that traders were caught up in a circle where profits were made on low turnovers but where little extra capital was generated.[59] Where capital accumulation was possible, as in the case of large *mercaderes*, the money went into foreign trade and agricultural investments.

In a trade structure where commercial institutions such as guilds and banks were underdeveloped or non-existent; where the volume of exchange was relatively small and constant, and where firms were synonymous with individuals, the *caraqueño* merchant should have been in an enviable position. The reality, however, was that the commercial sector of the *caraqueño* economy was less imposing than many of its counterparts elsewhere in the empire. Merchants in Caracas, unlike merchants in other colonies, were not the final arbiters of the economy or even necessarily its strongest brokers. It was not just that the comparatively smaller economy of the province precluded commercial activity on the scale of, say, Buenos Aires, or Veracruz and Mexico City. The commercial branch of our economy was an altogether weaker entity, even when considered solely in the provincial context.

This worked to the advantage of the political balance inside Caracas. The large merchants of the province, in the light of the limitations placed on their pursuits, turned to agricultural holdings to establish a broader base for their wealth. In the process they drew closer to the *hacendado* elite of the colony.

PART THREE

Politics

5

Elites

Introduction

Sociologists tirelessly point out the difficulties of defining a social class in any given society. In the present study we have seen how caste and ethnic considerations, occupational overlap and social and economic mobility were constantly affecting the surface distinctions of colonial society. Social alignments comparable to class differentiation were still clearly visible, but their character was not necessarily formed by their relationship to the means of production nor by an easily identifiable confrontational perception of other 'classes'. This social complexity was nowhere more apparent than among the upper groups of the white caste which dominated the life of the province. Recognizable ethnic and occupational divisions would not seem to have been distinct enough to create a strong consciousness of class. What may have evolved instead was a 'ruling class' perception held in common by the disparate groups at the top in relation to the rest of society.

While it is difficult to speak of classes among the higher echelons of white society in Caracas, it is relatively simple to speak of a ruling elite. This of course assumes that there was a cohesiveness, collective consciousness and unity of purpose among those who were members of the elite, which may not have been present. As Crane Brinton in his classic analysis of revolution and *anciens régimes* has pointed out, the ruling groups in those societies were 'divided and inept' on the eve of their revolutions.[1] Interestingly, the case of late-colonial Caracas provides an example of a pre-revolutionary society where the cohesiveness of elites actually existed, at least until it was put under severe strain after Napoleon's invasion of Spain in 1808. The following chapters will establish the extent to which the different interest groups forming the ruling elite at the top of colonial society interacted, were co-opted and co-operated in the formulation of reactions to the often-common experi-

ences they faced in the decades leading up to 1808. In the process of
analysis it will become apparent that the almost collective leadership
exhibited by the ruling elite of the province, was perhaps unique in the
empire.

There can, therefore, be no better introduction to a discussion of the
political unravellings of the late-colonial period than a closer look at the
functional and sectorial elites of the province whom we have already
met in passing. The socio-economic milieu in which they functioned
has been examined in earlier chapters. The emphasis now will be on the
composition and role of the elites, taking into account such formative
factors as status, ethnicity, wealth, power, kinship, intermarriage and
social mobility.

The usual roll-call of influential groups in an agricultural, colonial
society includes wealthy merchants and *hacendados*, higher royal officials, senior clergy, lawyers and important military personnel. All these
had a role to play in late-colonial Caracas, but their influence varied
considerably. In the wider societal context of the province the two most
important elites were the *hacendados* and the merchants, supplemented
by a small handful of royal officials, lawyers and clergy. I have accordingly grouped the above into three main categories: *hacendados*, merchants and the professional class. They will be considered in turn
below. The denomination of individuals as important merchants or
agriculturalists has been immensely simplified by the existence of Consulado membership lists.[2] Membership in the Consulado was limited to
those *comerciantes* and *hacendados* whose minimum personal worth was
30,000 pesos, which meant that only the wealthier members of each
economic group could belong.[3] It must be pointed out, however, that
the economic classification in the Consulado was only a measure of an
individual's predominant pursuit. It did not mean he did not participate to a greater or lesser degree in both activities. What the lists do
provide is a means of approaching the divisions in the economic elites.

Hacendados

The agriculturalists included in the Consulado were arguably the
premier status group in late-colonial society. That is, they perceived of
themselves, and were perceived by everyone else, as being at the pinna-
cle of the social hierarchy. Their numbers included the oldest and most
established local families, who represented the only hereditary aristocracy in Caracas. They virtually monopolized the nobility titles granted
to the province, ran most town councils and officered the militias. The
caraqueño landed elite also exhibited at least three noteworthy character-

istics: economic dynamism, an apparently easy-going willingness to take new blood in regularly and longevity or historical continuity. Several of the province's leading families traced their roots back to the late 1500s and early 1600s and, more importantly, had been powerful since then. The three-generation cycle of the rise and fall of family fortunes visible in other Spanish colonies was markedly less prevalent in Caracas.[4] Continued economic success was indeed the hallmark of many families in the province, and successful newcomers tended to add to the landed privileged rather than to take the place of aristocracy on the wane. In the last decades of the eighteenth century it is clear that a new group of families were becoming part of the *hacendado* aristocracy. The preceding observations can be substantiated by taking a closer look below at the individual members of the Consulado.

A large, perhaps predominant, number of the *hacendado* half of the Consulado was made up of representatives of the oldest families of Caracas. By these I mean those whose ancestors arrived in the province before the War of the Spanish Succession (1701–13); that is, before the enshrining of the Bourbons on the Spanish throne ushered in a new, inquisitive attitude on the part of the Crown towards an until-then-neglected colony. Of 45 individuals named in Intendant Saavedra's preliminary 1786 list of *hacendados* who might be included in a future Consulado, at least 25, or 55%, belonged to the old families of the province. The 25 were distributed among 13 family groups. The 1786 selection was meant by Saavedra to be only a representative sample, but significantly it was packaged as taking in 'one or two individuals of *all* the notable families'.[5] The presence of the old families remained formidable even in the complete 1805–6 lists of *agricultores*, where 169 individuals were mentioned at least once. Of these, a minimum of 70, or just over 40%, belonged to 20 old families (including the 13 of the 1786 list). The surnames would have resounded at several earlier points of *caraqueño* history: Alonso Gil, (Jerés de) Aristiguieta, Ascanio, Berrotarán, Blanco, Bolívar, Herrera, Ibarra, (de la) Madriz, Mijares (de Solórzano), Martínez (de Porras), Obelmexías, Pacheco, Palacios (de Sojo), Plaza, Ponte, Rada, Rengifo, Toro and Tovar.[6] The origins of these families may partially account for the apparent receptiveness of the *hacendado* elite to latecomers to the province, specifically those who arrived from the 1720s onwards. A substantial number of the established families originally came from either the Basque country (Aristiguieta, Berrotarán, Bolívar, Madriz, Mijares, Plaza and Rada) or from the Canary Islands (Ascanio, Blanco, Herrera, Ponte and Toro). These regions were precisely the areas the new immigrants of the eighteenth century were coming from, as we have seen earlier.

A second, smaller, identifiable group among the Consulado *hacendados* consisted of immigrants and their offspring who had established themselves in the province after 1700, primarily during the tenure of the Caracas Company (1728–84). At least 5 agriculturalists of the 1786 list and 34, or 20%, of the 1805–6 lists fall into the above category. The 39 were distributed among 23 families. They were: Anza, Berdú, Butrageño, Blandaín, Cocho de Iriarte, Clemente y Francia, Domínguez, Echezuría, Escorihuela, Fernández Leon, Gonzalez (Elias), Hernández Sanabria, López Méndez, Machado, Moreno, Muro, Mora, Paz del Castillo, Reverón, Ribas, Sanz, Vega(s) and Velez Mier y Teran.[7] The European origins of the founders of the new *hacendado* families were slightly more varied than those of the old. They came from three points: the Canary Islands (Domínguez, López Méndez, Machado, Paz del Castillo, Reverón and Ribas); the Basque country (Anza, Echezuría and Escorihuela); and from central and southern Spain. A noticeable number of the second wave of immigrants began their new lives in commerce-related activities. The López Méndez and Clemente y Francia families, for example, were the progeny of Caracas Company employees.[8] The trend for new agriculturalists to arrive via commerce was if anything becoming more accentuated in the late eighteenth century, as we shall presently see.

What made the *hacendado* families who composed the agricultural elite stand out? In a caste society supported by legalized status differentiation it might be assumed that wealth took a less prominent position in deciding the hierarchy. This was most decidedly not the case. Riches and status and power were inextricably linked in provincial society.

The following discussion of wealth is based primarily on information contained in the wills deposited in the notarial records for late-colonial Caracas. These include the wills (and/or their execution) of 22 (49%) of the individuals in the 1786 Consulado list, and of 38 (22%) of those on the 1805–6 lists.[9] In addition there is information on the wealth of 3 others (7%) for 1786, and 23 others (about 14%) for 1805–6 through the wills of their parents and wives.[10] The data are far from uniform. Few persons actually went to the trouble of enumerating the exact value of all their holdings. All the same, the revelations of the combined data bring us closer than ever before to gauging the economic strength of agriculturalists in the province, and on its own merits the information proves itself to be remarkably complete. Three clear ranges of wealth emerge from the data: over 200,000 pesos in assets, 100,000–200,000 pesos and less than 100,000 pesos. The two upper levels are worth examining in detail.

The wealthiest *hacendados* were predominantly drawn from the oldest families of the province.[11] Probably the single richest man in Caracas in the late eighteenth century was the third Marqués del Toro, Sebastían Rodríguez del Toro y Ascanio. In 1781 he was described by the Intendant as 'the richest *vecino* in this capital because of the large and numerous possessions he enjoys and because of the savings [he] . . . knows how to make'.[12] His annual income was estimated to be at least 25,000–30,000 pesos.[13] In 1800, when his property was divided among his heirs, his personal wealth was put at 504,632 pesos 7 reales.[14]

Below Toro, there was a small cluster of individuals of comparable wealth, nearly all, also, the scions of long established families. The most notable of this group was the first Conde de Tovar, Martín de Tovar y Blanco, who was without question the premier *hacendado* in terms of properties owned. His 1807 will listed 20 agricultural properties, 7 more than the Marqués del Toro.[15] Estimating from what can be validly read into the will, a conservative guess of his worth would be 200,000–300,000 pesos. Humboldt in fact calculated Tovar's annual income to be 40,000 pesos, or higher than that of the Marqués.[16] Others in this group include the first Conde de la Granja, Fernando Ascanio y Monasterios, who valued himself in 1796 at just over 200,000 pesos with a net annual income of over 13,000 pesos.[17] The third Conde de San Xavier, José Antonio Pacheco y Toro was also worth about 200,000 pesos.[18] Martín Eugenio Herrera y Rada was estimated by his heirs in 1826 to have been worth over 300,000 pesos before the wars after 1810 ravaged his extensive ranch-holdings.[19] Dr José Ignacio Moreno, who died in 1806, left just over 300,000 pesos to his beneficiaries.[20] Juan Vicente Bolívar's legacy was in the 1790s worth almost 350,000 pesos to his family, including the young Simón.[21] Seven additional persons should probably be counted with the above, including Feliciano Palacios y Sojo, Fernando Blanco y Mixares and Juan Ascanio from the pre-1700 families and Marcos Ribas, José Escorihuela, Sebastián Velez Mier y Teran and Antonio Fernández de León from the newer families. The last-mentioned was known as the Marqués de Casa León after 1809, and reputed to be one of the richest men of the province. He himself, in what is probably an exaggerated claim, estimated his annual income at about 50,000 pesos.[22]

It is highly unlikely that the aforementioned group would be a significantly expanded if the wills of all the Guild members were unearthed.

The same may be true for the second range of wealth, which encompassed persons worth 100,000–200,000 pesos, whose number was also small. This second wealth-range can in fact be more usefully considered as a downward extension of the first. Their numbers included Gerónimo Blanco y Plaza, Diego Moreno and Vicente Ibarra from older families; and Luis López Méndez, Juan Miguel Echezuría, Jose Vicente Machill-anda and Tomás Paz del Castillo from new families.[23] Not one of the above was likely to have had wealth in excess of 150,000 pesos. Probably ten to twenty names could be added to the above list, including members of the Ponte, Tovar, Hernández Sanabria, Mijares and Machado families.

Whatever the exact size of the upper echelons of the *hacendado* class, it is clear they were a very small group and probably getting smaller towards the end of the colonial period. The individuals we have examined represented in a real sense the swansong of concentrated wealth in the province. Quite simply, the old families which dominated the upper reaches of wealth in the province were in the process of witnessing the fragmentation of riches as an old generation died and their children divided their estates. The possible examples are numerous. The Marqués del Toro's fortune was divided into 10 parts, the largest being that of the new *marqués* at 111,700 pesos.[24] The biggest share of the Bolívar legacy went to Juan Vicente Jr, and was worth just under 120,000 pesos.[25] Pedro Blanco y Ponte's property valued at 114,114 pesos in 1766 was split among 8 heirs.[26] Gerónimo Blanco y Plaza left 118,745 pesos, which in 1800 was parcelled out to 4 brothers and sisters.[27] Miguel Jerés de Aristiguieta's 8 children took over his 107,498 pesos of net assets.[28] The Conde de Tovar's numerous offspring swallowed his properties.[29] Nor were the fortunes of newer families any more immune to the ravages of inheritance divisions: the offspring of J. M. Echezuría, Jose Escorihuela, Manuel Clemente y Francia, and Marcos Ribas, to name a few, were all likely to be markedly less affluent than their parents had been.[30]

Entail, keeping dead parents' goods undivided and the intermarrying of the rich probably did go some way to preventing family holdings from being whittled away to the bare bone. It is even possible that late-colonial society was undergoing a new phase of capital accumulation, with younger members of old families beginning to forge new economic foundations. If this was the case, the wars of independence interrupted the evolution, and the point becomes academic. What is apparent is that a younger and less wealthy generation of individuals was representing the old families as 1810 approached. The 1805–6 Guild lists are in fact heavily populated with the names of the children and heirs of those persons included in the original 1786 selection.

The composition of the assets of a typical *hacendado* was relatively straightforward, incorporating as a minimum a city house, an hacienda or two, personal and work slaves and miscellany such as jewelry, furniture, icons and the like. Additions to this basic structure were numerous in the cases of given individuals. I have already examined in some detail the participation of many large-scale agriculturalists in the overseas trade. Their non-farming pursuits extended to investment in real estate in urban centres. The Marqués del Toro possessed seventeen houses, the Conde del Tovar owned eight and many others had at least a couple.[31] There was also an inclination wherever possible to diversify agricultural holdings. *Hacendados* who owned two or more haciendas tended to invest in plantations growing different crops and on occasion in cattle ranches as well. The Conde de La Granja at one point or another had cacao-, indigo-, coffee-, sugar-cane- and ranch-holdings.[32] The Marqués del Toro among his properties had two sugar plantations, seven cacao haciendas, two *hatos* and a giant mixed farm growing cacao, sugar-cane and coffee.[33]

The liabilities and/or debts of the *hacendado* class were not particularly high. In an economy where agriculture was profitable, where *hacendados* were resourceful, where the Church did not hold extensive mortgages on rural properties and where the colonial government acted in the interests of the producers, the level of indebtedness was likely to be low. Such was in fact the case. The bulk of the debts carried by colonial *hacendados* were loans taken from the Church, usually in the process of being regularly paid back.[34] Properties were transferred to inheritors or sold to new owners together with the responsibility of paying both the interest and principal of the loans.[35] In other words, the borrowed sum was a calculated business risk, not a sign of financial mismanagement. Debt ratios to assets did, on occasion, rise to 40%–50% but these cases seem to have been the exception, not the rule.[36] Dr José Ignacio Moreno with 300,000 pesos of assets had only about 27,000 pesos of *gravamenes*, or less than 10%.[37] Furthermore it was not as though he could not have paid them off immediately; included in his assets were over 11,000 pesos in gold. Pedro Blanco de Ponte's liabilities in 1769 were less than 2% of his legacy of 114,114 pesos, and half of them were the result of the subtraction of the value of slaves he had freed.[38] These examples are not unique, and many families and individuals may have had no debts at all. They provide a healthy corrective to any attempt to portray the agriculturalists of our province as economic victims of anybody, be it merchants, priests, or officials. The *caraqueño hacendado* was a remarkably hardy species, especially when compared to his counterparts elsewhere in the empire.

One of the more noticeable sides of *hacendado* society was its obsession with status symbols. Among the planters, the old families, which as we have seen included most of the richest *hacendado* families, had something of a monopoly on the most visible of the symbols, the titles of nobility and membership in military orders.[39] The Marqueses de Mijares, Toro, del Valle, de Torrecasa and del Boconó, and the Condes de Tovar, La Granja and San Xavier were all members of established families. Only the Marqués de Casa León was a recent arrival to the province. A similar pattern held among the *caraqueño* members of the honorary military orders of the empire. The older Ascanio, Aristiguieta, Berrotarán, Blanco, Herrera, Ibarra, Mijares, Moreno, Ponte and Toro surnames outnumbered the newer ones of Casas, Barreto, Fernández León and Clemente y Francia.

It is difficult to know what importance to place on these titles. It can safely be assumed, in the first place, that they conferred prestige on the beneficiaries. Otherwise they would not have been sought. In the second place, they coincided closely with many of the richest men in Caracas and the oldest lineages, especially in the case of the titles of nobility. And so the holders became triply marked for distinction. All the same there was a sense of hollowness to the process, at least to modern eyes.

With the possible exception of the Valle and Torrecasa title, the others were bought, not inherited. Sometimes the grant was disguised as a transfer, as in the case of the La Granja title,[40] but the fact of the matter was that the privileges were being given to someone who could pay for them. If annuities to the Crown ceased, the favour lapsed, as occurred with Torrecasa.[41] Moreover the titles were of disconcertingly recent vintage: San Xavier and Toro were granted in 1732; Tovar in 1773; Boconó in 1787; La Granja in 1793; and Casa León in 1809. The membership cards in the military orders were also handed out rather late in the day (1770s–1800s) by an imperial government not averse to raising money by selling prestige.[42] It is not far-fetched to conclude that contemporaries were also aware of the character of the titled 'aristocracy' in the province. It is less easy to speculate on what they may have thought about it. Perhaps the combined weight of lineage, wealth and title made the dubiety of the honours a mute issue.

A wider group of *hacendados*, old and new, took commissions in the provincial militias in their search for visible prestige.[43] Prestige and a drain on personal finances were all they were likely to find. Whilst in New Spain and elsewhere the militias formed after 1763 evolved into a powerful arm of local interest groups, they remained hopelessly under-developed in Caracas. It is not even certain that the bait used in other colonies to attract native whites to the officer corps, the military *fuero*, functioned properly in our province.[44] The *caraqueño* elite seemed singularly uninterested in the proposed aims and needs of the militias, and of their potential as a coercive force which could be turned to their advantage. What attracted them, if the numerous petitions for military titles are any indication, was the right to call themselves officers and to wear uniforms.[45]

The *hacendado* class exercised considerable influence and control over the society it lived in. The primary interest of the *hacendados* at the paro-chial level took the form of three objectives: to maintain social order, to ensure a labour supply for their agricultural holdings and to protect their perceived social and legal rights. These aspirations could and did become intertwined with wider political issues affecting the imperial administration of the province, but on a day-to-day basis in local muni-cipalities they were dealt with by an influence network often quite removed from central colonial authorities.

The mechanics of the local influence network gave the *hacendado* elite extensive though indirect power over social, economic and political affairs throughout the province. Paradoxically, the most visible legal instrument of that network, the Town Council, played a relatively negative part in the political process of the late eighteenth century. Even the most cursory glance at the Cabildo records reveal the excru-ciatingly mundane nature of most of the issues dealt with by the worthy councils. Furthermore, the tendency to use the Ayuntamiento as the representative elite forum in co-ordinated responses to major issues, as had occurred in the past, may have been declining as our period advanced.[46] In the light of the preceding, the continued purchase of the *vendible* council posts by mostly *hacendado* individuals across the province requires some explanation. Part of the reason lies in the aforementioned need for the trappings of prestige. Individuals were willing to pay out from 100–200 pesos to over 1,000 pesos for titles which did not carry a great deal of power, in order to enhance the family name.[47] The councils did of course provide a means of influencing events in local municipalities; but perhaps the most important attrac-tion the councils held out was negative: by stacking the Cabildo memberships with their own, the *hacendados* prevented a potentially useful organ from falling into hostile hands.[48] In the case of the city of Caracas, the Council was largely and continuously dominated by a small group of individuals usually representing the richest families in the province.[49] The hegemony exercised by the important individuals and families in smaller towns was likely to have been even greater.

More immediate practical measures were at the disposal of *hacendados* interested in influencing or controlling local affairs. Their commissions in the militias gave them a potentially large degree of responsibility for and power over the policing of the province. They co-operated closely with the colonial authorities in sponsoring and funding initiatives to create para-military forces to deal with crime and runaway slaves. In addition, a significant proportion of planters took on the job of *tenientes de justicia* in the municipalities in which they lived. The post was probably the single most important representation of the colonial government at the local level, incorporating judicial, administrative and military duties. In 1789 the Justices of the Peace included in their numbers members of the well-known *hacendado* families of Gédler, Blanco and Palacios.[50] In another capacity, as *diezmo* collectors for the Church, planters were able to look after their economic interests. The right to gather this tax, which was the single largest levy on agricultural produce in Caracas, was auctioned off to the highest bidder. Not surprisingly, *hacendados* among others stepped forward to bid for the privilege. The *diezmeros* for 1802 included representatives of the following important families: Herrera, Toro, Ribas, Obelmexías, Blanco, Ascanio, Paz del Castillo, Vargas Machuca and Malpica.[51] Although there is little firm evidence that they manipulated the post to lower their own payments, it takes no imagination to recognize the opportunities for leverage in a collector's favour.

Another extremely useful avenue of influence was the indirect one offered by the system of *fianzas*. A whole gamut of official posts or concessions involved money-collection or rental, including the *tenientes de justicia*, *corregidores de indios*, *alcabala* collectors, Treasury officers, *aguardiente* vendors and public notaries. The government, to ensure honesty or its share, or both, required the appointees or licensees to provide surety. This commonly took the form of written guarantees by financial backers of the aspirants. These backers were usually well-off individuals and included numerous *hacendados* of our group. Thus the Conde de San Xavier proffered surety up to 1,000 pesos for Juan Jose Barandia, an appointee to the Treasury of the city of Margarita.[52] Juan Vicente Bolívar hijo covered for José de Aurioles, hopeful to the post of *teniente* of Victoria, Mamón and San Mateo in the Aragua valleys.[53] Dozens of other examples could be given but the point is made: a substantial number of petty and middle-level officials owed their jobs in part to the support of the very people they were supposed to tax and administer.[54] The influence wielded by *fiadores* in such an uneven relationship must have been great.

Of course politics in the province also took place in a sphere above the exigencies of municipalities and day-to-day rule. This realm was that of imperial affairs, where the wider economic, social and administrative needs of the province were considered in the context of the external nexus of the colony. At this second level *hacendados* shared power and influence more openly than at the local level, and they were ultimately subservient to the dictates and aims of the mother country, represented by resident, imperial officials. In addition, since so much of the colonial relationship revolved around trade, the small, resident, mercantile community and its interests became a much more integral part of the political process. Although *hacendados* were thus reduced to one third of the political equation, there was little danger of their being swamped by the other interest groups. As producers of the export crops they represented the economic *raison d'être* of the colony. It therefore made sense for both the government and the merchants to have an interest in their wellbeing; there was a strong communality of interest between merchants and *hacendados* and, as we shall see, royal officials throughout the 1790s and 1800s regularly consulted not just with the Consulado as a body, but with individual planters and merchants on matters as diverse as trade regulations, the structure of the tobacco monopoly, loans to the government and the remission of currency to Spain. Indeed, perhaps one of the greater influences the planters could expect to exercise was through personal contact with the royal officials who ultimately decided and enforced policy. Such contacts were not hard to come by in a province whose administrative and institutional centre was represented by just one moderately-sized city. One of the most important officials of the 1784–1810 period, the Intendant Esteban Fernández de León (1793–1801) was closely connected to the *hacendado* elite.[55] But he was not the only one. In 1796 the Town Council of Nueva Barcelona interceded on the behalf of Governor Emparán, later Captain-General of Venezuela, to get him reappointed as head of the province of Cumaná.[56]

The leadership of the *hacendado* class across the 1780s, 1790s and 1800s was remarkably collective in character. No individual stands out as an elite spokesman, unless it be the third Marqués del Toro, who died in 1787, or Antonio de León, the future Marqués de Casa León. But if no recognizable leader emerged from the ranks of the planters, or for that matter of the merchants, there is no question that the cream of both groups, at least as measured by wealth, was prepared to defend their interests actively and politically as social classes and as individuals.

Merchants

The merchant class represented in the Consulado lists differed from the agriculturalists in more than occupation: they were for the most part new immigrants to the province, limited in number and concentrated in just one city and its port. They were also less wealthy as a group, less inclined to have titles and less likely to participate in local affairs. Yet their socio-political marginalization was much less than might have been expected. Their economic importance ensured that they were heard whenever the wider issues affecting the province were decided. More significantly the *comerciantes'* ties to the planter class were stronger than they might seem at first glance. European merchants tended to marry locally and sire children who quickly became part of the *hacendado* establishment. Indeed the most striking feature of the *caraqueño* mercantile community was its overwhelming tendency to diversify into agriculture, to the point that these holdings could come to represent a greater portion of the merchant's wealth than commerce. In such an environment it becomes almost hazardous to speak of merchants as an occupational group distinct from *hacendados*. There was in fact a middle ground where the interests of several representatives of each group virtually coalesced.

The main source of information on the wealth of individual merchants is the wills of the notarial archives of the city of Caracas. These include the wills of 12 (36%) of 33 *comerciantes* on Saavedra's 1786 roll-call: of 6 (35%) of the 17 *mercaderes* of 1786 and of 20 (21%) of the 96 *comerciantes* on the 1805–6 lists.[57] In addition, we have information on several wealthy traders who did not appear on the above lists. I have, however, decided to simplify analysis by excluding the *mercaderes* from consideration as part of the merchant elite. The minimum property requirement for their entry into the Consulado was only half that of *comerciantes* and *hacendados*, so they were correspondingly a less important economic group. They took little part in the direction of the Guild, the town councils, the mercantile community's *juntas* and statements of intent on imperial policy. This is not to say individual *mer-*

caderes were not very successful, but the general profile of the group was likely to be lower than its counterpart among *comerciantes*.

The merchant elite of the late-colonial period lived mostly in the capital of the province, with small numbers stationed in La Guaira and elsewhere.[58] The La Guaira community, one day's journey away, was really just an extension of the one in the city of Caracas. There was nothing unusual about this concentration; as in other colonies, the merchants resided at the export and distribution centres of the economy. Immigrants made up an overwhelming majority of the merchant community. In our sample of 36, only 7 (19.4%) were creole.[59] Of the others, 15 (41.6.%) were Basques, 7 (19.4%) *canarios* and the other 7 from other parts of Spain. The sample is borne out by what we know of the nationality of other individuals on the list, and particularly by an 1802 Guild calculation of the origins of 47 resident *mercader* members: 91.4% were European.[60] The preponderance of immigrants was to some extent the product of the system of commissions and agents which may have marketed the bulk of the province's trade: this led companies in Spain to send out their own men to handle business. Furthermore, the Caracas Company had deposited during its tenure many capable merchants who stayed when the Company left.

'Foreigners' and immigrants the merchants may have been but they did not remain separate from their new environment for long. A measure of their level of integration is given by their rate of intermarriage locally. Of the 29 Europeans in the Consulado sample, 22 were married. Of these 18 married creoles and 4 Europeans.[61] Several of those who married creoles ended up by being affiliated to important and established *hacendado* families, such as Palacios, Aristiguieta, Garay and Urbina.[62] The pace of assimilation was likely to pick up as the new families' lineages became extended. The factors easing the integration of the immigrants were probably numerous. The pecuniary success of the newcomers was especially important. There are, after all, virtually no examples in the late-colonial period of established families marrying their daughters off to the many honourable, but less than rich, royal officials and military officers who were sent to the province from abroad. The new Europeans also had another major advantage working in their favour: they were *bona-fide* whites. To a painfully race-conscious creole class this attribute could not be valued too highly, especially when accompanied by money.

The immigrant merchants aided their integration by demonstrating a marked desire to become part of their new home, through solidly committing their financial assets to the province. Either through marriage or through outright purchase they became major landowners and slave-owners in their own right, so that many ceased to be considered merchants and were classed with the *hacendado* category.[63] Such was the case of José Escorihuela, the most important merchant of the 1780s, who in 1786 was listed as an *hacendado*. Francisco Xavier de Longa, a deputy for the merchant half of the Guild in the 1790s, was classified as a planter in 1805. Juan Miguel de Echezuría, a merchant in 1786, was an *hacendado* in 1805. The same occurred with José Joaquín de Anza, José de Elías Gónzalez and Luis Antonio López Méndez. Almost 60% or 21 of our Guild sample of 36 owned agricultural properties.[64]

The importance of haciendas in the assets of merchants becomes obvious, in examining the wealth of individuals, but so does the lesser prosperity of the merchant community as a whole *vis-à-vis* the planter class. If the examples in the wills are an indication, and I think they are, there were fewer merchants at the upper end of the wealth scale, and those that were there were less rich than their *hacendado* counterparts. The reasons for this are not hard to find. In the previous chapter I looked at the structural weaknesses of commerce in the province, and these naturally affected the capital accumulation of merchants. Many of their transactions both inside and outside the province were done on credit, so that at any given time a merchant's assets included funds that were not instantly realizable; it was wealth on paper. Earlier I referred to the extraordinary case of Domingo Zulueta and his accumulation of uncollectable debts in his favour of over 100,000 pesos. But he was only the most striking example of a common phenomenon. J. B. Echezuría, the richest merchant of our selection, at his death in 1801 left 20,800 pesos in *deudas incobrables*.[65] J. M. Echezuría in 1809 was owed over 12,000 pesos from goods he had exported for various companies.[66] Domingo Alejandro Pérez in 1819 was credited with over 60,000 pesos he had yet to receive.[67] Antonio Carballo in 1817 was owed over 20,000 pesos; J. J. Lander in 1817, 5,000 pesos; and Felipe Llaguno in 1789, 6,300 pesos.[68] Few if any merchants escaped the burden of this occupational hazard. It is no surprise that in an effort to secure their profits they turned to hard investments: haciendas.

The composition and value of the assets of the merchant class can be glimpsed to some extent through examining individual cases. At the upper end were individuals worth about 100,000–200,000 pesos. Juan Bautista Echezuría, who seems to have begun his career in the company of a major merchant of the Guipozcoana years, died in 1801 leaving about 200,000 pesos to his heirs, of which 115,000 pesos were in 3 haciendas, their slaves and other agricultural property.[69] He also had owned 4 houses in the city of Caracas worth a further 29,000 pesos or so. Felipe de Francia, who had been a *contador* of the Caracas Company, left over 160,000 pesos in 1785, of which 136,000 pesos were in 4 haciendas.[70] His transfer to *hacendado* status was almost complete by the time of his death, aided by his marriage to a Palacios. Manuel Clemente y Francia, a relation of Felipe and also married to a Palacios, left a more diverse inheritance in 1800.[71] In addition to 2 cacao haciendas probably worth in excess of 50,000 pesos, he had 32,000 pesos riding on an export deal to Veracruz, a tar mine in Maracaibo, houses in Caracas and *créditos activos*. No explicit calculation of his total worth is possible but it was likely to be in excess of 100,000 pesos. The López Méndez brothers, whose company in 1795–6 was one of the 10 largest of the province, were each probably worth about 100,000 pesos in the late 1800s.[72] The bulk of their assets by that time were in agriculture, and Luis Antonio had in fact been classified a planter in the Guild. José Vicente Galguera, another major wholesaler of the 1790s, estimated his net worth in 1823 at 80,000 pesos, part of which he accumulated across the war years.[73] Diego Rodríguez Nuñez, from the 1786 list, also skirted the 100,000 pesos range in the early 1790s.[74] Although he had over 20,000 pesos in outstanding *créditos activos*, he also had 56,000 pesos in haciendas and nearly 20,000 pesos in 2 city houses and their contents. Domingo Pérez in 1819 in addition to 63,800 pesos in money owed him, had a large coffee hacienda worth at least 30,000 pesos and a staggering 41 houses and *casas-tiendas* in the city of Caracas.[75] Not all merchants counted haciendas among their assets. Felipe Llaguno in 1789 left only commercial debts, stock in the defunct Caracas Company and over 20 urban properties.[76] But such singlemindedness was more likely to be exhibited by *mercaderes*. Only one of the six from the 1786 list had clearly diversified into agriculture by the time he wrote his will.[77]

Neither the close economic ties of most merchants to the soil nor their local marriages induced them to be particularly active in the day-to-day politics of the province. Their lack of visibility was of course in part due to their very small numbers and the fact that outside three towns their presence was negligible. But it also seems to have been a result of a conscious desire to be inconspicuous. Immigrants anywhere are unlikely to become deeply involved in the politics of a society they are only beginning to learn about; that level of integration is usually left to their children to accomplish.

Merchants did of course participate to some extent in local affairs and did make their contribution to the agencies of social control which helped protect and insulate the interests of the elites. In the system of *fianzas* described at length earlier, they acted as financial guarantors of posts, not coincidentally, connected with tax collections and commercial activities. Thus Joaquín Argos, a middle-sized wholesaler, acted as *fiador* in 1809 for Jesus María Franco, soon to be the head of the Coro Treasury.[78] He did the same favour in the same year for Pedro de la Sierra, who was to collect the poll-tax on tributary Indians for several towns in the Aragua valleys.[79] In 1786 Pedro Martín de Iriarte, one of the two or three largest wholesalers of the 1780s and 1790s, backed Juan de Emasabel, who had been appointed interventor of the Puerto Cabello treasury.[80] It would seem that merchants were exerting their influence on officials in their sphere of activity in much the same way that *hacendados*, through *fianzas* for J.P.s, were in theirs. Merchants also participated in the militias as officers. Manuel de Francia, Joaquín Castilloveittia and Esteban Otamendi were in the corps of the white militia battalion in Caracas City in 1786.[81] In this capacity, however, there is strong evidence that their dedication as a group was less than total. In 1793, representatives of the mercantile community asked for exemption from militia duty.[82] The then Captain-General advised the Crown against granting the concession to anyone whose *caudal de manejo* was less than 50,000 pesos, otherwise there would be an avalanche of such petitions.[83]

Their reaction to involvement in the Ayuntamiento of the city of Caracas, where most merchants lived, was equally lukewarm. After a major crisis over the lack of representation of Europeans in the Council, the Crown passed a law in 1776 reserving 4 of the 12 seats exclusively for the benefit of the immigrant population.[84] These posts would be filled by royal appointment of eligible individuals. The Europeans could also bid for the seats open to auction. The only problem is that this victory seemed to mark the high water of their interest. By the late 1780s and early 1790s the Captain-General was having trouble filling the seats, in that few individuals who were qualified, that is rich, European and white, seemed willing to serve.[85] Furthermore, few merchants showed an inclination to purchase the seats up for sale. Those who did, such as Joaquín Castilloveittia in 1770, Manuel de Francia in the same year, Antonio Egaña in 1778 and José Escorihuela in 1779, were well on their way to becoming *hacendados*.[86] In fact many of those who accepted the *vitalicio* posts, such as J. B. Echuzuría and Fernando Key Muñoz, were also strongly linked to agriculture in the province.[87] So the representation of merchants on the council was even more diluted than it might seem at first glance.

The merchants as a community clearly and voluntarily limited their involvement in local affairs to the necessary minimum. There was no socio-political need for merchants to defend their interests at the day-to-day level. They faced little social discrimination from the *hacendado* majority and without question shared the latter's views on the other social and racial components of the society. Their primary objectives therefore focused on general colonial policy affecting economic issues. To attain or defend these they operated much as the *hacendados* did: through the Consulado, through especially formed representative groups which tackled given issues, through personal contacts and, on occasion, through the Cabildo.

The professional class: an elite?

In other colonies the *hacendado* and *comerciante* elites were counterbalanced or paralleled by similar elites of successful miners, top-level royal officials, high clergy, senior military personnel and lawyers. It might be assumed that with the obvious exception of a mining class, the other occupational groups of the province of Caracas also formed, if not independent elites, at least a composite elite clearly distinguishable from the two leading economic groups. This was not the case, however. They were not sufficiently prominent in terms of prestige, power or wealth to act as much more than functional elites. That is, they were only important within defined occupational boundaries, in strong contrast to the *hacendado* and merchant elites, which transcended their functional supremacy to become a ruling elite. Most of the lawyers, priests and officials of the province were at best appendages to the ruling group, junior and subordinate associates in the running of society. At the top of the professional class there was a group of perhaps ten to fifteen individuals who wielded power and status by virtue of their occupations, which were arrived at mostly through imperial appointment. They were virtually synonymous with the institutions they headed, supported by the legal authority vested in them rather than by any influence derived from forming part of any special interest group or functional elite of the province. Pre-eminent among these individuals were of course the Intendant and the Captain-General. Together with the leading *hacendados* and merchants, they formed the ruling elite of Caracas.

It is possible to examine the preceding observations in relation to the three main occupational groups of the professional class: lawyers, clerics and royal officials. Each might have had a legitimate claim to forming part of the ruling elite; analysing their societal role it becomes clear why in fact they did not.

Lawyers in late-colonial Caracas, like lawyers in other parts of the empire, were kept busy by the numerous *pleitos* over financial matters, inheritances, land boundaries and water rights. In addition, the usual criminal cases added to their work-load. The individuals qualified as lawyers to deal with these problems were not particularly numerous. In 1796 there were only 56 lawyers listed in the *Colegio de Abogados*; in 1802 the membership had slightly increased to 61.[88] Their limited numbers combined with a litigation-prone population should have made lawyers indispensable and powerful brokers in provincial society.[89] Unfortunately for them, several factors were at work which lessened their importance. One was the mundane level of legal conflict in the province. Earlier we saw how, even in the Audiencia, the cases dealt with were hardly of major importance. The lack of weighty legal issues must have reduced many lawyers to the role of hired hands taken on by individuals too busy or too ignorant to resolve their minor imbroglios themselves. Furthermore, the creation of the Consulado in 1793, with a corresponding tribunal to decide commercial disputes, must have cut heavily into the business of lawyers now that merchants and agriculturalists could argue their own cases before their peers. A third factor working against *abogados* was the system of local justice in the municipalities, where often the *tenientes de justicia* decided day-to-day disputes of a potentially litigious nature.

It is not surprising in the light of the above that the typical lawyer was neither rich nor the member of a prominent family. The wealthy young men of the province tended to take degrees in law at the local university, but it is one thing to acquire a proficiency and quite another to practise it. Among the sixty members of the Colegio de Abogados in 1802 only about ten came from important families of the province. The majority of lawyers were men of modest means, by no measure poor but not by any measure rich. Lic. Miguel José Sanz, described by his wife as 'a lawyer of first rank and one [who] earned much [exercising] his profession', and recognized as such by his contemporaries, had only a quite paltry 3,000 pesos in assets when he married.[90] It was through his wife's inheritance that he acquired a cacao hacienda and his ticket to entry to the Consulado. Juan José Mora, another important lawyer of the late-colonial period, revealed himself in his 1809 will to be a middle-sized *hacendado*, again through inheritance.[91] Law, therefore, was not an exalted profession in the province. The lawyers who did stand out, made their mark not because they were lawyers but because they were scions of prominent families, or because, in the case of individuals like Sanz and Mora, their political activism and strength of personality made them impossible to ignore. The only practitioners of law who did acquire political importance were the four or five members of the Audiencia. As we shall see, the two Regents of the High Court became important members of the political factions of the province.

The clergy were another occupational category who might have been expected to form a strong interest group with political influence. Again, as occurred with lawyers, their role in provincial society was not as secure as it should have been. It was not just a question of their small numbers and comparative economic fragility limiting their influence. Unlike those in other imperial colonies, the clergy in Caracas had little opportunity to establish political legitimacy for themselves by fulfilling a role as socializing agents among the masses. The scattered nature of settlement in the province outside the Coastal Range valleys limited the possibility of exercising any kind of hegemony over the thinly-spread population. Solitary priests isolated in towns and hamlets could not derive the same strength or status as those clergymen who in other colonies served more concentrated and larger parishes. Nor could they possibly have adequately coped with the, at least in part, nomadic inhabitants of the Llanos, to whom the Church and its curates must have seemed a distant concern indeed. It is significant that it was not until after 1810, when the structure of colonial society began to fall apart, that any clergymen came to the fore of provincial politics.[92]

The central corps of royal officials in the province had a better chance of acting as an interest group than did lawyers and the clergy. Their occupation was well-defined and they were clearly distinct from the planters and merchants. Many of them held posts of high visibility and of consequence to the daily activities not just of the bureaucratic administration but of the economy. Among them, as among lawyers and priests, a functional elite existed. Once again, however, this functional elite did not really become a part of the ruling elite of the province.

The failure of the official class to mature into a serious socio-political force was not just a result of their lack of pecuniary success or of their apparent exclusion from the ranks of the local 'high society'. The authority and status derived from their official position should have insured their prominence without the need for props of a social kind. More detrimental to their potential importance was the nature of colonial administration and politics in Caracas. In a province where, as will be seen, the few burning political issues of the day were handled directly by the three or four senior imperial administrators, in consultation with *hacendados* and *comerciantes*, the function of most officials was reduced to the purely administrative. Thus even important posts, such as the heads of the four Treasury Centres of the province, remained unobtrusive branches of the bureaucracy, only coming to the attention of the wider public when tarred with the brush of corruption. The officer corps of the regular army units stationed in the province also lacked prominence. The regular army was tamely obedient to the dictates of the titular commander of the province, the Captain-General. Furthermore, the important *hacendado* and *comerciante* interests do not seem in the least to have coveted the few important posts handed to individuals sent from Spain. The officials of the administration, in short had little need or possibility to galvanize themselves into a formidable interest group. Their political neutrality was made explicit in the crisis years of 1810–15, when many royal bureaucrats served both insurgent and loyalist governments.[93] The flimsiness of the military wing of imperial administration was also revealed. The regular army, which represented a seventh of the military forces in the province, played little part in the royalist attempts to reconquer the colony in the years 1812 and 1814.

It cannot be said, then, that among the professional class there existed interest groups strong enough to stand alongside the leading elements of planter and merchant society. What did exist were imperial institutions and policies which the local economic, social and political interests had to come to terms with. Pre-eminent among the institutions were, of course, the Intendancy and the Captaincy-General. As we saw earlier, both governmental branches were created in 1776–7 to administer an area much larger than that of Caracas, but most of their business was destined to be concerned with the affairs of our province. Only the Intendancy really represented an innovation in the institutional structure of Caracas. The erection of the Captaincy-General merely upgraded the existing political administration of the province, expanding its power to incorporate the whole of Venezuela. In theory the Intendancy was to take charge of fiscal and economic matters; the Captaincy-General would deal with political, military and legal questions. In practice, the lines of separation were rarely to be so clear.

The comparative newness of the Intendancy and Captaincy-General makes their titular heads of greater relevance to the politics of the period than the institutions themselves. Of the two sets of imperial officials, the Intendants were probably the most important to *caraqueño* politics in the late-colonial period. So many of the affairs of the province revolved around political economy that even the Captains-General depended heavily on the skills of their Intendants to do their own job.

Perhaps more importantly, the Intendants who governed Caracas from 1777 onwards were far more imposing individuals than their Captain-General counterparts, who on the whole seem to have been an array of mediocrities. There were seven Captains-General between 1777 and 1810: Unzaga y Amezaga (1777–82); González (1782–6); Guillelmi (1786–92); Carbonell (1792–9); Guevara Vasconcelos (1799–1807); Casas (1807–9); and Emparán (1809–10).[94] As we shall see, they may have been able men on the whole but they acted more like bureaucrats than politicians. The Intendants, with their combination of forceful personalities and political skills, therefore had the edge over the titular heads of government for most of the period.

There were five Intendants between 1777 and 1808, three of whom were men of exceptional ability: Jose de Abalos (1777–83), Francisco de Saavedra (1783–8) and Estaban Fernández de León (1791–1802).[95] The three men, as we shall presently see, seemed to have had widely different ways of fulfilling their duties, but they did end up having a common experience: they were each unquestionably the most powerful men in the province during their tenure. Abalos was perhaps the most 'Spanish' of the three. As the first Intendant, he arrived as the harbinger of a new order, and religiously set out to establish it, irrespective of local sensibilities.[96] The irritated feelings he left behind were left to the conciliatory care of Francisco de Saavedra, a more flexible individual, who nevertheless was as competent as Abalos in safeguarding imperial interests in the province.[97]

The most fascinating of the three, and perhaps the most interesting personage of Caracas from 1777 to the outbreak of the independence struggle, was Esteban de León, fourth Intendant of the province. He held sway for twelve critical years which saw the economic prosperity of the early and mid-1790s, the depression of 1797–1801 and the major political strains caused by international wars and race difficulties inside the province. He was a member of an *extremeño* family in Spain, which had already sent two of its sons to Caracas by the time he arrived *circa* 1770.[98] He found his siblings well-established. Lorenzo, a priest, was also an *hacendado* and in the late 1770s was *cancelario* of the Ecclesiastical Council of Caracas. Antonio was well on his way to becoming one of the richest merchant-planters of the province and earning the title of Marqués de Casa León. With these connections and his patent natural abilities Esteban could not fail. He rose from Justice of the Peace in the 1770s to the Director of the tobacco monopoly in 1782 to Intendant in 1791. Once in power, he put his long experiences of life in the province to good use, promoting and preserving local economic interests even against the dictates of Spain.

6

Politics 1777–1808

Mention politics in connection with the late-eighteenth-century Spanish Empire and a well-defined general picture comes to mind: one of colonies struggling in the grasps of Bourbon reforms and Napoleonic Wars, experiencing the social, economic and political strains which accompanied the economic expansion, political centralization and military reorganization of the empire. Caracas, however, may have been an exception to the rule. No other colony, with the possible exception of Havana, experienced quite the combination of economic growth and internal political and social calm during the closing decades of the empire. In Caracas a relative harmony existed in practice between imperial and provincial interests, and indeed among the different components of the latter, which made the province not only an economic success, but also an example of what the Bourbon reforms might have achieved more widely throughout the empire if the circumstances which made the Caracas of our period possible had existed elsewhere.

I do not mean to suggest that late-colonial Caracas did not face problems and strains. It did, and some of the situations the inhabitants of the province confronted were grave indeed. But the issues the ruling elite dealt with cannot readily be seen in the usual light of a reaction to the imperial reforms and new demands from Spain, nor can they easily be seen as the reflection or result of internal divisions and rivalries among the components of the elite of the province. It is in fact more fruitful to look at late-colonial politics and society in Caracas not simply through the prisms of conflict and confrontation implied in the customary perspectives on our period, but also in terms of the cognizance of and resolution of issues.

The latter emphasis results in interpretations of the socio-political issues of the late eighteenth century quite different from the ones we have become accustomed to. Was there really a conflict of interests between the mother country and the colony? Can the relationship between merchants and producers inside the colony really be characterized as one of animosity? Did the landed creole elite really resent imperial administration, and *peninsulares* and *isleños* in general? Did they feel excluded from the political process? Was the racial tension between the whites and the other castes translated into insecurity among whites about their social supremacy locally, and doubts about the imperial will to protect that supremacy? The answer to all these questions is a qualified no.

1777–1783

The arrival of the first Intendant, Abalos, in August 1777 was probably the first tangible sign that change was in store for a province which had spent almost fifty years as a corporate colony. The innovations the Crown had in mind were designed to draw the region more tightly into the imperial net. It was not that Caracas was in any danger of slipping out of imperial control: since the 1730s the province had been one of the most strictly monitored colonies of the empire. Its commerce, and indirectly the whole economy, had been in the hands of a uniquely successful monopoly based in Spain, and the Captain-General of Caracas was one of the most powerful officials in the empire below the rank of Viceroy. Despite the erosion of the power of the Caracas Company since the late 1740s, and the apparent negligence of imperial administration in the colony, Caracas was still some way from requiring extraordinary measures to reset its course within the empire. What it was in need of were correctives, especially in the economic sphere. The emphasis of the reformist thrust during the Abalos years was accordingly economic.

The state of the province's economy in 1777 was not particularly healthy. The nominal manager, the Guipuzcoana, was in the unenviable position of having lent out over 2 million pesos in the province, a sum greater than the value of total annual exports and one which it had little chance of collecting.[1] Its forays into contraband did not seem to be solving its liquidity problems, and it was bungling its participation in the commerce of supplying slaves to the province.[2] The agricultural producers of the province and the merchants not attached to the company had also gone into contraband in their search for higher prices for their commodities and for cheaper and more plentiful imports. But contraband was no long-term solution to the needs of an economy still almost exclusively dedicated to the production of cacao, a crop not greatly in demand anywhere except in the mother country and New Spain. The latter market, which had remained outside company control

and in the hands of local agriculturalist-traders, was itself declining as
New Spain turned to other sources for its supply.

The first measures promulgated by the Abalos Intendancy were of
course dictates from Spain designed for the ultimate benefit of Spain.
Nonetheless one was of a nature to please local interests not tied to the
monopoly. The 13 June 1777 decree authorizing a limited trade by
locals with the foreign Antilles, reduced the need for contraband and
relaxed the restrictions governing the importation of slaves into the
province. The planters of Caracas, if they chose to do so, could now
personally bring in the slaves they said they needed for agriculture by
directly negotiating with the source of supply. By January 1778 one
major merchant-planter, Marcos Ribas, had applied for and received
permission to import 500 bondsmen at half-duty.[3] The Crown also
granted tax exemptions and the like to encourage the production of new
cash crops in the region.[4] For those planters thinking of diversifying,
these incentives were an indication that the new approach signalled by
the establishment of the Intendancy might work to the advantage of
local interests.

Not unnaturally, the Crown's new-found liberality had its limitations. The 1777 trade decree did not include Dutch-held Curacao
among the Antilles that Caracas could trade with, despite the fact that
Curacao was one of the islands most involved in contraband exchange
with Tierra Firme. Nor did the Crown see fit to suspend the 1774 free-
trade decree which allowed Ecuador's cacao free access to the New Spain
market, despite its adverse competitive effect on our colony and despite
continued appeals for protection across 1775–7 by the powerful *caraqueño* merchant-planter clique which had once controlled the trade.[5]
Perhaps worst of all, and perversely in the light of its upholding of free
exchange in the New Spain market, the Crown did not include Caracas
in the 12 October 1778 decree extending free trade virtually
throughout the empire. Abalos, however, worked hard to limit the
damage to provincial interests. Even before leaving Spain in 1777, he
was pressuring the Crown to grant some protection to the dwindling
Venezuelan share of the New Spain cacao market. His efforts were
rewarded by a quota system decreed in March 1778 putting a ceiling on
Ecuador's exports to Acapulco.[6] Abalos also argued unsuccessfully
against Venezuela's exclusion from the 1778 liberalization.[7] If his
intercessions did not always achieve positive results, they probably did
serve to keep alive a sense of expectancy among provincial economic
interests as to what might come with time through the reformist drive,
in addition to the gains already made.

Abalos himself, of course, could not always act as a sort of mediator between empire and colony. He was too much a representative and product of the imperial order, and sooner or later he would have to implement patently unpopular measures. The political atmosphere of the province in fact turned openly acrimonious in 1779. The Intendant, as the principal agent of imperial reform, was at the centre of most of the conflict. His reservoir of political goodwill among the local elites, if it ever existed as such, was dissipated when he set about establishing a state monopoly over the production and sale of tobacco in May 1779.[8] The Crown had for some time been interested in the commodity's revenue-producing potential, but would have been content to settle for an effective way to tax consumption. It had accordingly left it to the town councils of the Captaincy-General to find a solution. They knew what was in store if they failed to act but dragged their feet on the issue, perhaps not really believing a monopoly would be imposed. The local reaction when the *estanco* did come was one of anguished shock and protests against the low prices offered to producers.

The outcry was intense and widespread, but curiously shortlived. There is little doubt that many hundreds, even thousands, of small planters, rollers and retailers were hurt by the creation of the monopoly but they were not the ones with the political voice to cry foul. It was the *hacendado* elites of various districts who through the cabildos issued the public protests, though their ties with the tobacco industry were probably indirect. Significantly, resistance at the town-council level had diminished by 1780, and protest in the province did not reach the dimensions of armed rebellion as it did in neighbouring New Granada. The reaction of the elites to the whole issue from the moment it surfaced in 1777 was, in short, ambivalent considering the apparent provocation the shadow of the new monopoly represented. The spontaneous and vociferous outburst in 1779 can, at least hypothetically, be interpreted more usefully as the philosophical protest of the local elites against the extension of imperial economic control inside the colony rather than as the opposition of threatened tobacco 'industry' spokesmen *per se*. The immediate effect of the monopoly was therefore more political than economic, and it poisoned the probably already uneasy relations of the Intendancy and the provincial elites.

The Intendancy's policy on public lands and the sale of private ones must have been another rude jolt for the *hacendados* of the province, at least for those with ranch-holdings. For decades previously, they and their ancestors had been adding to their property seemingly at will, by moving into legally unclaimed land in the Llanos. A new government interest in populating the hinterland in an orderly fashion promised a new official approach to the distribution and use made of hitherto neglected public lands. A scheme was drawn up proposing the granting of land parcels to immigrants, a suggestion very much at variance with the slowly emerging latifundia of private holders.[9] Fortunately, from the point of view of the *hacendados*, little or nothing came of this and later proposals, and in any case the period of greatest land-appropriation was probably well over by the 1770s.[10] The planter-rancher families were more likely to be engaged in litigation to settle the boundaries of their large and ill-defined land claims. More ominous therefore was a new regulation of 8 June 1779, prohibiting the sale of more than 2 square leguas to one individual.[11] Though once again it was a measure – and intention – which had little impact over the ensuing decades, the reaction by local agriculturalists when it was announced could not have been favourable.

In June 1779 Spain entered the war then raging against Britain. The negative impact of the war on Caracas' economy aggravated the differences among the company, local interests and royal officials as the straitened economic and political circumstances made each faction more determined to secure its concerns. The worst of the political infighting now began.

Rumours of war had been current for months by the time Abalos informed the province in July 1779, of the official commencement of hostilities.[12] In anticipation of and in reaction to predatory attacks by British corsairs in the Caribbean, the traffic of ships from Spain slowed to a trickle and the province soon found itself short both of imports and of the means to ferry its exports to the Spanish market. The solution from the monopoly's point of view was to raise the price of the commodities it had already brought into the province, and conversely, to slow its purchase of local crops for export. The consumers and producers of the province thought otherwise: the prices of stored imported goods should remain at peacetime levels, and the company should fulfill its contractual obligation to buy all the crops set on its doorstep.[13] The matter of pricing already-imported goods was settled relatively promptly when Abalos, backed up by royal regulations limiting the company's freedom to change prices, and by his own prejudices, prevented the monopoly from pushing through exorbitant price increases.[14] The related questions of company purchases of local produce was not so easily solved. Abalos' attitude was once again the deciding factor, but this time he was forced to play a mediating role and to adopt a middle path himself, rather than casting the final vote in favour of one side or the other. After initially siding with the planters, he recognized that for all practical purposes the company was in no financial position to buy large quantities of goods for export even if it had wanted to.[15] Abalos apparently tried to stall or temper the producers' demands but without much success. He finally decided on a barter exchange of company imports for provincial exports, and devised a scheme whereby the Intendancy would itself purchase unspecified amounts of local produce.[16] The latter was the first case of several in the following decades where an Intendant, apparently acting on his own judgement, took imperial funds to protect and to subsidize the province's export-crop producers. It is not clear, however, to what extent the *hacendados* of Abalos' time appreciated the initiative. There is no question that it was better than having no aid, but its impact appears to have been meagre.[17] The innovation's importance lay more in its creating a precedent for such actions in the future.

More to the immediate liking of provincial agriculturalists and traders must have been Abalos' decision to anticipate the royal decrees of February and September 1780 which opened the empire to trade with neutral countries and their colonies for the duration of the war.[18] It is not difficult to understand why he did so: the problem of finding an outlet for the province's exports and the ships to carry them was becoming acute as transports failed to arrive from Spain. He began to issue licenses not only to the company but to independent traders as well, allowing traffic with the still off-limits Dutch island of Curaçao.[19] The unorthodoxy of his initiative was almost subversive in its implications. In the short run, it established the principle of competition between provincial merchants and the company. In the long run, Abalos set another precedent for future Intendants to follow: in times of economic crisis, bend the trade regulations of the empire to minimize damage to the provincial economy. In terms of immediate practical effects, the combination of Abalos' licences and the Crown's measures ensured that at least through 1780 and into 1781 the province was able to continue exporting, if at a more reduced volume.[20]

Once the Crown had passed its free-trade resolutions, Abalos went even further, allowing all locals to trade with the neutral powers in all products, including the previously-forbidden cacao.[21] Again, he was going beyond his role as the bureaucratic implementer of decisions taken by others, and becoming instead the initiator. This time the Guipuzcoana reacted violently: its fifty-year monopoly was being broken, and it would not idly stand by and await more normal times to put the situation right. For his part, Abalos had long been hostile to the continued existence of the Guipuzcoana. In his most famous condemnation of the company, in which he accused it of never fulfilling its function and impoverishing Caracas, he also observed the pernicious political effects it had on the population: 'The name of the King, of his Ministers, and of all Spaniards . . . [arouses among the inhabitants] tedium, aversion, and disaffection solely because of the presence of the Company which they see as the main source of their ills.'[22] Unfortunately for the company, it had few friends left in the Council of Indies, and the reports of its many critics in the province were reaching sympathetic ears. On 28 January 1780, a royal decree had already opened the colony to trade with all Spanish ports. This reform had little practical import in so far as direct trade between the colony and the mother country was virtually non-existent at the time, but it did serve as support for Abalos' more effective opening of competition from within Caracas. The company's attempt to force the issue only led to the formal abrogation of its contract, though not to its formal dissolution, in 14 February 1781.[23]

The political conflicts of 1779–80 left Abalos an embittered and possibly a defensive man. There is the appraisal of his successor, Saavedra: 'Abalos was not loved in Caracas, be it because of his austere and dry personality, or because the Intendancy had been created with blood and fire.'[24] Abalos' own correspondence with Spain reveals a similarly isolated and besieged man. His written attacks on the company, on the Caracas Town Council and on the Captain-General are sometimes couched in extremely emotional terms not entirely balanced by the facts. It was one thing to criticize the current state of the company, quite another to say that it had never fulfilled its duties to the Crown.[25] In criticizing Unzaga y Amezaga, he did not have to generalize about the dim likelihood of success of the Intendancy system in all of the American colonies.[26] It was fair enough to censure the Cabildo for usurping more authority than it was entitled to, but quite untrue to suggest it wanted to arouse *el pueblo* when it opposed him.[27]

The, by now, deep, personal antagonisms which characterized political relations in the province survived the demise of the company as a political force and carried over into 1781. Tension increased that year when a turn for the worse took place in the fortunes of war as far as Caracas was concerned. Until then the province had been able to survive economically by exporting to the neutral Antilles, which in practice had meant Curaçao. This outlet became imperilled however when Britain's declaration of war against Holland in December 1780 threatened an attack on Curaçao. Prices offered for Venezuelan goods fell sharply, and Caracas began to suffer in earnest from the effects of the war. An added complication, at least for the royal officials in the province, was the outbreak of rebellions inside the empire. The rebellion of Tupac Amaru in Peru from November 1780 to May 1781 and the Comunero revolt in New Granada, which reached its height in June 1781, attracted considerable interest in Caracas. To already-anxious imperial officials, and especially to Abalos, that interest meant potential treason, and they accordingly viewed manifestations of local opposition to government measures in this light.

The Intendant did not have to wait long for local displeasure to surface over another trade issue much aggravated by deteriorating economic conditions. Tariff duties on exports to foreign colonies were much higher than those on exports to places within the empire.[28] In view of the pernicious effects the war was having on trade, the third Marqués del Toro, who was both the wealthiest man of the province and that year's head of the Caracas Cabildo, requested in early June that the duties should be postponed or removed.[29] He was soon backed up by a chorus of other members of the Town Council.[30] In an unexpected, and not entirely clear political alliance the Captain-General Unzaga y Amezaga also joined the fray in support of Toro's demand.[31]

Abalos might not have given in to this formidable array against him, if news in early July of the truce in favour of the Comunero rebels in Bogotá had not begun to filter through.[32] The financial needs of the government and the defence of the province and region were growing, and he could ill afford to cut off a major source of revenue. He was even considering imposing an extra tax on trade to finance military expenditures. The temporary capitulation of the royal authorities in New Granada shook him out of his intransigency. Fearing the contagion of a rebellion which had featured the abolition of the tobacco monopoly and of extraordinary taxes in its programme, Abalos decided to compromise. Before July was out excise duties had been lowered and the introduction of the special tax was postponed.[33]

Abalos' fears of the neighbouring rebellion spreading were greatly exaggerated. True, its economic objectives were not without local appeal, and there were indications that the Bogotá insurgents were attempting to draw in regions of the Venezuelan province of Maracaibo with some success; but Abalos' accusation that 'the natives in this country, or at least those of this capital . . . do not cease to manifest . . . the love they nurture toward liberty and independence' was, if not an outright lie, a gross overstatement of the issue.[34] That there was sympathy for the rebellious elsewhere is without doubt. Local curiosity was

also wide enough to follow not only the course but the substance of the
rebellion of the thirteen British colonies to the north. A translated copy
of the 1774–5 Philadelphia Proclamations was in the possession of a
leading *caraqueño* in 1777.[35] All the same, the sympathy and interest
seem to have stayed latent, even dormant. In the first place, the Caracas
elite singled out by Abalos must have been aware that it had little in
common with the largely Indian rebels of Peru, or with the *mestizos* and
Indians who made up the bulk of the Comuneros in New Granada. In
the second place, they never really stepped outside the boundaries of
legal opposition in pressing their objectives, even when the tobacco
monopoly was established. Perhaps most revealing about the actual
mood in the province was the content of a private letter sent to Spain by
the second *alcalde* of the Caracas Cabildo. He protested the loyalty of
the province's inhabitants against the 'pernicious designs' of the Bogotá
rebels and spoke of the *caraqueño* reaction to the news of the defeat of the
attempt to spread the movement into Trujillo in southern Maracaibo:
'The joy and satisfaction of all the citizens of this capital, on learning of
the generous deliverance of their *co-provinciales* [countrymen] is without
bounds.'[36] So wrote José Cocho de Iriarte, named by Abalos as a co-
conspirator of Toro's.[37] Toro himself, the storm blown over, received a
licence in 1782 from the Intendancy to take a merchant ship of his to
Spain.[38]

While he clashed with the elites over trade, the heightened military
alertness required in 1781 as the British fleet in the Caribbean moved
onto the offensive, led Abalos into conflict, with the Captain-General
and the military over how much should be spent on preparations. The
decline of the economy and the subsequent inability of producers and
traders to pay taxes cut heavily into available revenue, and Abalos
across 1781–2 became increasingly concerned with reducing expenses.
He maintained that the mass of military costs was unnecessary and
railed against the demands of the Captain-General and of the military
governors of Guayana, Margarita, Cumaná and the port of La
Guaira.[39]

The cessation of open warfare towards the end of 1782 and early 1783
seems to have had a cooling effect on the province. The economy began
to recover in 1783, at least partly because Abalos continued a liberal
policy on trade in spite of Crown attempts to close the channels it had
opened during the exigencies of the war. Perhaps as a corollary to the
end of the war and economic recovery, no new controversial issues arose
to bedevil the politics of the province. More significantly, several of the
leading participants began to take their leave: the company had been

out of the picture since 1781; a new Captain-General replaced Unzaga y Amezaga in 1782 and Abalos, asking to be discharged from duty, left the province in August 1783.[40] A new reign could now begin, under new men and new circumstances.

These first years of the Intendancy and the Captaincy-General were a watershed period in the history of Caracas. It cannot be emphasized enough that our province was the only American colony left under corporation rule in the late 1770s, and that therefore the demise of the Caracas Company represented a significant change in its economic and political makeup. That change was carried out by the imperial government and was accompanied by official measures liberalizing the trade structure of the province in other ways. The combination ensured that the era of Bourbon reforms got off to a good start in our area, lessening rather than increasing tensions. In the more strictly administrative sphere, the tightening of imperial control did not really threaten the socio-political position of the local elites, as occurred elsewhere, and the new imperial administration was showing itself more responsive to provincial needs than its predecessors. If the political acrimony characteristic of these years was real, and it was, it was acrimony resulting from natural reactions to change within a long-established *status quo* and from the inordinate strains created by coping with war. By 1783 the local elites were in a stronger position than they had been for decades, with the company removed and with an intendancy system essentially designed to promote the economic potential of the province. With the departure of the abrasive Abalos the transition could be said to be at an end. The consolidation of gains could now begin.

1783–1796

The signing of peace in September, 1783, ending Spain's hostilities with Britain, did not find Caracas in the best of circumstances. The political aftershocks of the conflict-laden Abalos years were still being felt, and the new Intendant, Francisco de Saavedra, described the province as economically impoverished.[41] The gloom, however, was destined to be shortlived. The following decade or so was the most stable and prosperous period of the post-1777 years, and indeed may have been the crowning moment of Caracas' 300 years inside the empire. As is usual with periods of comparative peace and prosperity, it is easier to look at the events of 1783–96 in terms of general developments.

The economy

Exports reached or surpassed pre-1777 levels in 1784 and had nearly doubled in value by the mid-1790s. The rapid economic recovery from the war-induced depression and the formal abolition of the Caracas Company in 1784, did not mean that serious problems and major structural deficiencies did not continue to plague the economy. As the crisis over the monopoly receded, other long-standing questions came to the fore.

One of the most vexing problems facing the producers, traders and administrators of the colony was the seemingly continuous shortages of ships to carry provincial exports and imports. This was not the one-sided issue it appears, nor was it a simple question of correcting the imbalance between supply and demand. The shortfall was connected to the larger question of imperial regulations of the province's commerce. Changing the legislation became a prime consideration for provincial interests throughout the 1780s. The 1778 exclusion of Caracas and Venezuela from the imperial free-trade system would appear to have been at the root of the shipping problem. Other reasons can be adduced, including the need of shippers to adjust to the rapidly increasing exports from the province, and the enforced, problematic transition period required to restructure the commercial skeleton from one based on monopoly control to one composed of many traders. But the central complicating factor remained the imperial limitation on the number of ships allowed to enter the province's ports.[42]

The new Intendant, Saavedra, could have contented himself with following royal dictates, but in the tradition established by Abalos he actively searched for the best way to overcome this obstacle to the economic development of the province. In the day-to-day administration of the economy he adopted measures to mitigate or eliminate the negative effect of trade restrictions. By delaying for nine months a request for instructions on what to do about the admission of all ships owned by Spaniards into *caraqueño* ports, a practice he found to be policy upon his arrival in late 1783, he, in effect, extended well into peacetime the life of free trade that had been granted only under the pressures of war.[43] In 1784 he confirmed the policy inaugurated by the 1777 decree, by permitting the export of indigo and hides to the foreign Antilles in return for specie and slaves.[44] In 1785, in the face of an unusually severe scarcity of ships from the Peninsula, he sanctioned the exports of all produce through the foreign colonies, including cacao.[45] In 1786–7 he sent most of the province's tobacco exports out via Curaçao.[46] Not one of these measures was taken in consultation with Madrid but, significantly, not one of them was overturned. The Crown finally gave in to various pressures and extended free trade to New Spain and Venezuela by royal decree of 28 February 1789.[47] The scarcity of transport for exports to Spain ceased to be an issue in peacetime.

The successive intendants of these years also made sure that the legal avenue to the foreign colonies was kept open. It was not that the 1777 decree was in danger of being rescinded, but sometimes its rules needed imaginative interpretation to make them of practical use. We have seen how Saavedra sensibly stretched its provisions in 1785, allowing the province's exports to be sent out through the Antilles. Even more unorthodox was the various intendants' occasional practice of permitting the importation of basic commodities like flour and textiles from the islands any time supplies from Spain lagged. This was an open breach of imperial regulations, which for strong economic reasons expressly limited imports from the Caribbean to specie, slaves and agricultural tools. In 1785 Saavedra opened the gates when imports did not arrive from Spain. In September 1790, the Captain-General, Guillelmi, who was temporarily doubling as his own Intendant, acknowledged an order from Spain ordering him to stop granting licences to import flour from the foreign colonies.[48] But the most blatant floutings occurred under León in the early and mid-1790s. He apparently permitted a small group of merchants to trade unrestrictedly with the islands, outside the legal exchange permitted by the 1777 law.[49]

In matters concerning imperial trade regulations, developments were largely dependent on the initiative of the intendants. On other economic problems of the province the intendants worked more openly in conjunction with others. A case in point was the handling of the anaemic state of the New Spain exchange. The Veracruz connection really had no hope of being resurrected by the mid-1780s, but this did not prevent *caraqueño* economic interests and the Intendancy from joining in an effort to prevent any further erosion of the Venezuelan share of the market. The Intendant Saavedra, both in his capacity as economic overlord and as a sympathetic supporter of individual requests by the planter-merchants involved in the trade, pressured Madrid for favourable measures. While urging in his official communiques that Venezuela's supremacy in the cacao trade should be reasserted at the expense of Guayaquil producers, he backed the separate demands of major traders like the Iriarte brothers and Diego Moreno for tax and trading concessions of an often very privileged nature.[50] The combined efforts to save the Veracruz trade were not successful of course; in June 1789 the Crown lifted the restrictions it had imposed a decade earlier on Guayaquil exports to New Spain as a protective measure for Venezuelan cacao.[51] But the urgency had gone out of the issue by then. The continued decline of the exchange across the 1780s had not, after all, led to the negative economic consequences anticipated by the *caraqueños* and their Intendants. The growing market in Spain largely compensated for the drop in demand from the Veracruz *ferias*. And from the point of view of the Intendants, who were primarily concerned with the now-acute shortfall in the circulation of hard currency inside the province, royal concessions in 1786 and 1792 ensured that Caracas could continue to receive at least some specie from New Spain even without the formal commercial exchange of cacao for cash.[52]

The worsening liquidity shortage in the 1780s was also dealt with collectively. The local economic interests and royal officialdom banded together to find a solution to the currency drain caused largely by the transfer of tobacco monopoly profits to Spain. Across a series of meetings in early and mid-1791 senior officials and *juntas* of wealthy *hacendados* and merchants discussed the issue, presenting proposals and counter-proposals.[53] There was no alignment along occupational lines behind one proposed solution or another. There were instead two currents of opinion. The majority opinion was a surprisingly heterogeneous group including as it did the resigning Intendant Rafael Alcalde, Juan José Mintegui, who was the Cía Filipinas representative in the province, and Juan Bautista de Echezuría, Juan Esteban Echezuría, Isidoro López Méndez and José Eschorihuela who were all major wholesalers and planter-merchants. Their suggestion, that the surplus specie should be given by the Treasury to solvent locals engaged in commercial or agricultural pursuits in return for promissory notes payable by established merchant houses in Spain, was opposed by the new Intendant, Esteban de León, and by the fourth Marqués del Toro. The former feared such a measure would concentrate the limited currency in the hands of too few individuals; the latter preferred the Crown to invest the available surplus in buying provincial commodities at guaranteed prices. The majority opinion won out, and their proposal proved to be a success in practice during the next few years. Once again the objectives of resident royal officials, planters and merchants turned out to have meshed almost uncannily. Traders had an extra source of currency to buy commodities from producers. Producers had greater prospects of selling their crops, and the wealthier among them in effect had access to the equivalent of a lending bank for production purposes.

Finally, royal officials and the Crown did not run the risk of unrecoverable specie being seized or sunk at sea on its way to Spain. Instead the Imperial Treasury in the mother country received its payments safely via promissory notes issued against companies in its own backyard.

A corollary to the attention given to trade and financial matters inside the colony during the 1780s and 1790s was the care taken to stimulate the economy's production sector. The fiscal branch of the provincial government actively involved itself in the promotion and protection of local agriculture, investing both financially and politically in the future of the sector. The most notable examples of the financial commitment the colonial administration was ready to make occurred in the mid-1780s. In one case the government underwrote the importation of 4,000-plus slaves between 1784 and 1787, and then sold them on easy credit terms to local buyers, many of whom happened to be wealthy planters.[54] In a separate issue roughly contemporary with the slave-deals, the Intendant in 1786–7 used the funds from the prosperous tobacco monopoly to rescue the indigo planters of the province from the effects of falling prices caused by the crisis of overproduction.[55]

The royal officials who acted on these and other questions cannot be said to have anticipated all the problems which surfaced, or for that matter to have come up with all the solutions. The decision to finance slave imports was taken in part after prolonged and steady pressure from local economic interests counselling the need for more labour for the plantations. The salvage operation mounted for indigo planters was a direct reaction to their vociferous demands for help. All the same, had imperial policy as carried out by resident officials inside the province not been in principle protective and supportive of *caraqueño* agriculture, it is inconceivable that local *hacendados* could have had such a relatively easy time getting the kind of handouts they received. The late eighteenth century was, after all, a time when the emphasis was on extracting money for Spain, not on additional, long-term expenditures in the colonies themselves. Indeed, the pattern of implementing economic policies beneficial to the export economy of the province characterized most of the years between 1783 and 1796. And with the co-optation and co-operation of the local economic interests into and with the decision-making process, imperial policy was ensured an acceptance inside Caracas which was probably highly unusual in the context of the tensions of the late-colonial empire. The one discrepant note during these years was caused not by policy, but by the differences surfacing between planters and merchants inside the province. The rivalry of the two economic groups is discussed below.

During the rule of the Caracas Company the small group of independent merchants outside corporate control were largely indistinguish-
able from the local *hacendado* community. Indeed in the one major
sphere of activity not in company hands, the Veracruz cacao trade, a
combined merchant-agriculturist group handled the exchange. The
demise of the corporation in the early 1780s altered this close relationship between local merchants and *hacendados*. The monopoly which had
excluded both parties from the province's trade with its major market,
Spain, gave way to a reasonably competitive commercial structure. The
result was the appearance of a distinct merchant community which, for
all its ties to the province, naturally had interests to look after separate
from those of the agriculturalists.

Clashes between merchants and planters were therefore inevitable in
the years after 1784. The ensuing friction did not mean that sharp
differences developed between the two. In the case of differences over
trade legislation and markets, for example, the positions taken by the
two economic groups were characterized more by different points of
emphasis than by a clear ideological split between local producers
wanting to trade outside the empire and Spanish merchants trying to
maintain their hegemony over a colonial market. As stated elsewhere,
Spain continued to be the primary consumer of *caraqueño* commodities
throughout the late-colonial period, so there could be little question of
provincial producers seeking their fortune solely outside imperial
boundaries. Nor, conversely, were the resident peninsular merchants
adverse to partaking of the trade with the foreign colonies. In addition,
it must be remembered that the commercial community which served
Caracas after 1784 was composed of many disparate elements, a diversity which diminished any tendencies it may have had toward developing a monolithic personality *vis-à-vis* the planters.

The differences between planters and merchants in the 1780s and
early to mid-1790s were all actually resolved or contained with comparative ease and did not in any way signal a major split between the two
groups. Many of the difficulties encountered were temporary, the result
of structural problems arising from the changeover from a monopolistic
to a competitive trade system. Not unnaturally, planters in the
mid-1780s worried about the lack of regular shipments to and from
Spain, and about the apparent inability of firms in the mother country
to supply their *caraqueño* agents with enough funds to purchase local
commodities. Worse, the heralded age of competition did not seem to
be materializing, as a handful of buyers in the province established an
apparently strong hold on the market. Yet, as we have seen, the prob-

lems were shortlived. As the Spanish companies established provincial contacts, as they learned the needs of the province and as competition developed, planter complaints about the trade structure declined and had virtually disappeared by the early 1790s.

Significantly, there was only one real conflict over commodity prices between merchants and producers in this period. The differences were brought on by the crisis of the overproduction of indigo in 1787 and therefore the fall in prices was largely self-induced.[56] The merchants do seem to have pressed their bargaining advantage to a fault, giving the planters the excuse they needed to protest publicly against the prices they were offered. Their case was strongly worded in *representaciones* which reached officials in Spain. The then Intendant of Caracas, Saavedra, was ordered to look into the allegations. Saavedra for his part realized the seriousness of the crisis, which involved far more than price discrimination on the part of wholesalers, who could not begin to purchase the whole of the harvest, even at the reduced prices. The state became an interested third party as Saavedra mounted a rescue operation, later sanctioned by the Crown, whereby he appropriated funds from the tobacco monopoly to purchase the excess indigo at pre-1787 prices from producers and even from wholesalers acting as agents for groups of small planters. Although the solution pleased no one – the producers felt not enough was being done, the wholesalers wondered if they were being closed out – the crisis eased, possibly as early as 1788. Certainly no more was heard from the indigo-planter faction after that date, as Spain consumed more and more *caraqueño añil* in the following years.

The undeniably harsh language used in the mutual accusations by merchants and planters – Saavedra spoke of the 'continuous war [of words] between one and the other class' – cannot be taken too seriously.[57] The diatribes employed by both sides more likely represented a tactical weapon aimed at reinforcing the righteousness of one position at the expense of another. Not one of the differences between *comerciantes* and *hacendados* turned into a long, simmering feud. Each conflict of interest was over a specific issue, usually resolved and of short duration. The one apparently major confrontation, that of 1787, was primarily the result of producer overconfidence in market possibilities rather than a *bona-fide* clash of economic sectors. Merchants were just as capable of bringing themselves to the brink of ruin independently of their dealings with planters, as was the case in 1786, when they flooded the province with two years' worth of imports, only to find themselves unable to sell their goods.[58]

Indeed the examples of co-operation and mutual interest during these years were always more important than the differences which surfaced. In 1787, the year of the indigo crisis, the planter-dominated Caracas Cabildo was requesting tax breaks from the Crown on cacao exports on behalf of both merchants and producers.[59] We have already seen how the two co-operated with the colonial administration to confront the serious liquidity shortage of the province and the decline of the Veracruz cacao exchange. In the mid-1790s they acted in concert again to demand protection for commercial fleets when war with France broke out.[60] It cannot be emphasized enough that the two groups had many problems in common and a similar interest in seeing them solved.

The one problem which could not be done away with, and bedevilled the lives of both planters and merchants, was the presence and role of the Filipinas Company in the province's commercial life. The company was formed from the remains of the Caracas Company in 1785 and, though its main trade was to be with the Philippines, it was given the right to carry about 40% of Spain's exchange with Caracas under the regulations which excluded our province from imperial free trade until 1789.[61] It was not an enlightened royal decision. Until 1789, when all restrictions on Caracas' trade within the empire were lifted, it seemed that the province had exchanged one master for another, and a less capable one at that. To planters and merchants indebted to the old Caracas Company, the new company was an unpleasant reminder that they still collectively owed over 200,000 pesos, which the Filipinas Company now laid claim to.[62] More generally, and more onerously, the new corporation exercised considerable control over the province's trade in the middle and late 1780s. Taking over the remaining infrastructure of the old Caracas Company gave the new corporation an advantage over its Spanish competitors, who were still feeling their way and in any case were burdened by the *toneladas* restrictions.[63] The company's undue preponderance did in fact slow the development of the competitive commercial network which eventually emerged. The company was also at least partially responsible for the shortages of transport and commercial capital affecting the province's trade structure in the middle and late 1780s. The corporation never did solve its financial problems. It somehow prevailed upon the Crown to permit it to take funds from the province's tobacco monopoly in return for promissory notes payable in Spain.[64] The *libranza* system was thus inaugurated in 1788 for the sole benefit of providing liquidity for the operations of the main trading concern of the province.

Fortunately for all concerned, the Filipinas Company's primacy did not last long. Spain finally included Caracas in imperial free trade in

1789. This decree removed the company's guaranteed share of the province's trade and its share of the annual commerce quickly plunged. By 1795 it carried less than 5% of the total.[65] Disagreements over the money the company took from the tobacco funds resulted in the suspension of the privilege in 1791,[66] and thereafter the corporation became only one of many bidders as the *libranza* system was opened to all reputable merchants and *hacendados*. All the same, and even in its much-diminished role, the company continued to be a part of the province's commercial network capable of arousing the antagonisms of many in Caracas. As we shall see, it was the company's representatives who sparked the bitter verbal confrontation between merchants and planters in 1797, when both groups were striving to prevent the economic collapse which was threatening them.

The race question

Race relations in late-colonial Caracas are usually discussed as though there were some undercurrent of animosity which made the tension in the hierarchical caste structure of the province potentially more explosive than elsewhere in Spanish America. What these analytical efforts seem to represent is an after-the-fact explanation of why the violence of the independence struggle in the 1810s was so extreme and so tinged with the hue of caste warfare. The tendency, therefore, is to view every sign of antagonism between the castes before 1810 as a portent of what was to come in the near future.

In reality Caracas before 1810 probably had more stable race relations than most other colonies in the empire. In New Spain and Peru, social and economic oppression of the Indian and *mestizo* masses across the eighteenth century created the volatile environments which in Peru led to the Tupac Amaru revolt in 1781 and in New Spain bred urban riots, social banditry and the rage which led to the general massacre of whites in Guanajuato in 1810. In New Granada the *mestizo* population of the region was politicized enough by their sense of grievance to launch, in 1781, a tax rebellion mobilizing as many as 20,000 people. In Chile constant warfare with the numerous Arauco Indians required the maintenance of a military apparatus out of proportion to the colony's economic importance and strategic vulnerability to external attack. By comparison, as we shall presently see, the situation in late-colonial Caracas was relatively calm. It is true that the dominant white caste was in general defensive *vis-à-vis* the rest of the society. It is also true that elements of the *castas* were in our period resorting to violence in an unfocused reaction to their unpalatable lot. There was nothing unusual in either of these manifestations, however. In every colony where whites were a clear minority, a similar siege mentality was exhibited; and in all colonies, as in all historical periods, endemic poverty and repression led to social and criminal banditry. It is in fact misleading to focus on the attitudes of castes towards each other to explain racial tensions. These were likely to have been antagonistic from the time the racial hierarchy first evolved in the sixteenth century. What is of much greater interest in determining the level of racial tension in our province and in our period is the number, the kind and the impact of the disturbances which affected and strained the by then long-standing *status quo* which accommodated and regulated the coexistence between the castes. By this measure it cannot be said that racial friction in Caracas was increasing unduly as 1810 approached.

The political side of race relations in Caracas involved three of the four principal castes of the province: the whites, the free-coloureds and the black slaves. The Indian segment of the population was by the late-colonial period marginal to *caraqueño* society, no longer a military threat and now more of a neglected administrative charge than an active participant in the daily life of the province. The same cannot be said of the free-coloureds and the slaves, who could not be relegated to the shadows of colonial existence, the *pardos* because of their large numbers and the slaves because of their importance to the export economy. Their presence and role in society were a constant preoccupation of the minority whites who ruled the province.

The central relationship of caste interaction in the province was the one between whites and free-coloureds. It was certainly the most problematic one for whites in the late eighteenth century. The place of *pardos* in society was not as neatly contained by legal restrictions and the strength of social tradition as the whites might wish. The ambiguity was created by the blurring effects of miscegenation itself, by the nature of societal organization in the province and by imperial measures in the second half of the eighteenth century which accorded greater rights, on paper, to the coloured castes of the empire. It will be remembered that *caraqueño* society was unusual in that it allowed the mass of free-coloureds a degree of economic and spatial mobility. Imperial reforms enhanced this relative freedom. From 1760 onwards free-coloureds were permitted to participate in the militias, hold officer positions and enjoy *fuero* rights.[67] In 1795 the *castas* were granted the legal right to purchase dispensations from colour, illegitimacy and the like.[68]

The white caste was remarkably successful in stemming the readjustment which may have been threatening the caste *status quo* in the late 1700s. There was little that was dramatic in the manner by which the containment was achieved. In the case of the formation of the *pardo* militias there was never that much of a threat to the racial hierarchy in the first place. *Pardo* militias were officered at the highest levels by whites.[69] Free-coloured officers and soldiers did not receive the same salaries or array of privileges as their white counterparts.[70] *Pardo* units were kept strictly segregated from white companies to discourage ideas of equal status.[71] Furthermore the militarization of free-coloureds was comparatively and absolutely smaller than that of whites in the province.[72] There is no evidence of *pardo* militias being disruptive to the life of the province before 1810. In the light of the lack of noticeable controversy over their presence by the 1770s, it is possible to suggest that their existence was accepted by whites, and what is more was serving the purpose of co-opting free-coloureds who might otherwise grow disaffected with the white regime.

The complaints about the *pardo* militias contained in the Caracas Cabildo's 1796 protest of the royal *Gracias al Sacar* decree must therefore not be taken solely at face value. The allegation that the militias encouraged arrogance among the lower classes by granting them a dignity they did not have, was only one of several reinforcements of the case then being made against the royal concession of 1795 allowing the free-coloureds to buy dispensation from the stigmas of colour and illegitimacy. The potential significance of the measure was not lost on the white caste. Once freed of the colour bar the *castas* could compete on a more equal footing with whites for any number of occupations and privileges previously denied them. The vociferous and virulent public protest to the Crown of 28 November 1796 has become justly famous as the embodiment of white fear and loathing of the possible encroachments upwards of the lower castes.[73] Among many other things, they accused *pardos*, mulattos and *zambos* of being 'men of infamous and twisted lineage, uneducated and easily moved to commit the more horrendous of excesses'. It was strong language indeed, but whether it can be said that white attitudes had ever been any different is difficult to say. What this *informe* may represent in retrospect is the visceral defence of the caste system by those who had most gained from it and who now were forced to put their sentiments on the matter into writing in confronting the gravity of the threat which was apparently being posed.

It could be asserted that this *informe* of the Caracas City Council represents the clearest sign that whites in the province were on the defensive, and that a crisis of confidence was emerging as to whether the Crown would continue to guarantee the supremacy of whites in colonial society. The facts of the case just possibly suggest the opposite. There is no question that the creole and Spanish leaders of the white caste were highly apprehensive, but they still felt secure enough to appeal to Madrid for redress, and redress of sorts they received. Their hyperbolic expressions of anxiety found support in a Court which had never meant to promise equality to the castas. The articles granting colour dispensation in the 1795 decree were only a few of the 71 dispensations which could be bought by whites as much as by any other caste.[74] The Crown's overwhelming intention had been to raise money and only incidentally to provide the semblance of reward to deserving free-coloureds. To resolve the controversy it had stumbled into, the Crown adopted the middle course of continuing to pay lip service to the idea that some individuals of the *castas* were worthy of honours by not rescinding the offending clauses, while in practice it raised the costs of purchasing colour dispensations and obstructed, or allowed the obstruction of, attempts by free-coloureds to take advantage of the decree.[75] Diego Mexías Bejarano, head of a wealthy *pardo* family of the city of Caracas, bought his 'whiteness' in 1796 only to wait five years for royal confirmation.[76] When his son Lorenzo tried to enter the priesthood via the university in the early 1800s over strong white opposition, the Crown expediently decided the *gracia* it had granted Diego did not extend to his children, thus violating the spirit if not the letter of its own laws.[77] In more general terms, restrictions on the offices free-coloureds could occupy, the institutions they could enter and the clothes they could wear were maintained, and intermarriage between whites and non-whites continued to be virtually prohibited by a whole series of imperial decrees on the subject. If the whites of Caracas had been initially shocked by the wording of royal measures, they could not but feel comforted when the imperial authorities continued in practice to reinforce the hierarchical structure of their society. Tangible social advancement was virtually as closed off to free-coloureds in the decades before 1810 as it had ever been.

The *castas* themselves did not push particularly strongly on the legal front to assert their apparent rights. The more educated among them were certainly aware of the hypothetical potential of royal decrees on race. In a 1797 *informe* to the Crown asking that the 'laws of dispensation' should be maintained, the Gremio de Pardos of Caracas queried '[what] inconvenience does the Caracas council find in [a measure] which concedes to free and honourable *pardos* the dispensation of their colour? ... All the [measure] does is to draw us nearer to them, providing the means [for us] to ... unite and come to form and constitute ... one Family alone.'[78] Nevertheless the *pardos* were lethargic in trying to make this dream come true. During the lifetime of the *Gracias al Sacar* there were only eight attempts by free-coloureds in the province to seek dispensations of any kind.[79] To be fair, the chances of success, even for the hardy few who tested the law, were slim. Most eligible *pardos* probably realized the futility of the endeavour and the limited value of benefits which were only won at the expense of a public, bitter and humiliating struggle against the opposition of the white elite. The tenacity of the Bejaranos in pursuing the rule of law seems to have been the isolated exception, not the rule. Perhaps the most limiting factor at work on the potential militancy of the *pardos* was the small number of those well-off enough to take advantage of the legal reforms.[80] It is possible to suggest that this is why the few who ventured to make claims were so easily isolated and countered by white pressure.

The antisocial activities of the not-so-tractable mass of free-coloureds were not so easily checked; but then they never represented the threat to the *status quo* that the assertion of rights through legal means seemed to be. The problems of a floating population living in communities outside the pale of white society and engaging in acts of lawlessness had existed for at least a century, and what is more had been accommodated by the social structure. The difference in our period was that although the issue was not new, the seriousness with which the whites now treated it was quite a departure from the comparative *laissez-faire* of their attitude in earlier decades. The whole question, so easily open to misinterpretation, requires a closer examination.

To the orderly elements of the white caste, the floating population referred to was made up of individuals who 'having removed [themselves] ... from their towns and [Indian] settlements [and] retiring to unpopulated and untilled [places] where [criminals] ... vagrants and malcontents of all classes [gather] ..., foment and undertake every kind of atrocity.'[81] It was, as we shall see, in the interest of the white caste to portray illegal communities, a migrant population and criminality as part and parcel of the same phenomenon. In reality of course, the 'problems' were not necessarily interrelated. In the Coastal Range region, where over a third of the free-coloured population lived and where unsanctioned settlements formed outside the law were most prevalent, there is little indication that crime or vagrancy were much of a problem. In the Llanos further inland, however, where roughly another 40% of the free-coloureds in the province lived, crime and vagrancy may have been more pronounced.

The formation of settlements in the coastal valleys outside the boundaries established by the Spanish urban network, is a manifestation of colonial life we still know only a little about. The tendency has been to view these communities as conglomerations of runaway slaves, created by the latter as a means of providing sustenance, abodes and group protection against recapture.[82] There is no question that many *cumbes* were founded and maintained by runaways, but the evidence is that they attracted a considerable number of free-coloureds, Indians and even whites. It is at least hypothetically possible that by the eighteenth century the *cumbes* sheltered more freemen than fugitive slaves. A 1716 royal order to the Governor of the province ordered him to subdue 'the Spaniards, mulattoes and free blacks who wander as fugitives in the mountains'.[83] In 1770 a Tuy valley *cumbe* was described as containing 'Indians, whites . . .' as well as runaways.[84] In 1776 a *rochela* in Cata, down the coast from Puerto Cabello, was populated by '*zambos*, blacks and mulattoes'.[85] Why freemen were attracted to these settlements is not entirely clear. Some may have been escaping punishment for real or alleged crimes, and this would probably be especially true of the whites present. Nonetheless the fact that these communities were set up with an air of permanence in reasonably well-populated areas easily accessible to harassment from local authorities suggests that fear of the law was not the primary motive in their creation.[86] Rather it would seem that elements of the free-coloured and Indian population were seeking to escape the yoke of white society by living in greater but ordered freedom on its boundaries.

The life of free-coloureds in the Llanos on the other hand, was less structured and more violent. The combination of the recent and scattered nature of urban settlements on the open plains, of an economy built around the movement of livestock to pastures and markets and of the existence of an at least partly nomadic population which tended the herds bred a frontier environment where lawlessness was encouraged. It is not too far-fetched to speculate that the region, because of its vastness and lack of structural development, attracted the hardcase criminals and fugitives of other regions, compounding the crime problem. As we have already seen, rustling was so widespread that it seriously affected the functioning of the livestock industry. If the dangers to personal life and property were exaggerated in contemporary accounts as one historian plausibly suggests,[87] it is still safe to say that the Llanos were the least peaceful region of the province and that members of the *castas* with no fixed habitat were predominantly responsible for the mayhem which did occur.

How many free-coloureds were involved in either the *cumbes* or outright lawlessness is probably impossible to establish. One estimate of the total population living outside the pale in the 1780s put the number at 24,000, including individuals of all castes and men, women and children.[88] What is certain is that the problem in its totality was proportionately and absolutely no worse than it had been since the beginning of the eighteenth century. What had changed by the 1770s were white expectations of what could be done about the relatively large population of disaffected *castas*, and about the mass of the free-coloured population as a whole.

The attempt by whites, both Spanish and creole, to come up in the 1770s, 1780s and 1790s with a way to police the *castas* and to tie down the rural free-coloureds to fixed abodes reflected changing social circumstances and the hardening of white attitudes. In the Coastal Range the presence of semi-anarchic communities in the midst of a developing urban and economic network must have seemed less and less tolerable across the 1700s to colonial authorities and *hacendados* who had never accepted their creation in the first place. Once removed from population centres, the illegal settlements now found themselves in close proximity to what their inhabitants had once fled from. The same factors were at work in the Llanos as new towns sprang up, as new *hatos* were established and as the open spaces of the plains were laid claim to by *caraqueño hacendados*. Squatter and nomadic rights became particularly unacceptable to planters and ranchers in search of land and labour. The colonial bureaucracy and the *hacendados* did not, however, entirely agree on the measures necessary to achieve their apparently similar objective of public order. For Crown officials it was a question of discouraging illegal settlements by violent means if necessary, or returning runaway slaves found in these communities to their owners and of patrolling the province more carefully to deter crime. The *hacendados* however preferred to see the relatively contained problems of the *cumbes* and the wandering population of the Llanos as proof of their argument that everyone would be better off if the *castas* as a whole were more tied down. Their motivation, examined earlier in another light, was simple: to reduce the free-coloureds to indebted servitude on the haciendas and *hatos* of the province. Their most brazen attempt at instituting a pass-system occurred in the early 1770s, when a group of major *hateros* suggested a new legal code for the Llanos, granting leading ranchers of different localities the right to police the population and the livestock of their districts, and in the process usurp the authority of already constituted local officials.[89] The most they were able to achieve, however, was the creation of special military squadrons for police work in the Llanos and later in the valleys of the Coastal Range.[90]

In retrospect, the greatest threat to peaceful race relations in the province before 1810 was latent rather than actual. The practical gains made by *caraqueño* whites in protecting their supremacy and in imposing greater social control of the mass of free-coloureds were small enough not to alter the *status quo* significantly or to seriously increase the potential for friction in the province. The majority of free-coloureds more or less settled quietly within the confines of white society, general coexistence being facilitated by a degree of economic and social mobility, the absence of famine and the failure of the whites to implement some of their more extreme plans for curtailing the already limited freedoms of the *castas*. In these plans, however, lay some of the seeds of the virtual race wars of the 1810s. The white elite of the province clearly had every intention of taking a more active part in law enforcement in rural areas and of introducing a pass-system for free-coloureds sooner or later. Stronger economically and socially than ever before, they could now think of formalizing their domination of the lower castes. When they finally did try in 1811, they helped overturn the delicate balance of caste relations in the colony.

By comparison, the relations between whites and black slaves were a much less complex affair. The total subjugation of the bondsmen was never in legal question in the late-colonial period. The Crown did try rather feebly to humanize the institution by introducing a new slave code in 1789, but violent protests from Caracas and other parts of the empire insured that the reformist Código Negro was never applied.[91] Slaves in Caracas could still appeal against mistreatment by their owners in court as well as hope for manumission at some stage in their lifetimes.[92] Neither avenue offered much chance of redemption from their condition. The number of slaves who could even consider pressing their grievances legally must have been infinitesimally small, and the prospect of manumission, as we have seen, was remote. The only real recourses open to slaves pushed beyond the limits of their endurance were either to become runaways and join the *cumbes*, or to rebel openly and violently against their masters. Slaves did both in our period, but whether their actions were symptomatic of deeper than usual master–slave tensions, is another matter.

Runaways were without question a problem for slave-holders in our province in the late 1700s. There was nothing original about this phenomenon, however: fugitive slaves have always been a feature of slave systems at any time and in any place. If a 1721 estimate is to be believed, better than one out of every three slaves in the province that year was a runaway or *cimarrón*, living in *cumbes* or otherwise scattered across the countryside.[93] Historians have projected forward from the 1721 figures to arrive at an estimate of around 30,000 *cimarrones* for the late-colonial period against the 60,000 slaves held in captivity.[94]

Neither estimate of the fugitive slave population is convincing enough to be taken at face value. If the incidence of runaways was indeed as high as the figures suggest, it would have been extremely unprofitable for planters and others to continue purchasing new slaves if as many as a third of the bondsmen were likely to escape. Indeed owners would have quickly fallen into debt, lost the labour and thus the means to recoup their considerable long-term investments. Yet the evidence is that across the eighteenth century many more tens of thousands of slaves were imported into the province, almost surpassing the combined total of imports in the previous two centuries;[95] and furthermore the new slaves were sold at prices higher than ever before.[96] Unless the business-minded *caraqueño* planters enjoyed throwing away money, the above would suggest they had every expectation of holding onto their purchases for a long time.

Quite apart from the issue of whether it was worthwhile holding slaves who were going to flee sooner or later, the estimates of runaways imply the existence of a continual insurrectionary situation. This was clearly not the case in Caracas. In the face of what should have been an intolerable strain, local authorities and *hacendados* did little to confront the threat to public order and the economic losses implicit in having a third or more of the slaves of the province continually on the run. The danger was even greater than it appears if we consider that the majority of *cumbes*, which are seen by historians as primarily communities of *cimarrones*, were located in the midst of the Aragua and Tuy valleys, which were the plantation–agriculture and population centres of the province. The incitement to slaves under bondage to follow course is obvious. Yet there is only one documented example of a serious attempt being made by colonial authorities and *hacendados* to attack these communities flourishing in their own backyard and to round up the runaways they contained. This effort took place in late 1794 and for most of 1795, and netted 300 or so slaves.[97] If indeed the illegal settlements had been the population centres for a large proportion of the alleged 30,000 or so runaways and their offspring, it is inconceivable that so small a number were actually apprehended and that no lives were lost in the process of recapturing them.

What then was the real status of the runaways problem in our province? I would suggest, in the first place, that *cumbes* and the like were not the large gatherings of slaves that has been supposed. Without doubt they acted as magnets to slaves brave enough to dare escape in our period, and fugitives may indeed at times have tried to found new ones. Yet the evidence as examined earlier points to the more settled and permanent *cumbes* as being populated largely by free-coloureds of one kind or another. This would help explain the relative tolerance exhibited by the white leadership to their continued existence in the proximity of white-owned plantations worked by slaves. In the second place it would seem that the actual number of *cimarrones* in Caracas was much lower than has been estimated. This contention gains strength when we consider the confusion which has clouded the forward projections made on the 1721 figure. Not a few historians have mistaken the 1780s estimate of the *vago* population as the number of *cimarrones* at large in the Llanos alone.[98] As we have seen however, the 24,000 figure applied to the *población volante* as a whole and appears to be the estimate for the province and not just one region. We have also seen how runaways were often spoken of by contemporaries in the same breath as other supposed vagrants. It is at least hypothetically possible that Olavarriaga's 1721 estimate also covered the complete range of the floating population.

In marked contrast to the recurring incidence of runaways, only one open slave rebellion occurred in Caracas in the late 1700s and early 1800s. Although white apprehension increased after the black-slave revolt in Haiti in 1791, the fear of a violent revolt far exceeded the actual threat. The slave revolt which took place in the *partido* of Coro in May 1795 was the exception which proved the rule.[99] Fascinating as the genesis and course of the three-day uprising is, its significance should not be overestimated. Both the rebellion and the region had special characteristics which could not have been easily duplicated elsewhere in Caracas. Coro, in the north-western corner, was well removed from the economic and population centres of the province. An atypical slave society had evolved, based primarily on livestock ranches, in addition to a smaller number of cash-crop plantations.[100] The *hatos* and haciendas were worked largely by a tenancy system in which not only free-coloureds but also slaves participated.[101] As a consequence *pardos*, *negros libres* and slaves probably mixed more freely and openly than elsewhere in the province. The racial composition of the population was also unusual: the number of whites was only little more than half the provincial average.[102] Although slaves were proportionately no more numerous than elsewhere in Caracas, indeed even less so, the white minority in Coro may have felt more under siege in the heavily *pardo*, black and Indian population.

The attempt by authorities in the 1790s to squeeze taxes from the production of the large free-coloured tenant class increased whatever racial tensions already existed in the district. In the Curimagua region, south of the city of Coro, the resentment coincided with the appearance of two charismatic individuals: the free *zambo* and tenant farmer José Leonardo Chirinos and the free black and mystic José Caridad González. Both were influenced by what they had managed to learn of the French Revolution, of events in Haiti and of the Código Negro. The proximity of Coro to the information conduit of nearby Curaçao facilitated the transference of the subversive influences these two men picked up. In Curimagua, a centre of plantation agriculture in Coro and probably an area hard hit by the new taxes, Chirinos and González found an audience. On 10 May 1795 the slaves and free-coloureds they had influenced rose in revolt, proclaiming among their goals the abolition of slavery and taxes.

Considering the explosive mix of ingredients the conspiracy represented, uniting as it did the aspirations and frustrations of free-coloureds and slaves, the revolt was a curiously isolated and small-scale affair even within the confines of Coro. Of a possible 15,000 slaves, *pardos* and free blacks in the district, only 200 to 300 joined in the rebellion. Less than a score of whites were killed and the unrest did not noticeably spread beyond the limited boundaries of the Curimagua region. Within Curimagua the revolt was crushed in less than 3 days, and in the ensuing months at least 170 slaves and free-coloureds paid with their lives for the audacity of the rebels. Worse, the sacrifice was in vain. There was no ripple effect of measureable significance either in Coro or the rest of the province of Caracas. No leaders, no comparable pressures and no alliance between free-coloureds and slaves developed elsewhere to spark another revolt.

Administrative and local politics

In the relatively peaceful and prosperous climate of the 1780s and early 1790s there was more than the usual scope allowed for the administrative questions and power intrigues of a lesser nature which make up the bulk of political activity in any society. The problems of day-to-day administration, jurisdictional disputes between governing institutions, power plays by one royal official against another and the incidence of corruption attracted considerable attention from the politicians of the province even as they dealt with more important matters. To analyse this lesser political world in depth would require more space than I can allow here, but its character is still worth outlining, not least because it helps place the greater issues of the day in a broader perspective of the political environment as a whole.

It was perhaps inevitable that conflicts over jurisdictional responsibility should develop. Many of the institutions in the province including the Intendancy, the Captaincy-General, the Audiencia and the Consulado were either created in these years or were only recent additions to the colony. Boundaries of authority had yet to be clarified on paper and by practice. I have already examined some of the tension this caused between intendants and captains-general but friction affected all levels of inter-institutional relations. In 1784 the Bishop of Caracas, the Intendant and the Cabildo clashed over the naming of stewards on the newly-formed *juntas de diezmo*.[103] In 1785 the Captain-General complained that the Audiencia of Santo Domingo, to which our province was subject until 1786, was not adequately informing him of its proceedings and was usurping his authority over a legal case by turning it over to his Intendant.[104] In 1786 a representative for the public notaries of Caracas condemned the interference of Treasury Officials in the discharge of notarial duties.[105] In 1789 the ministers of the Treasury claimed that the Intendant was curtailing their right to name their own subordinates.[106] In 1790 the general auditor of the province made the same charge against the Captain-General.[107] In the same year the Caracas Ayuntamiento argued that the *junta* of the Real Hacienda could not void an appointment they had made to a city post.[108] After 1793 the Consulado petitioned for the right to judge boundary and water disputes between *hacendados* which, if granted, would have left the fledgling Audiencia of Caracas with little but criminal cases to prosecute.[109] The attempt by Captain-General Carbonell in the 1790s to reform and centralize the administration of the *tenientazgo* system met the opposition of other officials and *hacendados* zealous to preserve their influence over the appointment procedure.[110] The most remarkable, documented example of conflict affected the *tenientazgos* of the important indigo-producing district of Maracay in the Aragua valleys. Across a period of almost thirty years the powerful *hacendado* Antonio Fernández de León managed to have at least two Justices of the Peace ousted from their posts in the 1780s and 1790s, and their successors in the 1800s were described as being his hand-picked men ready to do his bidding.[111]

The incidence of corruption and scandal in these years preoccupied the political class of the province somewhat less than their differences over dividing power. This is not to say that corruption was not a constant problem. Fraud in the keeping of Treasury accounts was regularly uncovered in one branch or another. The employees of the tobacco monopoly in general were described in 1792 by their ex-head and present Intendant Esteban de León as having a 'disordered propensity to enrich themselves'.[112] In 1789 and 1792 the tax offices of *temporalidades* and *bienes de difuntos* were respectively suspected of fraud in their account-keeping.[113] In 1792 the engineer in charge of building fortifications for the port of La Guaira, Fermín de Rueda, managed to siphon off thousands of pesos with the apparent collusion of senior officials, including the Intendant León.[114] Further afield, the military garrison of the province of Guayana found 15,000 pesos to be missing from its expense allocations in 1789.[115] Matters were hardly more in control in other spheres less obviously connected to fiscal collections and expenditures. Captain-General Guillelmi in 1786 and the Audiencia in 1794 complained of the widespread dishonesty of Justices of the Peace.[116] The sale of lesser public offices was plagued by bribery and attempts to underpay the Treasury for the real value of the posts, especially in the case of notarial positions.[117] In 1791 the price-tag of *escribanías* was revised upward in an unsuccessful effort to ensure their orderly sale and purchase.[118]

The documentation on the conflicts of jurisdiction and on corruption reveals something about the formation of political cabals in the colony. The connecting thread through the 1780s and the 1790s was the participation of the León brothers. Both Antonio, the merchant-agriculturalist based in Maracay, and Esteban, the future Intendant, began their rise to political influence and power under the Intendant Saavedra and the Captain-General Guillelmi in the mid-1780s.[119] Whether the brothers' ties to the then-senior officials in the province were the product of friendship or of mutually convenient political alliances is difficult to establish. Esteban's successful directorship during the 1780s of the pivotal tobacco monopoly on which so much of the administration's finances rested, and Antonio's position as one of the wealthiest merchant-*hacendados* of Caracas, and his strong connections with the creole elite, could not but have assisted their climb to power once they gained a foothold. The arrival from New Spain in 1787 of Antonio López Quintana to head the newly-created Audiencia of Caracas added a further reinforcement to the Leóns. A friend of the family since their days in Spain, he was to prove a staunch political ally in the coming years.[120] The connections with figures in high places soon paid big dividends when Esteban became Intendant and economic overlord of the province in 1791.

During the 1790s, with their power formalized by Esteban's promotion, the León brothers and their allies ruled the province with something approaching dictatorial powers, if their many enemies are to be believed. The Captain-General between 1792 and 1799, Pedro Carbonell, was certainly not much of a match for them, being as he was old, suffering from ill health and overly absorbed with personal affairs.[121] Along with other León critics he saw the courts, justice in general and the fiscal branches of government as being in the brothers' hands.[122] The opposition was probably correct: an alliance including the Leóns, Quintana, the fourth Marqués del Toro (another friend of the family), the lawyer of independence fame, Dr Francisco Espejo, the very wealthy *hacendado* Dr José Ignacio Moreno, as well as assorted members of the Caracas Cabildo and the Audiencia was a formidable political entity indeed.[123] The León group was labelled at least on one occasion as anti-European, and it would be easy to consider it as a creole, *hacendado* clique except for the fact that it included senior Spanish officials and immigrant *hacendados*.[124]

1797–1802

The years at the turn of the century were perhaps the most difficult ones Caracas went through in the decades before 1808. Spain's new war with Britain between 1796 and 1802 raised the spectre of the province's direct involvement in military hostilities for the first time since the early 1740s. The revolutionary ferment affecting France found a disturbing echo in Caracas with the Gual-España conspiracy of 1797. Most unsettling of all was the severe economic depression which the war brought in its wake. The not always compatible attempts by planters, merchants and officials to confront the sharp downturn of the economy seriously strained the political balance inside the colony.

The preliminary phase to these hard times was the mildly negative experience of Caracas during Spain's war against republican France between 1793 and 1795. Even before hostilities began, rumours of an impending war led to a 'notable fall' in the prices of the province's export commodities.[125] The Intendant León appears to have immediately permitted greater leeway on trade with the foreign colonies, and once war was declared in March of the same year he responded favourably to a Caracas Cabildo suggestion that public funds should be used to purchase the crops of needy *hacendados*.[126] A system of convoys was introduced to protect merchant ships leaving from the province, which operated for the duration of the war.[127] These emergency measures were successful. In spite of the occasional depredations of French corsairs and a probable increase in the level of contraband, the province's trade with Spain continued to flourish through the two years of the war against France.[128]

More problematic than the war's effect on trade was its impact on the province's administrative finances. The Crown did what it usually did in times of war and requested of the colonies in general special 'donations' over and above the customary remissions to Spain. In Caracas' case that translated into sales and excise duties on economic activity in the province, the appropriation of funds from corporate bodies like the Church and obligatory contributions from the salaries of public employees.[129] The rise in the real or perceived defence needs of the province was even more detrimental to the health of the colony's finances. In the first three months of war 300,000 pesos went on extraordinary expenditures, and this in a province where annual tax receipts were usually under 1,500,000 pesos and where normal expenses equalled the intake.[130]

The fiscal crisis was aggravated by events in the Caribbean theatre of the war. Spain joined forces with Britain in an ill-judged assault on Haiti aimed at rescuing whites from the slave rebellion then raging, aiding royalist Frenchmen on the island against French republican forces and reinstalling order, if possible through annexation.[131] The Spaniards used their half of the island, Santo Domingo, as their military base but soon found it necessary to involve more of its neighbouring colonies. Caracas was called upon to supply money, men and arms.[132] The fleet at Puerto Cabello became a combination of convoy service for merchant ships and a logistical backup for the forces in Santo Domingo.[133] The province itself became a temporary repository for some 700 French republican prisoners, and 200 slaves from the French colonies.[134] The financial strain on Caracas was considerable: 240,000 pesos were sent to Santo Domingo for the war effort; 600,000 pesos were supplied in one form or another to the Puerto Cabello fleet; and 160,000 pesos were spent for the maintenance of the *émigrés* and prisoners, and on their transport out of the province.[135]

The war with France ended in July 1795. At the time it must have seemed to contemporaries that Caracas had come through relatively unscathed. The province's economy had escaped a serious downturn and the colonial administration's finances, for all the demands placed on them, had proved resilient. The potentially subversive influence represented by the presence of hundreds of republican French prisoners held in the province, ended when the prisoners were removed.[136] No new political rift had appeared inside the colony because of the external hostilities. Accordingly, across 1796 life in Caracas regained much of its normal pace, but in the mother country the threat of renewed hostilities hung unremittingly in the air. Under pressure from both Britain and France, Spain decided to throw its fortunes in with Napoleon and in October 1796 went to war against Britain.

The negative consequences for Caracas of the new war soon made themselves felt. The gravity of the crisis was recognized early in the merchant circles in Cádiz which traded with the province. The number of ships sent from Spain to La Guaira dropped from 43 in 1796 to 7 in 1797 with a corresponding decline in imports into Caracas from just over 3,000,000 pesos to less than 100,000 pesos.[137] Traders in Caracas were slower in acknowledging the dangers inherent in navigating seas patrolled by an enemy that also happened to be the major maritime power in the world. At least 20 of the 28 ships sent out from La Guaira to Spain in 1797 were sunk or seized by the British with losses totalling 600,000 pesos worth of exports.[138] The disastrous downturn of the economy was complicated by the British conquest of the Venezuelan province of Trinidad in February 1797. Royal officials feared with good reason that an invasion of sorts might be launched against mainland Venezuela, if not against Caracas then at least against its neighbouring province of Cumaná.[139] The aborted Gual and España republican conspiracy uncovered in La Guaira in July 1797 only heightened the atmosphere of crisis. Defence preparations intensified, and a determined search began to find the means for buying armaments and paying for the mobilization of militias and the refurbishment of fortifications.

One source which could not be turned to was government income from taxes. The sharp contraction of economic activity devastated government finances. The Intendant León was forced to consider extraordinary measures to raise money. Among the actions he took was the opening of the province to unrestricted trade with friendly or neutral foreign powers and their colonies.

As early as 22 December 1796 León was informing the Crown of requests by the Caracas Ayuntamiento and the Consulado for convoys as well as the right to export the province's commodities in neutral ships.[140] Among the signers of the Cabildo petition were two of the most important merchants of Caracas, the Spaniard Juan Bautista Echezuría and the creole Luis López Méndez. León in forwarding the request may have been doing no more than fulfilling his official duties, but the likelihood is that he was paving the way towards opening the province up. He was no enemy to commerce with the Antilles and in the previous emergency of the French war he had relaxed the province's trade regulations before seeking authority from Spain to do so. As economic conditions deteriorated and fiscal needs increased in early 1797, León won over the Captain-General, Carbonell, who had initially opposed the idea.[141] León then sought the opinions of the merchant and agricultural halves of the Consulado on how best to promulgate the measure. Both interest groups favoured free trade for exports, but a schism appeared over what to do about imports, with most merchants favouring restrictions on what could be brought in on foreign ships and agriculturalists opposing any limitations. The merchants' apprehensions were only natural: they derived much of their profits from importing foreign goods via Spain and felt they would suffer serious losses if imports began to come more directly from the source of manufacture; but notwithstanding merchant objections, and in recognition of the growing shortage of essential imports, León authorized unrestricted free trade and lower excise-taxes in April 1797. He received royal approval for his decision in October of the same year.

It would seem, as I will presently explain, that most merchants soon accepted the April free-trade decree and set about benefiting from it. What did incite the anger of the mercantile community as a whole was León's proposal to sell almost 1,000,000 pesos worth of tobacco, stored by the state monopoly, to foreign trading firms in the Caribbean, in return for munitions, cash and necessary imports.[142] León actually did first approach *caraqueño* merchants, asking them either to lend the administration 400,000 pesos or to take charge of selling the tobacco themselves. Probably because of lack of funds, no local traders came forward, and León went ahead and arranged a tentative contract with Eckard and Company of the Danish island of St Thomas, in effect barring the *caraqueño* merchant community from an extraordinarily large business enterprise.

When León informed the Consulado of the arrangements with Eckard in October 1797, part of the merchant block moved in opposition. Four men were appointed to investigate the merits of the impending contract. They were Bernardo Larrain, Martín Baraciarte, José de las Llamosas and Juan Esteban Echezuría. In their 19 October report these men went far beyond the pros and cons of the Eckard deal and launched a tirade against free trade with foreign parts under any circumstances.[143] They openly questioned the Intendant's assertion that there was a fiscal crisis and argued that the military threat of the war was receding. Apparently not knowing yet of the Crown's approval of León's measures, they accused him indirectly of violating royal prohibitions on trading with the enemy by permitting commerce with foreign colonies which were nothing more than emporiums for British goods. This concession would ruin forever Spain's hold on the province's economy. It was better to let the tobacco and other commodities rot than to give foreign firms the chance to penetrate the market, an inroad which once gained would never be lost.

If the case made by the four deputies was intended primarily to discredit the giant Eckard contract, which could legitimately be perceived as a threat to local trading-interests, they succeeded to some extent. The delaying and obstructing tactics discouraged Eckard, and in January 1798 he backed away from buying the 40,000 available quintals of tobacco and agreed to purchase only 14,000 quintals, on terms not entirely favourable to the Caracas Treasury.[144] However, if the four deputies had been hoping to mobilize merchants and the Crown against the free-trade concessions, they failed. León appealed to the Consulado for its true opinion on the subject. Only two of the six merchants on the eleven-member governing council of the Guild categorically rejected free trade.[145] They were Domingo Zulueta and Juan José Mintegui. The latter had been one of the officials of the deceased Guipuzcoa Company which had once controlled *caraqueño* commerce. At the very least it can be said merchant opinion was divided on the issue.

The matter was not allowed to rest there. The *hacendados* of the Consulado, fearing the merchant *representación* might reach receptive hands in the Court, issued a lengthy rebuttal on 25 January 1798.[146] It was co-signed by four of the wealthiest men of the province: Martín Herrera, Manuel Felipe de Tovar, Martín de Aristiguieta and the Conde de San Xavier. Without question they acted with the collusion of the Intendant León, who may even have gone as far as helping to draft the document.[147] Whoever wrote it, the *hacendado* report was a savage, double-edged counter-attack against the previous paper. At one level, it was a defence of León's open-trade policies. With relentless, if rambling, logic the agriculturalists confirmed the existence of a fiscal crisis and the need for totally unrestricted trade. They pointed out that the Antilles exchange could not become a replacement for trade with Spain but that what it did provide was some relief from the economic collapse facing Caracas.

The *hacendados* of course already knew of the Crown's confirmation of free trade. The real thrust of their message was expressed at the second level of their *representación*. They delivered a scathing diatribe against the group of merchants they felt were behind the 1797 report, the old and new representatives of the old Caracas Company. The planters charged that adventurous merchants had already transferred their interests to the foreign colonies and were making a good business of it. In fact, they said, the majority of merchants favoured free trade. Even among those who complained, there were individuals who were buying consignments of imports from foreigners and reselling them at high prices. These same men bought up commodities for export and sold them profitably to foreign traders. If the validity of free trade was not really the issue, what then had been the motivation of the merchants' report? The agents of monopoly wanted to reassert their control and sensed the opportunity had presented itself in the current crisis. The *hacendados* reviewed the history of the Guipuzcoana from the 1730s through to its reincarnation as the Filipinas Company. They pointed out how the latter had continued to stifle competition until 1789 and had tried to manipulate prices in the downturn of 1793, thwarted of course by León's contingency measures. And it was the ghost of the monopoly which was now behind the present controversy.

Did the cabal the planters referred to actually exist? The evidence is that it did. The planters' *representación* mentioned by name Juan José Mintegui, Juan José Echenique and Joaquín de Anza, all of whom were ex-employees of the Caracas Company. They were supported by the Filipinas Company's representative in the province, Simón Mayora.[148] Their ties to the four deputies who co-authored the October report are less clear. It should be pointed out that across 1797 and 1798 Echenique, Anza and Mintegui held executive positions in the Consulado and were thus able to choose, or at least influence the choice of, the deputies picked to examine the Eckard deal.[149] In the poorly-attended Guild meetings such manoeuvrings would not have been inconceivable. León was later to say that the report's authors 'are not, as they call themselves, representatives of the merchant body'.[150] Appointed for a very specific purpose, they had far exceeded their authority.

In short the merchant report was probably as unrepresentative of wider merchant opinion as the planters said it was. It is highly significant that major traders like Key Muñoz, the López Meńdez brothers and the Iriartes did not rush to publicize their support for the Guipuzcoana group, either during the controversy or when Mayora and the rest appealed to the Council of Indies to censure both the *hacendado* tract and León's conduct during the episode. In July 1799 the Council, while agreeing that the document was libellous and that León had been less than impartial, recommended that the incident should be forgotten as soon as possible.[151] This was probably what occurred. When the Crown decided to rescind the free-trade concessions in the same year, the authors of the 1797 controversy, Larrain, Llamosas, Echenique, and Mintegui, joined the united offensive by officials, planters and merchants to convince the Crown that it should reopen the ports of the province.

By 1799 no one inside Caracas was really questioning the need for free trade. The economy had managed to keep afloat only because of the exchange it had carried on with the foreign Antilles, and even with this outlet exports were down to roughly half their pre-war levels. This time there was no controversy when León arranged another million-peso contract exchanging tobacco for guns and *viveres* with Robinson, Phillips and Corser of Curaçao in November 1799.[152] The economic situation was desperate and, unlike the case in 1797, every interest group in the province recognized it as such.

In April 1799 the Crown, under pressure from the Cádiz Consulado, revoked the free-trade privileges in all the colonies.[153] The news was made known in Caracas in July and general consternation broke out. León may not even have bothered enforcing the new decree. In November, and working with the new Captain-General Guevara Vasconcelos, León suspended the royal prohibition. He did not inform the Crown until 14 December. The delay was beneficial to the province, but ultimately futile. The Crown in an order dated 13 February 1800 reaffirmed the prohibition. By June the new trade regulations were being enforced.

A concentrated effort now began in earnest to regain the lost concessions. The Consulado was formally asked by the Intendant to gather the statistical documentation proving the necessity of free trade.[154] On one occasion fourteen merchants including Echenique, Mintegui and Larrain allowed themselves to be interviewed on the causes of the deteriorating situation and several recounted their own negative experiences.[155] On another occasion ten leading *hacendados* went through the same ritual.[156] Even the Church abetted the effort, pointing out how the intake of tithes had dropped markedly since 1797.[157] All information was presented in the guise of requests for the resumption of free trade. Meanwhile the Intendancy renewed its wartime policy of purchasing limited amounts of the province's export commodities at market prices in an attempt to provide some relief from the worsening crisis.[158]

Sometime in 1800 during this critical juncture León fell ill and his place was temporarily taken by his old political ally Quintana, the Regent of the Audiencia.[159] The quest for free trade moved slowly thereafter. We can hypothesize that Quintana was more cautious politically, and that the fall of Curaçao, the major outlet for Venezuelan goods in the Caribbean, to British forces in mid-1800, may have made the matter of free trade almost a non-issue. By the time the documents petitioning for free trade were ready, in early 1801, the Crown had already decided to restore open commerce till the end of the year. In Caracas the new grace period went into effect on 22 May 1801.[160] León, back in the saddle again, again acted independently of Spain and in October informed the Crown he had extended the concession until July 1802 or until peace was achieved.[161] The latter came first. Although the Treaty of Amiens with Britain was not signed until March 1802, peace talks between the two nations actually began in October 1801. León was ordered to suspend free trade and on 22 December 1801 this was what he did.[162]

The difficulties which beset the economy and government finances in this period were compounded by other kinds of problem. Most were also directly related to the course of the war. The near-constant military threat posed by the British takeover of Trinidad in 1797 and of nearby Dutch Curaçao in 1800 led to a renewed concern with upgrading the defence capabilities of the region. Caracas once more became involved in the traffic of refugees. As the British conquered more islands, more *émigrés* came to the province. When Toussaint's Haitian blacks overran Spanish Santo Domingo, a further 1,500 refugees arrived in 1801 alone.[163] The captains-general of Caracas not surprisingly spent much of their time monitoring events in the Caribbean. The revolutionary ferment still alive in the area was especially worrisome. From Trinidad the new British governor, Thomas Picton, did his best to spread inflammatory propaganda to the Venezuelan mainland, urging the local population to rise against their king. Picton, through no fault of his own, actually did manage to become a supporting actor in the one subversive movement which did materialize: the unsuccessful Gual and España conspiracy.[164]

The conspiracy had its roots in La Guaira, the province's principal port, at one day's ride from the city of Caracas. As early as 1794 a small group of men had begun discussing the possibility of a republican revolution. They were headed by two longtime Spanish residents of the province: Manuel Gual, a retired captain of the regular army, and José

María España, a local *hacendado* and *teniente justicia* of the small Indian village of nearby Macuto. What may have been no more than the small-talk of armchair revolutionaries was given encouragement in 1796 with the arrival in La Guaira of four convicted conspirators of the foiled Ruy Blas republican complot in Spain, who were then in transit to their places of permanent imprisonment. Their transfer was delayed and across the following months the loosely guarded prisoners were in almost daily contact with local inhabitants. Among their visitors were Gual and España who, under the influence of one of the prisoners in particular, Juan Picornell, planned an uprising in the province along French republican lines. In June 1797 Picornell escaped and made his way to the foreign Antilles. At the same time authorities in Caracas learned of the conspiracy through the carelessness of one of the organizers. In mid-July the few dozen conspirators were rounded up. They were tried, some were absolved and the rest given lenient sentences in accordance with the long-standing royal policy in Caracas of discouraging subversion by basically ignoring it. Gual and España, however, managed to escape and in 1798 found themselves in Trinidad where, with Picton's aid, they began to plot new adventures on the mainland. It was not to be: Picton had no logistical support to offer them and there were hardly enough revolutionaries in exile to attempt an invasion. España nonetheless returned to Caracas under cover in early 1799, resolved to start the revolution by inciting a black uprising. Betrayed by one of his own servants, this impractical radical and idealist was finally arrested by the authorities in his own house. There was to be no clemency this time: his actions were deemed far too serious to ignore. As was the case of Coro in 1795, when race war was also the issue, the guilty were executed. España was accompanied to his death by five of his co-conspirators.

Whatever the significance of the Gual and España episode, it is certainly not derived from the course events took. The conspiracy was an isolated and badly organized affair and the evidence suggests it would never have taken on even the modest proportions it did if it had not been for the oversight of royal officials in the port and in Caracas. La Guaira, though the major point of entry into the province, was a small town of some 4,000 inhabitants plus several hundred military personnel. It had been at the very least a questionable decision in 1793 to concentrate up to 1,000 French republican prisoners for the better part of two years in a place where they temporarily came to represent one-fifth of the population. Worse, supervision over their movements was not as strict as it might have been. The same relaxed custody then characterized the stay of Picornell and company. León and Quintana later blamed the aged and infirm Carbonell for permitting a situation to develop where subversive influences could spread.[165] In defence of Carbonell, it must be said that the Crown's leniency, first with the captured French and subsequently with the Ruy Blas conspirators, must have lulled the Captain-General into thinking matters were under control.

Once the conspiracy was aborted it was discovered to have only limited dimensions. Of seventy-two persons implicated, twelve were entirely cleared of charges and forty-two were exiled but then amnestied. Of those involved, twenty-five were Spaniards, fourteen were creoles and thirty-three were free-coloureds. Forty-one of the seventy-two were members either of the regular army or of the militias. The odd mix should surprise no one acquainted with the course of attempted coups. The large number of free-coloureds can be explained by senior officials involving subordinates who were probably not very sure of the reasons for the conspiracy. The light sentences they received confirms this hypothesis. Nor should too much be made of the fact that among the whites there were planters, merchants, lawyers and even a priest. No major planter, merchant or official was incriminated and Carbonell congratulated himself that 'the strongest and most illustrious of these loyal [*caraqueño*] vassals have remained untainted [by the conspiracy]'.[166] Indeed the scions of leading local families rushed to offer the Crown their support, including the fourth Marqués del Toro, the Conde de Tovar and Antonio Fernández de León. It would seem Spain had more to fear from the actions of Spaniards ingesting too liberally the ideas of the French Revolution than from the actions of restless colonials.

The wider significance of Gual and España lies on a more philosophic plane than its tragicomic trajectory would seem to allow: it was firm evidence that republican ideals were having an impact, however limited, on the province. The educated classes of Caracas had, of course, been aware of their existence since the American Revolution in the 1770s. Across the 1780s and 1790s literature inimical to the basis of much of colonial society circulated with a surprising degree of freedom, including works by Thomas Paine and by the French philosophers, as well as the revolutionary *Declaration of the Rights of Man* from the French Revolution.[167] It is one thing, however, to be abreast of the latest currents in world politics and quite another to take them on as a banner for political action. The *caraqueño* elite across the decades rejected all practical applications of disruptive ideologies and stood by the Crown with only slightly varying degrees of steadfastness through the Comunero insurrection of 1781, the 1797 conspiracy and the republican-inspired invasions of 1806.

The danger for royal officials therefore lay elsewhere: in the occasional conversion to the new ideals of apparently marginal individuals. Francisco Miranda, the greatest of all the precursors of the 1810 revolutions in Spanish America, was one such man. Born and raised in Caracas, he left the province in the late 1770s and saw military service under the Crown during the American Revolution.[168] By the 1790s he was in England plotting the overthrow of Spanish rule in America. Gual and España were other such converts. So to some extent were the leaders of the Coro rebellion. Members of the maturing new generation of creole aristocracy were also probably being won over to the new ideological currents across the 1790s and 1800s. The problem, of course, is that all of these men were politically isolated. For revolutionary ideas and men to prosper, circumstances would have to create a revolutionary situation.

Esteban de León retired from the *caraqueño* political scene in the middle of 1802. His departure was not forced on him: he had requested a transfer back to Spain as early as 1798 on the grounds of ill-health.[169] Whether it was his physical or political wellbeing which was at stake is hard to tell. His considerable political capital seems to have begun to dwindle in the harsher circumstances of the late 1790s. In the Council of the Indies' decision on the battle over free trade at least one *fiscal* asked for León's recall, and the Council as a whole decided León had been overly partial to the *hacendado representación*.[170] His steady contravention of imperial dictates could not have pleased Court legislators even while they recognized the need for flexibility. Inside the province the weak and ineffectual Carbonell died and was replaced by the more vigorous Guevara Vasconcelos, who was credited by one contemporary observer with breaking the Quintana–León axis.[171] In addition, León's integrity came under a cloud when he was accused of trafficking in the flour shortage which affected the province in 1801 and of favouring the export of coffee over the more important cacao because he was a coffee planter himself.[172] Upon his returning to Spain his freedom of movement was restricted to his home town, while the Council of Indies reviewed the legal cases pending against him, involving over 250,000 pesos.[173] Yet this man proved to be a remarkable political survivor. In January 1810 he was one of five men initially called on to form the emergency Regency which then governed Spain.[174]

1802–1808

Caracas was not allowed a measured recovery from the ravages of the 1796 war. During the years between the Peace of Amiens in March 1802 and Napoleon's usurpation of the Spanish throne in May 1808 the province was subjected to a new war with Britain, two attempted invasions in 1806, heavy and crippling fiscal demands from Spain, a depressed economic outlook and a run of droughts, floods and plagues which severely affected agricultural production. As significant was the fact that the two royal officials who governed the province during these years were ill-equipped to deal with the difficult period they were part of. Guevara Vasconcelos, the Captain-General from early 1799 to late 1807, and Arce, the Intendant from early 1803 to mid-1809, showed none of the imagination and little of the flexibility which characterized Abalos, Saavedra, Guillelmi and León during their tenures in office. Guevara and Arce seem to have functioned adequately as administrators but the times demanded much more than that. Neither man proved very responsive to the challenges they faced, preferring to await royal orders to the more dangerous course of initiating policy. It is highly illuminating that the two men, though hardly political allies, were openly critical of León's previous tampering with trade regulations.[175]

Peace in 1802 found Caracas in an extremely weakened state. The producers of the province's two main exports, cacao and indigo, had been hard-hit by the war. As many as two thirds of the indigo plantations had temporarily ceased production.[176] The merchant community was scarcely better off, having suffered heavy losses of consignments and ships. Moreover it was afflicted by an acute shortage of capital which dimmed the prospect of a rapid recovery.[177] The provincial Treasury was also in bad shape: it was carrying a deficit of over 2,300,000 pesos or double the annual intake of taxes in normal economic times.[178]

The economy did not return to normality, however. Although demand in Spain for imperial commodities in general was very strong in the post-war period, trade between Caracas and its principal market languished between 1802 and 1804. Cacao imports into Cádiz remained at about half their pre-war levels, and indigo fared badly also.[179] The reasons for this stagnation seem to have been related to conditions in Caracas. Droughts and insect plagues more than halved the annual harvests of cacao across 1802–4.[180] In the case of indigo, though demand from Spain may indeed have begun its long-term decline, the structural collapse of the industry in the province during the war was probably the determining factor limiting indigo exports. Even tobacco production, which was seemingly immune from the vagaries of economic cycles, went into a tailspin in 1803–4, when drought cut the size of the harvest.[181] Tobacco had to be imported from Virginia to supply the province's needs.

Arce's first response to this grim panorama was to suspend virtually all foreign trade shortly after his arrival in March 1803.[182] It will be remembered that the Crown had already prohibited commerce outside the empire in late 1801, but Caracas, as it had since 1777, escaped the full brunt of the suspension through a legislative loophole which allowed it to trade with the foreign Antilles in times of peace. Arce suspended this privilege. In justifying his action he argued correctly that the trade with the foreign Caribbean for slaves, specie and tools in exchange for any provincial commodity except cacao had served as a cover for the clandestine importation of foreign goods. He also pointed out that in the present circumstances there would not be enough exports left to fill the holds of Spanish ships if foreign trade were permitted.

Arce's motivation may have been primarily political rather than economic. In the spirit of imperial administration throughout the empire after 1801, Arce was probably trying symbolically to reassert imperial control and discipline in order to counter any impression that ties to the mother country had been permanently loosened by the experiences of the war years. Surprisingly, his prohibition of the trade aroused little open opposition in the province at the time it was announced. It is possible that the economic stagnation then current reduced the measure's impact, but only temporarily. When the economy finally began to recover in 1804 it did so only to find itself facing the outbreak of another war and the renewed interruption of trade with Spain. With commerce severely limited by circumstances and law, contraband once again flourished along the coasts of the province.

In late 1804 Spain's running conflict of interest with Britain intensified again and in January 1805 a new war formally began. Caracas immediately plunged afresh into a war-induced depression from which it did not emerge for the better part of the next four years. The same tired issues resurfaced in provincial politics: reviving commerce, forestalling the military threat from abroad and finding emergency funds for colonial administration and defence preparations. The imperial context in which they were handled by the province had changed considerably, however, from that which had prevailed in the comparable crises of 1779–83 and 1797–1801. The shift in Spanish attitudes and policies towards the participation of the colonies in its war efforts had a strong impact on Caracas and is worth examining, however briefly.[183]

Spain at earlier stages in the history of its wars with Britain had been inclined to find ways for the empire to continue functioning as normally as possible. If this meant temporarily opening the empire to trade with foreigners to ensure that traffic in commodities, manufactures and specie continued, so much the better, as long as the exposure remained controlled and temporary. Stress levels were kept to a minimum outside of the considerable immediate problems caused by the war at hand. As military expenditures mounted in the 1790s, however, Spain's internal economic resources and borrowing possibilities in Europe began to exhaust themselves. The colonial treasuries with their tax collections and remittances, which in peacetime supplemented the income of the mother country, now became a basic source of financing for the wars. By the time the Crown reopened the colonies to neutral trade in the late 1790s it was clear that royal priorities had begun to change. The aim was no longer solely 'to provide vital supplies for the colonies [and to] sustain some level of Spanish exports to the Indies'.[184] Rather, it was also to find a new means of financing the war effort. In conjunction with the first moves to consolidate the Spanish internal debt, the Crown began selling bills of exchange to neutral foreign merchants payable against the treasuries of given colonies. This money-raising measure joined the longer-standing manipulation of the American market represented by the sale inside Spain of monopoly rights to supply given colonies with their flour needs. At roughly the same time the Crown made its first serious attempt to squeeze money out of the colonial Church by requesting a percentage of tithe collections as a war donation.

Spain's finances had still not recovered when the country was drawn back into war again in late 1804. This time the fiscal needs of the mother country took precedence over every other consideration, and the Crown ruthlessly exploited every available avenue to raise money. The most spectacular of the measures adopted was the appropriation of all Church funds, but it was not the only one. The Crown began trafficking not only with the surpluses of colonial treasuries but with the bulk of colonial trade as well. Instead of allowing a straightforward neutral trade to make up for the lack of Spanish ships, the Crown began selling virtually monopoly-carrying rights to the trade of individual colonies to major, neutral, commercial firms, especially from the United States. It even considered stepping in and taking over the new flour monopoly it had granted in 1803 to the Marqués de Branciforte. At the same time a relentless pressure was put on colonial officials to increase remittances to Spain.

The new measures had a pronounced impact on Caracas. The first effect of the war on our province was, as usual, the near-cessation of commerce with the mother country. Unexported commodities began to accumulate on the wharves of La Guaira and in February 1805 the governing body of the Consulado and the Caracas Cabildo requested of the authorities that free trade should be permitted.[185] Arce, in what was to become typical of his reaction to emergencies, stalled, but by late May recognized that the situation was becoming desperate. In collaboration with the Captain-General, he opened the province to neutral and friendly ships on 29 May 1805.[186] Shortly thereafter Arce received royal orders informing him that the Crown in December 1804 had granted exclusive trading-privileges for Venezuela to the John Craig Company of Baltimore.[187] Without publicly explaining the reasons, Arce quickly reversed himself and on 11 June again closed the ports of the province.[188] The fiscal situation, however, deteriorated with the lack of commercial activity, and in November 1805 Arce was forced to petition the Crown for free trade. He did not only offer financial reasons: he spoke of the 'excessive and scandalous' contraband which could only be contained by allowing neutral trade.[189] By early 1806, and not having collected much in the way of tax revenues for the past year, Arce was prepared to act unilaterally and reopen the province, but he was opposed by Guevara who, fearing an imminent invasion, censured Arce's move on security grounds.[190] Undeterred, in March 1806 Arce again argued the need for free trade, reassuring the Crown that it need not harbour any doubts as to the loyalty of the province's inhabitants.[191] Meanwhile Craig's ships finally began to arrive after over a year's delay but his company's services were dismissed as insufficient and dangerously monopolistic by both Arce and the local merchant community.[192] The latter again petitioned the Crown in April for free trade.[193] On 25 June 1806 Arce with Guevara's accord reopened the province to neutral trade, only informing the Crown three months later on 20 September.[194] Coincidentally, Madrid had come to the same conclusion that its innovative concessions to neutral traders had failed. Anticipating the *caraqueño* officials' decision by ten days, the Crown declared the colonies open to unrestricted trade on 15 June 1805.[195]

This time open trade did not prove to be the expected panacea for the province's commercial ills. Unlike the experience with free trade between 1797 and 1801, foreign ships did not rush in to ferry out exports and bring in imports.[196] This was not surprising given the extreme gravity of the international situation. Curaçao, one of the province's principal outlets in the Caribbean, fell to the enemy British in 1806, just when neutral trade was being sanctioned. Perhaps more importantly, U.S. merchants kept their distance from Caracas. The 1807 American embargo on commerce with the belligerents of the European war placed a serious obstacle in the path of trade with the province's second major foreign market. The *caraqueño* economy, therefore, did not revive and by April 1808 Arce was warning the Crown to 'expect losses of major proportions in [the province's] agriculture'.[197]

With all commerce hindered in one form or another a scarcity of essential imports developed. One scarcity, however, may have been largely artificial: that of flour, the grain mainstay of the province's white population.[198] In December 1806 Arce, in response to royal orders, began enforcing Branciforte's monopoly right to be the sole supplier of flour to the province. The Consulado immediately protested that the concession would interefere with the flow of neutral commerce, in that flour was one of the principal goods brought in by North American merchants. Arce refused to act on the matter, accusing the Guild of impugning royal intentions in an effort to have the monopoly overturned. Once again, however, economic realities intervened to force Arce's hand. Branciforte's agents were unable or unwilling to supply the province, and a severe scarcity of bread resulted. In October 1808 Arce was forced to suspend the monopoly. Again, almost coincidentally, the Crown did the same.

One salutary development in the generally negative evolution of events during these years was a new willingness on the part of the local merchant community and the Intendancy to work together on what might be called government contracts, in spite of their differences over first free trade and then the Branciforte monopoly. It will be remembered that in the late 1790s local traders were either disinclined or unable to handle the export of the state tobacco monopoly's surpluses in return for armaments and essential imports. This situation was radically reversed in the 1800s. In 1803–4 local merchants contracted with the administration to import U.S. tobacco when a shortfall in domestic production occurred.[199] In 1806 they took over the export of new tobacco surpluses.[200] By 1809 *caraqueño* merchants were involved at all levels of government dealings: exporting *tasajo* to feed Spanish armies in the Península, importing weapons and uniforms through agents in Britain and co-operating in the transfer of Treasury funds to Spain.[201]

The provincial Treasury was in fact the main casualty of the economic hardships of the period. The strains of the earlier British war had hardly worn off when the costs of new military preparations and extraordinary remittances to Spain presented themselves. Provincial finances were simply not capable of meeting these demands. In early 1805 Arce asked for a 500,000 pesos loan from the Consulado to cover rising expenses but met with a cool response.[202] By September he was informing the Crown he would not in the future be able to honour *libranzas* issued against the Caracas Treasury.[203] As defence preparations increased in 1806, in response to two attempted invasions of the province, the situation deteriorated further. In August 1806 Arce informed Spain that because the Treasury 'has absolutely . . . no money to pay for the extraordinary expenditures [demanded] . . . and because neither the tobacco monopoly nor [taxes from] the open trade with neutrals can supply it' he was taking over Church funds in the form of a forced loan.[204] By August 1808 the situation was worse than desperate: total bankruptcy loomed. Caracas had an outstanding current debt of over one million pesos and only 300,000 pesos, which had been set aside to send to Spain, to cover it. The tobacco monopoly on which the province had been subsisting since at least 1803 was described as 'extremely debilitated' and useless as a source of income. More seriously, the Spanish Treasury, assuming that the alienation of Church income was proceeding according to plan, as laid down in the December 1804 consolidation decree, allowed 700,000 pesos worth of *libranzas* to be issued against the near-broke Treasury of Caracas.[205] The Crown was warned that unless the situation changed quickly the 300,000 pesos marked for transfer to Spain would have to be 'consumed'.[206]

In 1806 the long-standing threat of a British-backed invasion of the province finally became reality. Francisco de Miranda tried twice that year to invade the province.[207] This revolutionary had convinced the British that an uprising of sorts was possible in Caracas, and they accordingly supplied him with ships and men for the enterprise. Secrecy was not the strong point of this conspiracy and the *caraqueño* coastguard was alerted by the time the first invasion was attempted, in April 1806, with 3 ships and 150 men. The landing just west of Puerto Cabello was foiled with the loss of 2 British ships and 60 members of the invading company. Miranda tried again in August, this time with 10 ships of varying sizes and about 500 men. He landed just north of Coro, spent some days trying to win over the local population, which had fled, and himself took leave when local militias began firing at his men.

At the time, these outings by Miranda must have seemed a strong indication that a full British attack against the province was possible, especially if seen in conjunction with Popham's invasion of Buenos

Aires in the same period. In fact 10,000 men were being mobilized across 1807–8 for a full attack on the province when events in Spain forestalled the planned invasion.[208] Guevara's temporary mobilization of 8,000 men was therefore no overreaction to the larger threat. Significantly, the royal officials in the province showed no signs of fear that Miranda's clarion might find an echo inside the province. Nor should they have: in spite of the harsh experiences being undergone because of the war and concurrent royal policies the local planter and merchant elite enthusiastically welcomed the defeat of Miranda and donated men and money against any further incursions of that 'abominable monster'.[209]

The virtually uninterrupted hardships which afflicted the province in the years after 1797 took a particularly heavy toll on its economy and finances and strained the balance of political forces inside the colony, but, if anything, the political environment improved between 1802 and 1808. The open disagreements between merchants, planters and officials over trade policy and government contracts in the late 1790s had faded. Race was no longer the issue it had been in the mid-1790s, when royal initiatives and the Coro slave revolt had temporarily aroused white fears and antagonisms. The republican threat seemed even more distant than it had during the aborted Gual and España episode of the late 1790s. Merchants and agriculturalists were not in conflict over any major issue, and Arce, if not as co-operative as previous intendants, was certainly trying to meet the needs of the province. Significantly, the economy, for all the difficulties it confronted, had not caved in. What the province proved unable to confront was the shock to the entire imperial structure resulting from Ferdinand VII's abdication at Bayonne in May 1808.

7

The balance overturned 1808–1810

Introduction

Napoleon's takeover of Spain in 1808 did not simply trigger the events which in Caracas led to the struggle for independence: it caused them. There was little presage of the conflict to come in the pre-1808 Caracas which has emerged in this study, nor was there anything inevitable about the collapse of the colonial order after 1808. Caracas during most of the late-colonial period had grown, prospered and matured as a society within the confines of the empire. The province's ruling elite had not broken up into warring factions defending inimical economic and political interests. Internal political, social and racial tensions were, if anything, on the decline when the crisis of 1808 and its ensuing ramifications destabilized Spain and the rest of the imperial order.

This is not to say that a potential for conflict did not exist in late-colonial Caracas. Tensions of all kinds – economic, social, racial, political – can be found in any society. The question is whether they are so strong that they throw the given society into disequilibrium, or whether they are contained enough by the fabric of commonly held social, political and cultural values to be seen as no more than part of the normal give and take of societal interaction. By the latter measure, and certainly in comparison with other Spanish possessions in the same period, late-eighteenth-century Caracas was a well-balanced and relatively tranquil society. This is not to say that the balance could not be disrupted; but when it was, from 1808 onwards, the principal catalysts were not internal tensions or latent liberationist, separatist or nationalist tendencies inside the colony.

In Caracas the major and the fundamental destabilizing factor leading to and conditioning the eventual destruction of colonial society was the political confusion arising from the collapse of traditional authority in Spain in 1808. It is hard to overemphasize the negative impact

146

of this development on the empire at large. In the process of their reaction to the crisis, divisions appeared among Spaniards in the mother country, among Europeans in the colonies and even among the creoles of the Americas. Very soon the conflicting reactions to the French occupation created a revolutionary situation in both Spain and most of the colonies. Ill-defined political differences hardened into antagonistic dogma, and new currents and men came to the fore who in more peaceful times would not have been heard from in quite the same way. In Spain the latter were represented by the forces and leaders of constitutional liberalism, decentralization and militarism; in the colonies by the ideals and men of separatism, nationalism and republicanism. While in Spain the minority radical tendencies were temporarily defeated by the forces of tradition and conservatism when Ferdinand was restored, in most of the American colonies, in contrast, where the revolutionaries were also in a minority, the new currents won out. In Caracas, the radicals, aided by events and their own extraordinary willpower, transformed what began as an autonomist movement into a fullfledged revolution and achieved their ultimate objective of independence from Spain.

The collapse of established authority 1808–1810

The crisis of 1808 had its genesis in Spain's faltering participation in European wars from 1793 onwards.[1] Spain unsuccessfully waged war first on revolutionary France and then on Britain for over twelve years of the sixteen-year span. The toll taken by the near-continuous hostilities was predictable. The country's commerce with the American colonies, on which the prosperity of much of the domestic economy depended, was regularly disrupted. The Crown was reduced to fiscal penury and was driven to find ever more extreme measures to raise money. The country's military capabilities were drained by loss of life, defeat and a decline in morale. The Spanish navy, on which the mercantilist theory of empire depended for survival, was laid low by losses at sea, and more specifically by the spectacular defeat at Trafalgar in 1805. These negative reverberations affected the American Empire as well. The colonial economies were placed under severe economic strain, and some colonies were drawn directly into the military conflicts: Santo Domingo and Trinidad were more or less permanently lost in the 1790s and Buenos Aires temporarily succumbed to a British invasion in 1806. In short, the crisis of the empire's (mother country's and colonies') international position increasingly threatened its stability from the 1790s onwards.

The wear and tear on Spain across the years 1793–1808 was measurable in more than physical and economic losses. It was the country's, and the empire's, misfortune to be presided over by a relatively weak king, whose system of rule by favourites undermined the capable ministerial apparatus built up by Charles III. The 'Prince of Peace', Manuel Godoy, governed, if not malevolently at least corruptly and inefficiently, in the name of Charles IV (1788–1808). Their misguided attempt to come to terms with Napoleonic France by keeping alive the system of alliance between Spain and France which had held sway when both countries were under Bourbon sovereigns, led to the wars with Britain and their disastrous consequences. The at turns hesitant and desperate policies devised to confront the successive crises pleased no one in Spain; and clerical conservatives, Carolingian reformers, liberals, Cadiz merchants and Catalan industrialists found themselves increasingly at odds with the Godoy-administered Court.

The depth of the political crisis in Spain was revealed early in 1808, *before* Napoleon's coup at Bayonne in May. The supporters of the crown prince, Ferdinand, engineered a riot in front of the royal palace at Aranjuez on 17 March, which by 19 March had led to the fall of Godoy and the abdication of Charles IV in favour of the future Ferdinand VII. The significance of this event has perhaps been underestimated: for the first time ever, since Spain was unified in 1492, a monarch had been forced off the throne. The net result was the discrediting of the absolutist authority of the Crown which Charles's predecessors across the eighteenth century had carefully cultivated. Ferdinand was not given the opportunity or the time to undo the damage: on 10 May he was forced to abdicate his crown at Bayonne in favour of Napoleon's brother, Joseph. Many established authorities across Spain therefore hesitated when faced with the choice of recognizing the French surrogate and carrying on as before, or rising against Napoleon in the name of Ferdinand. The choice was made for many of them by the extent of the hostile public reaction to the French coup. Even as the Council of Castille was making up its mind, the Spanish War of Independence (1808–14) began on the streets of Madrid.

The monarchy was saved by the insurrection against the French, but Ferdinand, prisoner as he was, had no impact on the war waged in his name except as a rallying symbol. This was perhaps just as well. The events of March–May unleashed forces which called into question the foundations of the monarchy as it was structured before 1808. These forces were in the ascendant up to 1814, and in the light of Ferdinand's later intolerance of change, his physical presence during the war might have caused divisiveness on a scale grand enough to break the back of Spanish resistance to the French. As it was, the general patriotic unity exhibited by all classes and regions in the face of the invaders poorly masked the political struggle carried on by constitutional liberals and regionalists to transform the legal structure of government and indeed of Spanish society.

The disintegration of Spain's political as opposed to national fabric became apparent in the months following the popular uprising of 5 May 1808 in Madrid. A relatively large group of fearful and disaffected government officials, the *afrancesados*, immediately threw their lot in with the French for the duration of the war. The majority of the country's national and local ruling elite, however, rushed to gain control of the mass movements against the French in their respective provinces before they could turn into social revolutions. Across Spain provincial *juntas* were set up to direct local war efforts, and in the process the anti-centrist regionalism the Bourbons had tried to bury was revived. Those *juntas* that could, legitimized their rule with local elections, creating the odd spectacle of conservative landowners, officials and the like appealing to *el pueblo* for support. The autonomist tendencies of the *juntas* delayed the establishment of a central national authority until September 1808, and then the only agreement which could be reached was on a weakly empowered, federalist Junta Central to co-ordinate the national defence.

The Junta Central which in its short life was forced by the French to retreat south from Aranjuez to Seville to Cadiz and finally to the Isla de Leon, off Cadiz, dissolved itself in January 1810 in favour of a five-man Regency. Almost oblivious to the French troops then laying siege to Cadiz, and with the centrifugal tendencies of the provinces temporarily in abeyance, the Regency turned its attention to the reformist issues which had been simmering in the background since March 1808. Incredibly, in the midst of a national struggle for survival, it called into existence the Cortes or General Congress of the Spanish peoples. The move was the equivalent of Louis XVI's gesture in assembling the States-General in 1789, except that it was made in much more extreme circumstances. Imperfect elections were duly held where it was possible to hold them and on 24 September 1810 the Cortes was opened on Isla de Leon. For the next year and a half, with a war raging around them and with an empire beginning to crack at the seams, the nominal leaders of the country thrashed out legislative matters of little immediate practical importance. With the constitutional liberals and social reformers in control of the Cortes, if not of the Regency, the radical

Constitution of 1812 was drawn up, promising a curtailed monarchy, representative government, an enfranchised electorate, and the abolition of special class and corporate privileges.

The spectacle and example of the mother country overthrowing a king in 1808 and then simultaneously toying with notions of local autonomy and representation while collapsing into a virtually ungovernable mess about to be swallowed by the French invader, must have had a profound impact on the body politic of all the American colonies. The revolution begun in Spain in fact soon found an echo overseas. In the case of Caracas the reaction to the events in Spain between 1808 and 1810 closely paralleled the reaction and course followed by the Spanish provinces and political groups. The difference, of course, was that the radical element in the colony advocated not constitutions but independence.

Before 1808 there is little if any concrete evidence as to what the *caraqueño* ruling elite thought of the way Spain and the empire were run under Godoy and Charles IV. The local planters and merchants and imperial representatives, in the face of the increasingly difficult times thrust upon them after 1796 by Spain's European wars, limited their public dissent to attempts at respectfully protesting against or ignoring royal decisions harmful to the interests of the province. However, this polite silence on the greater matters at hand probably carried with it a sharp, hidden edge of growing hostility to the politically decaying regime in Spain. It must have seemed to *caraqueño* that the hesitant and inconsistent emergency policies being drawn up in Spain to salvage its economy and the war effort were tending less and less to take into consideration the colony's needs in similarly straitened circumstances.

News of the abdication at Bayonne first reached Caracas in July 1808. The story of what then happened is well known.[2] The population at large and the majority of the social and economic elite enthusiastically pledged their support to the Spanish resistance in Ferdinand VII's name. The new Captain-General, Juan de Casas, at first hesitated in choosing sides, as his sympathies clearly lay with the *afrancesado* faction in Spain supporting Joseph I. The intensity of the popular reaction in favour of Ferdinand, however, quickly convinced Casas that it would be more politic to follow course. Then, for reasons which have never been satisfactorily explained, Casas suggested the formation of a *junta* along the lines of those being formed in Spain to confront the emergency at hand. The Caracas Town Council replied with a suggested composition for the *junta* of eighteen persons, including the Captain-General, the

Intendant, the Archbishop, the Regent of the Audiencia, military commanders and representatives of the Caracas Town Council, merchants, planters, nobility, the clergy, the university, the Lawyers' Guild and *el pueblo*.[3] The almost simultaneous arrest of three men on republican conspiracy charges may have frightened Casas off:[4] for whatever reasons by the end of July and early August he had dropped his proposal. A significant number of the provincial elite, however, refused to let the matter rest. On 24 November a new petition was submitted to Casas requesting the formation of a *junta*. Casas's reaction was swift: all forty-odd signatories were arrested. All were freed in the next few months and for the time being the initial excitement generated by Bayonne seemed to die down.

The calm was deceptive. The developments of July–December reveal in no uncertain terms that the abdication of May set loose disruptive forces in Caracas similar to those unleashed in Spain, albeit tailored to the local environment. The difference, of course, was that the individuals who led the patriotic reaction in Caracas, with expectations of reforming government in the process, were already part of the central ruling elite of their 'country', whereas it was largely the provincial elites in Spain which formed the focuses of reformism and of resistance to the French in their country. In Caracas, in other words, the political split of July–November was among the heretofore-unified ruling groups of the province.

Whatever else the proposal for an emergency ruling *junta* represented, it was not an exclusively creole initiative or bid for power as contemporary enemies of the motion and later historians would have us believe.[5] It should be re-emphasized that the *junta* idea was not a local, nativist response to the imperial crisis. The precedent for the formation of *juntas* was set by the numerous provinces of Spain and moreover it was the Captain-General Casas who first openly suggested the formation of one in Caracas. Furthermore, there were royally sanctioned antecedents in the province's own history which had resulted in the Ayuntamiento of Caracas, that is the local elite, sharing directly the responsibility of administrative government in periods of crisis.[6] The example, therefore, already existed when the *caraqueño* elite began seriously contemplating the creation of a *junta* in late July 1808.

Once the *junta* movement did materialize in the province, it incorporated Spaniards, *canarios*, creoles, planters and merchants.[7] The prime instigator of the petition for a *junta* which was delivered to Casas on 24 November with forty-eight signatures was none other than the *peninsular* Antonio Fernández de León, the ex-Intendant's brother and the future Marqués de Casa León and a confirmed royalist. At least twelve merchants, most of them Spaniards, signed the *juntista* document, and many more Spaniards and merchants were drawn into the official investigation which followed Casas' clamping down on the movement.[8] Moreover, many of the signers were among the most important representatives of the colonial elite: the Condes de Tovar and San Xavier, the fourth Marqués del Toro, León, the Ribas brothers, Andrés Ibarra and José Vicente Escorihuela for *hacendados* and merchant-planters; J. J. Argos, Fernando Key Muñoz, José Vicente Galguera and Martín Tovar Ponte for merchants and planter-merchants. One man who did not sign the petition but promised to support it was the Spanish ex-Regent of the Audiencia, Antonio López Quintana,[9] and it is possible other senior royal officials were in sympathy with the project. To round out the dimensions of this formidable alignment, it should be pointed out that, although several key men of 1810 did not sign the document, in the light of their later revolutionary actions they must have at least partially approved of the initiative. This group included the Bolívar brothers, the López Méndez brothers, Miguel José Sanz and Vicente Salias. Finally, among the members of the exploratory commission suggested by the proposal were the two remaining holders of Caracas noble titles who also had not signed the petition, the Conde de La Granja and the Marqués de Mijares.

In short it would have been difficult if not impossible to find a more respectable and representative cross-section of the province's ruling elite than the one which signed or backed the 24 November petition. It must have seemed to the men involved that it was not entirely out of the question that the Captain-General might respond favourably to a request from such a reasonable, moderate and influential group. This was not to be, however. Casas was an incompetent, weak-willed, querulous Francophile and into the bargain old and sick, out of sympathy with the developments in Spain and likely to resist any full-hearted attempt to follow course in the province.[10] His only political ally was the equally disliked but far more able *regente visitador*, Joaquín de Mosquera, a native of neighbouring New Granada, who had superseded López Quintana as senior man in the Audiencia.[11] Neither was inclined to compromise with the *juntistas*. In their defence it can be said that the implications of the formation of a *junta* were serious. It meant that the province was placing itself on a par with the provinces of Spain, using the same rights to protect local interests. In other words, the leaders of the province were implicitly rejecting its status as an administered dependency and claiming recognition as an integral part of the Spanish nation. This move towards autonomy, however, was not yet explicit or radical enough to necessitate the measures Casas employed to halt it. Unlike the situation in colonies as diverse as New Spain, Quito, Chile and Buenos Aires, where appointed Captain-Generals and Viceroys were overthrown in 1808 and 1809 by one political faction trying to thwart the ambitions of another, the *junta* proposal in Caracas was presented through legal access to the Captain-General by moderate men representing most interests in the colony. Furthermore, the plan openly accepted the continuity of the Captain-General as titular head of the government, if with his powers somewhat circumscribed.

The Captain-General's coup seemed to provide the desired results in late 1808 and early 1809. The arrest orders, most of them of short duration and leniently applied, frightened several of the petition signers into denying their involvement, and the wind seemed to be taken out of the *juntista* sails. Casas and Mosquera may have hastened the apparent submission of malcontents by threatening to mobilize *pardo* support against any seizure of power by the local white elite.[12] By May 1809 the last individuals under house arrest had been freed.

Casas' triumph was illusory, however. By taking away the civil liberties of the most illustrious men of the province and treating them as if they were a political rebel fringe, he broke the political consensus and dialogue which had existed among the ruling groups of the province. It is difficult to find a parallel anywhere in the empire to Casas' incarceration of virtually the entire leadership of provincial society, and this in a region where local elites had more often than not co-operated with the royal officials sent to govern them. The practical impact of Casas' measure was to weaken severely the already-shaky symbolic strength on which the Captain-General's authority rested, by revealing the local imperial executive to be as arbitrary as the already-discredited monarchical regime he represented. Among the province's elite, the mostly moderate men, who up to 24 November 1808 had thought dialogue and consensus were still possible, gave way to the advocates of a more radical solution to the imperial crisis of government.

The year 1809 was something of a hiatus in Caracas between the ferment of 1808 and the explosion of 1810. It began well enough. News arrived at the province of the major Spanish victory over the French at Bailen and of the Junta Central established to conduct the war effort. Both events were welcomed with a genuine enough patriotic fervour in January and seemed to ease the accumulated tensions inside the province.[13] The Junta Central helped matters along by raising colonial hopes of an imminent reform of the imperial system with the declaration that the colonies were 'an integral part of the nation'.[14] This suggestion of equal status with the provinces of Spain was given more substance when the colonies were invited to hold elections to send representatives to the Junta.

Inside the province the contentious Casas and the reputedly corrupt Intendant, Arce, were replaced by Vicente Emparán as Captain-General and Vicente Basadre as Intendant in May 1809.[15] Emparán, who for over a decade was Governor of neighbouring Cumaná, was well known as a competent and flexible administrator and had ties of friendship with members of the *caraqueño* elite. The political transition, which was initially well received in Caracas, coincided with a remarkable recovery in the economic fortunes of the province. With the cessation of the maritime war with Britain, 1809 turned out to be a record year for *caraqueño* exports. The resurgence was strongly aided by the decisions by Emparan and Basadre to keep the ports of the province open to foreign trade in spite of imperial orders to the contrary.[16] Arce, before departing, even went as far as lowering the tariffs on non-imperial commerce to encourage foreign traders to come to the province.[17] In 1808–9 the intendants, admittedly in an attempt to send remissions to Spain, revived the *libranza* system and proceeded to hand over large, individual sums of Treasury funds to selected merchants and planters, including among others Simón Bolívar and the recently freed and newly ennobled Antonio Fernández de León.[18]

A *rapprochement* might have begun to seem possible but for the numerous signs of continuing tension just under the surface. The state of the economy was no longer the dominant issue in the colony, the situation in Spain was. The fate of the mother country and of the political issues raised since the abdication were foremost in everyone's minds, and the only hope of a significant appeasement of the tensions in the province was the combination of a successful outcome to the war against the French and the promulgation of reforms in the imperial order. The situation in Spain, however, deteriorated across 1809. The victory at Bailen proved to be the high point of the organized Spanish resistance to the French invader, and thereafter the military defence of the unoccupied parts of the country crumbled in the face of the advancing enemy. Meanwhile the surviving provincial *juntas* continued to feud among themselves, thwarting the attempts of the Junta Central to run an efficient war effort and to establish a legitimate central authority for the country and for the empire. Moreover the Junta Central while tolerating the divisiveness of regionalists, centralists, reformists and conservatives in its midst, began to exhibit a marked coolness to similar manifestations in the American colonies.[19] It also outlawed the open trade which had been practised in the colonies since 1806, on the grounds that the British war which had led to the concession had ended.[20] Undeniably true as this was, Spain was in no position to resume fully the responsibilities of imperial trade. The prohibition was a firm indication to the colonies that Spanish liberals were as closed to the economic reform of the empire as diehard mercantilist conservatives were.

The negative developments in the mother country no doubt contributed strongly to keeping alive in Caracas the desire to form an autonomist *junta*. Inside the province Emparán could do little to re-establish confidence in imperial authority. His predecessor Casas, in a last devastating blow at the legitimacy the Junta Central was trying to build up, manipulated the election of the local deputy, so that the unrepresentative Mosquera was sent to Spain as the regional delegate.[21] Emparán avoided controversy of this nature but he became entangled in a number of petty jurisdictional disputes with local corporate bodies, which added to the general sense of unease.[22] In the economic sphere there were political problems too, in spite of the return of prosperity. Basadre, in a partial attempt to meet the imperial prohibition on foreign trade, raised the duties Arce had lowered only to find himself opposed by a combative Consulado.[23] The Guild's reaction may also have reflected a wider rejection of any measure curtailing the island trade while Spain's economy was not fully restored to its pre-war levels. The province was having its first taste of economic wellbeing since the mid-1790s and was probably in no mood to brook interference with one of the main sources of that prosperity. All these disagreements were hardly major but in the context of the time they were particularly unwelcome.

The senior imperial officials in Caracas in effect found their authority increasingly undermined by events in Spain across 1809. Casas did, of course, make a notable contribution to this erosion by his extreme reactions in 1808, but with or without him it would have occurred. The imperial system these officials represented in a sense no longer existed by 1809, and would not resurrect until 1814. The whole hierarchical chain of authority from which they derived their positions had been disrupted from the centre outwards. The provincial *juntas* in Spain and the Junta Central were no substitutes for the deposed monarchy and in any case they brought into play political concepts contrary to the imperial government as it had been structured. The *caraqueño* officials must have suffered from a growing loss of confidence and sense of purpose as the system they once represented turned upon itself and succumbed to the

French usurpers. With the decline of morale came a loss of the will to hold onto power and to use the province's armed forces to defend their authority.

In Emparán's case his *afrancesado* tendencies made it unlikely that he was more than a lukewarm supporter of the imperial system as represented by the divided Spanish resistance. His loyalty was, in fact, sufficiently in doubt to merit an investigation into his tenure as Captain-General when he returned to Spain after 1810.[24] His political ambivalence seemingly also extended to his relations with the *caraqueño juntistas*, several of whom were his friends. When, in December 1809 and again in March 1810, conspiracies were afoot to install a *junta*, he did little more than try to dissuade the conspirators quietly from their purposes.[25] In short he was not the man to defend the old imperial system when the challenge came.

By early 1810 the military situation in Spain had deteriorated to such an extent that organized Spanish resistance under the Junta Central was reduced to a foothold at Cadiz in the southern tip of the country. The Junta Central's resounding failure at both the military and political levels led to its dissolution in favour of the five-man Regency, to be legitimized by calling it a Cortes. A fatal sign of the revolutionary blindness gripping Spain at the time, was the invitation to the colonies to form part of the Cortes with the inciteful words: 'From this moment, Spanish Americans, you see yourselves elevated to the status of free men . . . your destinies no longer depend on ministers, viceroys, or governors: they [the destinies] are in your hands.'[26] The provincial *juntas* in Spain did not rush to recognize the new central authority, and neither did the American colonies when they learned of the rearrangement. The long-restrained *juntista* forces in Caracas took immediate and decisive action only four days after news first arrived of the developments in Spain. On 19 April 1810 Emparan was peacefully deposed and replaced by the Junta Suprema Conservadora de los Derechos de Fernando VII, which refused to recognize the Regency in Spain.[27]

The radicalization of conflict 1810–1811

The most striking aspect of the coup of 19 April was the active support it received from the overwhelming majority of the political groups of the province.[28] The creole-Spanish-*hacendado*-merchant elite of Caracas rushed to fulfill government duties with a civic zeal which contrasted strongly with their past history of lethargic participation at the institutional level of politics.[29] The secondary, and even some senior, administrative officials and military officers of the royal bureaucracy and armed forces stayed on in their posts and accepted promotions in the new order.[30] The Archbishop of Caracas ordered his priests to preach support for the new government.[31] From around the province local municipal councils, with the important exception of Coro, transferred their loyalty to the Junta Suprema.[32] As a consequence of the general acceptance there were no preventive arrests of potential enemies in the first weeks after the coup and only nine officials of the old regime were deported.[33]

Clearly at this early stage of the revolution the majority of the political population did not feel an illegal usurpation had taken place. With the multiple examples to be had of insurrectionary provinces in Spain, and increasingly in the empire, and with the added incentive of the political uncertainty of the previous two years and the apparent collapse of the Spanish resistance and government the residents of Caracas had sufficient reason to form a *junta* of their own as an emergency protective measure. Most of them, anxious only to partake more fully of the reformist and autonomist currents sweeping the mother country and the empire, also had little cause to see their small movement as outside the mainstream of the times. In a sense the *caraqueños* were only following the oblique advice of the Regency and throwing off the remaining vestiges of the past regime.

What was unusual about the *caraqueño* reaction to the two-year-old imperial crisis was the categorical rejection of the centrally constituted government in Spain. Again, however, it is unlikely that many in Caracas initially felt they were doing more than recognizing the state of affairs in the mother country. For them, the denial of the legitimacy of the Regency was not a first step towards independence. This is perhaps difficult for us to understand when we look back at a period in which events followed upon each other with a startling rapidity and in which it became apparent fairly quickly that Spain was not going to collapse and that the struggle for independence had indeed begun. Nevertheless at the time of the formation of the Junta Suprema in Caracas there was a very real sense that the central imperial government had ceased to exist. Two years of living through the uncertainty of two abdications and the influences of revolutionary currents, and of witnessing the successes of the French invasion and the anarchic antics of governments in Spain seemed to reach their culmination in the discrediting and dissolution of the Junta Central and the apparently imminent French triumph. Rejecting the authority of another makeshift Spanish government in the form of the Regency and creating a local *junta* must have

seemed the only sane course the province could take for its own protection.

Anybody doubting the impact of the 1808–10 crisis as a whole on
the mentality of the *caraqueño* elite need only look at the propaganda
put out by the Junta Suprema in its first few months in power.[34] The
overriding justification given for its creation was not based on depicting
the evils of colonial rule as it could well have been and would be later,
nor was it derived from eighteenth-century theories of social contract
and the natural sovereignty of all peoples. Instead the justification argument proffered was built basically on references to events in Spain and
by appeals to what was held to be Spanish law and practice. The argument was developed in the following way. The colonies were by law
Crown properties and not subject to the authority of intermediary or
interim powers. The abdication at Bayonne had therefore for the time
being dissolved the strongest ties between Spain and her colonies.
Caracas nonetheless had shown its continuing loyalty to Spain when in
1808 it recognized the Junta Central established by the provincial
juntas to co-ordinate the struggle against France. The Junta, however,
had exercised secretive, corrupt, inefficient and unrepresentative
government. When it fell it was 'not by French arms but by the Spanish
pueblo which had no confidence in it'.[35] The conclusions drawn were
obvious. A Regency established by such a Junta could have no legitimate right to authority. So until Ferdinand VII was returned to the
throne, Caracas as an integral part of the nation had the same rights as
the peninsular provinces to establish a *junta* to provide for its security
and interests.

The peacefulness of Caracas in the first four or five months after the
19 April coup can only really be understood in the context of this prevailing sense that it had been a legally correct act justified by the circumstances and by the fact that loyalty had been maintained to the
symbol of imperial unity, the monarchy. The Regency in Spain contributed to lulling potentially conflicting tensions in the province by not
taking a firm stand against Caracas for months.[36] Moderates and royalists in the colony, who as we shall see represented the political majority
in the province, could thus delude themselves that nothing but a reform
of government and a measure of practical expediency had taken place.

There had of course been a change of fundamental importance. At the
level of provincial politics one third of the ruling elite disappeared from
one day to the next. Among the nine individuals deported from La
Guaira after 19 April were the Captain-General, the Intendant, half the

lawyers of the Audiencia and senior military officers of the colony.[37] Apart from demonstrating that the presence of the Crown in the province had been almost entirely symbolic, rather than institutional or numerical, the deportation forced the realization that the planters and merchants had to come forward to assume the formal responsibilities of directing government and day-to-day administration.

The *hacendados* and *comerciantes* were more than willing to take on the trials of government but in the process of doing so they showed they had no intention of being simply a caretaker government awaiting the return of their king. The Junta Suprema legislated a number of measures it assumed would become permanent fixtures of a reformed colonial order.[38] Open trade was declared and the *alcabala*-tax was either lowered or abolished on many products. The tributary tax on Indians was done away with and the slave-trade was prohibited. The Audiencia was abolished and replaced by a High Court of Appeals.[39] Agents were sent to the foreign Antilles, to the United States and to Britain to inform their governments of events in Caracas and to secure their support, trade and, if necessary, arms.[40] In June the ground rules for elections for a Congress to rule in the name of Ferdinand VII were established.[41]

It would be wrong to assume that these first measures, radical as they seem, were divisive. As in Spain, the general wish for reform was widespread in Caracas and touched most if not all segments of the ruling elite. The twenty-three-member Junta Suprema was a highly representative body of the surviving two thirds of the local ruling groups.[42] José de las Llamosas, who in the late 1790s had been one of the instigators of the merchant–planter conflict of those years, now served as one of the three heads of the revolutionary Junta Suprema. He was a merchant and a Spaniard. His fellow leaders were respectively the major *canario* merchant and planter, Fernando Key Muñoz, and the creole merchant Martín Tovar Ponte of the wealthy and numerous Tovar clan. Key Muñoz also shared the responsibility of the ministry of the Treasury. It is true that the composition of the rest of the Junta was creole and *hacendado* but at this stage of the revolution this reflected the creole majority in the white population as much as anything else. Interestingly, the old creole families represented in the Junta by such surnames as Tovar, Palacios and Ascanio were balanced by the members of newer families only once removed from their immigrant origins such as the Clementes, the Ribas and the López Méndez. The success of co-opting most of the local elite can be seen at other levels of government too. The future royalist Marqués de Casa León headed the new Law Court; the *granadino* Francisco Berrio, formerly of the Audiencia, took over the Intendancy; and future royalist collaborators, such as the Spanish merchants Francisco Aramburu, Simón Ugarte and Gerardo Patrullo, took on jobs in the newly constituted Tribunal de Policia.[43] In short, the political decisions taken in the first few months reflected a consensus of the merchant-planter-Spanish-creole elite of Caracas, carried out with the aid of the largely intact secondary levels of the colonial bureaucracy.[44]

This facade of unanimity could last as long as the illusion of a lingering loyalty to the empire was maintained, and as long as no hardships, economic or otherwise, followed on the coup and its accompanying legislative innovations. Yet even in the first phase of the revolution it was clear that a serious split existed in the ranks of the local *juntistas*. The division was not as yet, as might be expected, between royalists and separatists. It was between the moderate majority which had carried out the coup and the radical minority which had supported it but was prepared to carry the coup to its logical conclusion of a full declaration of independence. This minority included the individuals referred to earlier as the isolated idealists and would-be revolutionaries of the pre-1808 world, men such as Simón Bolívar. Their number had been augmented considerably by the crisis in progress since 1808.

Developments after mid-1810 in the province are probably best understood in terms of the retreat of the moderates who carried out the coup of 19 April and the ascension to power of the radicals. We already know what the composition of the moderate group was: the social and economic elite which held sway in the province in 1808. The men in this faction were probably on the whole older and more established than the comparatively younger members of the radical sect.[45] The differences between the two groups, however, went far beyond two generational outlooks, one conditioned by the prosperity of the 1780s and 1790s and one by the hardships suffered by the province since 1797. What also separated the two groups was a pronounced difference in their class composition. True, men like Simón Bolívar, José Félix Ribas and Isidoro López Méndez in the radical faction were drawn from the highest echelons of the local elite. Their sympathizers also included prominent men like the Marqués del Toro and his brother Fernando, both now in charge of the province's armed forces.[46] Later, when other regional and provincial elites of Venezuela entered the fray, more aristocratic revolutionaries, like Antonio Nicolás Briceño and Cristóbal Mendoza, made their presence felt.[47] Nevertheless the fact is inescapable that many, and maybe the plurality, of the radical activists were not part of the colonial elite I have been studying. Men whose roles as constitution-makers, agitators, politicians and generals would be crucial in the coming months and years through 1814 came largely from the middle ranks of the province's society. Included in this category are the eternal revolutionary and later general of the patriot forces in 1812 Francisco Miranda; the radical Chilean priest José Cortes Madariaga; the lawyer and Secretary of State (1811–12) Miguel José Sanz; the *ad hoc* merchant, doctor, secretary, and newspaper editor Francisco Isnardi; the lawyer, constitution-maker, journalist, Secretary of Foreign Relations (1811) and Vice-President of Venezuela in 1819, Juan Germán Roscio; the lowly notary Rafael Diego Mérida, who in 1813–14 was in charge of justice in revolutionary Caracas; the lawyer José Rafael Revenga, one of Bolívar's right-hand men at Angostura in 1819; the small-time merchant and planter Fernando Peñalver, a deputy in the Constituent Congress of 1811 and future statesman of the Venezuelan republic; and the one-time secretary to the office of the Captaincy-General and future Venezuelan man of letters Andrés Bello.[48] To this list could be added others, not to mention all the obscure men from the free-coloured caste who later rose to fame and power in the military theatre of the independence struggle.[49] The radical group in 1810, then, was a curious mixture of elite revolutionaries and their middle-class cohorts.

The radicals were still at some remove from the centre of power in the first few months after 19 April. They did, of course, participate in the overthrow of Emparán, and a few of them, notably Roscio, José Félix Ribas and Madariaga, did manage to force the moderates to enlarge the Junta Suprema to include them.[50] Nevertheless there seems to have been a subtle attempt by the moderates to keep the real subversives under control. In June the Bolívar brothers, Bello and Revenga, were sent on missions to the United States and Britain and it is hard not to speculate that the choice of envoys was made to weaken the radicals in the province.[51] In October, when news first reached Caracas of the murders in Quito of *juntistas* by Regency royalists, Félix Ribas took to the streets of Caracas urging the expulsion of local Spaniards from the province, only to find himself expelled from the Junta and temporarily exiled.[52] The same month, having learned that Simón Bolívar intended to bring back Francisco Miranda with him from London, the Junta prohibited the re-entry of the old revolutionary into the province.[53]

The moderates were fighting a losing battle, however, as the pace of events around them outstripped their cautious reactions and eroded their sphere of control. Their middle position of respectful separatism was severely undermined when the Regency in Spain revealed at long last that it intended to halt the *juntista* movement in the colonies, by violent means if necessary. In November the plenipotentiary of the Regency in the Caribbean, Antonio Cortabarria, demanded that the province should recognize the authority of the Regency and Cortes in Spain in addition to accepting a new Captain-General, the re-establishing of the Audiencia and the disbanding of any militias organized since April.[54] It goes without saying that the Regency made no concessions on the free-trade matter. Negotiations between Cortabarria and the Junta Suprema carried on through December, but it was clear that even moderates were not yet willing to countenance the clock being turned back as far as the Regency planned to. The talks broke down, and in January 1811 Cortabarria began a naval blockade of most of the Venezuelan coast.[55]

The escalating crisis in external affairs was mirrored by the growing difficulties the Junta Suprema had in asserting its authority and legitimacy locally in the face of resurgent regionalism. The reader will remember that Caracas was the administrative, institutional and economic centre of the six provinces which had made up the Captaincy-General of Venezuela. For reasons which are not entirely clear, but which may have been as basic as securing the strategic flanks of the revolution, the *caraqueño* elite responsible for the coup of 19 April felt it necessary to continue to represent their province and their government as the political centre of the region. At first it seemed as if they would succeed. They had little trouble winning over most of the former Captaincy-General to the *juntista* principle, and only half of the province of Maracaibo and the Coro district of Caracas remained loyal to the Regency.[56] Both areas were relatively isolated geographically from the rest of the colony and neither had a significant population or military base with which to threaten the *juntistas*. The *caraqueños*, if they chose to, could more or less ignore the existence of the loyalist areas and this is what they more or less did across 1810 and 1811.

The problem for the Junta Suprema then, was not so much containing loyalists but rather getting the *juntista* provinces to follow its lead. Paradoxically it was the coup against Emparan which most weakened *caraqueño* pretensions of leadership. The political authority that the *caraqueño* elite might have wielded in the disbanded Captaincy-General had been almost exclusively based on their province's pre-eminence in the region's economic and political ties to Spain. They certainly had few connections to the other provinces of the Captaincy-General, other than those superimposed by imperial institutions. The other provinces coexisted in a more or less autonomous relation to Caracas, having separate micro-economies, different societal makeups and independent local elites over which those in Caracas had very little influence or control. Contrary to what might be expected, the city of Caracas did not act as a magnet to which all elites were drawn from the interior. Regional elites chose rather to remain powerful, relatively wealthy and dominant away from Caracas.[57] Nor did the *caraqueño* elite counter this tendency by branching out itself: it owned and controlled little that was outside the boundaries of Caracas.[58]

The net result was that after 19 April the Junta Suprema found that Caracas was no longer automatically accepted as the political centre. In the absence of the imperial authorities who had imposed administrative unity on the region, the other provinces now claimed political autonomy *vis-à-vis* Caracas. Nor was there much in the way of pressure Caracas could bring to bear on its fellow *juntista* provinces. In an effort which both recognized the force of regionalism and yet represented an attempt to install a legitimate central government led by *caraqueños*, the Junta in June 1810 called for the election of a Constituent Congress to meet in Caracas. The elections were duly held in October and November 1810 and the Congress was convened in March 1811.[59]

The events of October and November 1810 marked the turning-point of the balance of political power in Caracas, with momentum shifting in favour of the small radical faction. The arrival of Cortabarria and the promotion of Governor Fernando Miyares of Maracaibo to Captain-General of Venezuela gave the local loyalist opposition to the *juntistas* a symbolic weight and a focus which it had previously lacked. Representing as this did the hard line adopted by the Regency towards the rebellious colonies, and coinciding as it did with the news of the massacre at Quito, the quiet approach pursued by the moderates began to lose ground. Internally, the excitement surrounding the congressional elections confirmed the drift towards federalism and disunity among the *juntista* provinces.

Although there is no hard evidence to offer as proof, it seems probable that the military expedition mobilized against Coro in November 1810 was one of the last efforts made by the moderates of Caracas to retain control of the movement they had started.[60] This contention gains credibility if we observe that no effort had been made before then to subdue Coro and none was made afterwards. The attack was meant as a symbolic gesture to placate public opinion and the radicals, as well as to assert the primacy of Caracas within the *juntista* alliance. The message would hopefully be that Caracas alone had the means to defend the *juntistas* against its outside enemies. It is also significant that it was

Coro, small and technically part of the province of Caracas, rather than Maracaibo, the real centre of loyalist resistance, which was the target of attack. The Junta Suprema clearly hoped to score an easy, not too costly, propaganda victory. As it turned out, however, the initiative was a disaster. The Marqués del Toro at the head of the small, 3,000-man *caraqueño* army retreated after his first serious encounter with the enemy led to casualties, and the project of subduing Coro was abandoned. The political impact of the attack was to weaken further rather than strengthen the position and the morale of the moderates.

The clearest sign of the decline of the moderates after the November fiasco at Coro was the more or less unchecked rise in the revolutionary activities of the radical faction. These centred on the Sociedad Patriótica de Agricultores y Economía founded in August 1810 by the Junta Suprema.[61] The Society was originally conceived of as a predominantly apolitical body subordinate to the government, created to encourage the development of agriculture, commerce and education in the province. Unfortunately for the moderates, however, it became a repository of discontented radicals, including Antonio Muñoz Tebar, Vicente Salias, Miguel Peña, Fermín Pául and others. In December, Simón Bolívar and Francisco Miranda upon their arrival in Caracas also became members, and from then on the purpose of the Society became expressly political: to become a mouthpiece for the extreme separatist forces in the province. During the first six months of 1811 the Society became a formidable pressure organ and source of pro-independence propaganda. Its leaders held open meetings, organized parades and attended and disrupted the sessions of the Constituent Congress, which began to meet after March.[62]

The pressure tactics of the Sociedad were supplemented by the very aggressive use made of the press in the province. It should be said that the press in Caracas was actually limited to the press in the capital city, and that it had only been in existence since 1808.[63] It is therefore all the more surprising and remarkable that across 1810 and 1811 five newspapers vied for the attention of the reading public of the city and the province. That readership was not as comparatively limited as might be thought. The main newspaper, the *Gazeta de Caracas*, seems to have had a run of 500 copies per issue at its height which compares favourably with the circulation of an average newspaper in the many-times-larger Paris of the 1790s.[64]

The newspapers in Caracas were entirely in the hands of the radical faction.[65] Why the moderates should have given their enemies such a powerful weapon without even a struggle is something of a mystery. All sides, including the Junta Suprema, which used the *Gazeta* to publicize its dictates, considered the press an integral part of the political process as it was evolving. Whatever the reasons the pro-independence spokesmen ran the newspapers. In the first six months of 1811 the three papers then in publication, the *Gazeta*, the *Semanario*, and the *Mercurio* increasingly argued the case for a complete break with Spain.[66] It is not to be assumed that this propaganda was the co-ordinated product of like-minded individuals. Roscio, who edited the *Gazeta*, represented the conservative wing of the radicals and was openly opposed to the antics of the Sociedad Patriótica.[67] Sanz, the editor of the *Semanario*, was on the other hand closely allied with Miranda and seems to have attended meetings of the Sociedad.[68] Whatever their differences, however, the effect of their separate efforts was to help condition the political climate for the declaration of independence to come in July 1811.

The strategic advantage of the radicals was aided by the formation of a leadership cadre in early 1811. The return in December 1810 of Francisco Miranda, the revolutionary precursor of Spanish American independence bar none, gave the pro-independence forces a weighty symbol to rally around as well as an effective spokesman.[69] At the same time, Simón Bolívar re-entered provincial society, and although he as yet did not command any real political allegiance locally, his close personal ties with the influential Toro brothers among others ensured the adherence of important elements of the provincial aristocracy to the radical cause.[70] In April 1811 another revolutionary aristocrat, the street agitator, José Félix Ribas, returned from his exile in Curaçao to resume his demagogic activities.[71]

By early 1811 the radicalization of events inside the province and outside it were also working in favour of a revolutionary takeover. In January the Regency blockade of Venezuela began. That Spain, still very much involved in a life-or-death struggle with the French, could also find the resources to commence hostilities against a colony which until recently had contributed to the Spanish war effort must have made a profound impression on the province. It can at least be speculated that the Spanish move shocked the moderates into acquiescing to radical demands that the colony's anomalous constitutional position should be clarified. In March 1811 the province of Cundinamarca in neighbouring New Granada showed how this could be done by declaring itself an independent republic.[72] The development was applauded by radicals in Caracas but again it is more than probable that it also influenced moderates in the province by breaking the psychological barrier to a full declaration of independence.

The transformation in March 1811 of the local *juntista* government marked the fall from power of the *caraqueño* moderates. That month the delegates elected the previous November by the *juntista* provinces met as the Congreso General de Venezuela.[73] The Junta Suprema resigned, to be replaced by a three-man executive body named by the Congress.[74] In addition ministers of government were replaced and the makeup of the Law Court was altered.[75] A glance at the names of the new leaders of government shows to what extent the moderates had been pushed aside. In the Congress the presence of the representatives of other provinces substantially diluted the dominance of the Caracas elite which had been so apparent in the composition of the Junta Suprema. Among the *caraqueño* delegates a combination of elite radicals and their middle-class allies prevailed: the likes of Fernando Toro, Isidoro López Méndez, Luis Ribas and the Marqués del Toro were joined by Roscio, Fermín Pául, Alamo and, later, Francisco Miranda. In the government Sanz replaced Lino Clemente as Minister of War, Roscio replaced the merchant Key Muñoz at the Treasury and took over the Justice Department as well. The *hacendado* lawyer, Francisco Espejo, replaced the Marqués de Casa León as head of the Law Court. Three relatively obscure men became the new Poder Ejecutivo in place of the Junta Suprema. The moderates had not, of course, disappeared entirely, but it is clear that a fundamental power shift had occurred.

In retrospect it can be seen that the political defeat of the *caraqueño* moderates was not just the product of circumstances beyond their control and of the strength of the radical opposition to them. They contributed to their failure by demonstrating a pronounced lack of resolution and resourcefulness in the face of political adversity. Part of the reason is what one author has called the 'almost organic weakness in the position of the moderates' in any revolutionary situation.[76] Our moderates found themselves caught in the middle between the system they were trying to reform and the extremists in their own ranks pressing for a total transformation. Yet occupied as they were with carrying out administrative reforms, ensuring public order and fulfilling the routine needs of government at a time when the legitimate authority had ceased to exist, the moderates had little inclination to fight the political battles they should have fought to cement their position. It should also be remembered that our moderates, in effect the *caraqueño* planter–merchant elite, had not seized power with any revolutionary intentions. True, they had implemented measures which were in principal inimical to the continued inclusion of Caracas in the Spanish Empire as it stood, but in 1810 they had not expected the empire to survive the Napoleonic invasion in its old form, if it survived at all.

When it became clear that much more was under way than an attempt to reform the imperial system, and that military confrontation was in store for the province, the moderates not surprisingly found themselves on the defensive. They were not frightened enough by Regency threats to return to the imperial fold: their reformist sentiment was too strong to allow that. Yet at the same time they could not conceive of joining the regionalist and radical currents which were threatening to destroy their world as they knew it. The result was political inaction and, ultimately, political abdication. Rather than forcefully asserting their considerable authority over the divisive influences at work, they allowed the radicals to promote their objectives almost at will. The radicals for their part, unencumbered by the responsibilities of government, small in number, well-organized, confident as to their priorities, and favoured by the hostility of the Spanish reaction, which made polarization and conflict inevitable, were thus able to wrest power from the confused and dispirited moderates.

After March 1811 it was only a matter of time before independence was declared. With the radicals in control and with the growing need to define Venezuela's ambiguous political status, the debate in the Constituent Congress shifted from constitutional concerns to the question of the colony's continued loyalty to the mother country. The proponents of an immediate declaration of independence argued persuasively that, until the ambiguity of Venezuela's loyalties was cleared up, no constitution could be promulgated, no advantage could be taken of relations with Britain and the United States, no sense of direction could be given to political proceedings in the colony and no halt could be put to seditious loyalist activity in the *juntista* jurisdiction, acting under the cover of Ferdinand's name. On 5 July 1811 the Congress declared the area under its control independent of Spain.[77]

It is extremely interesting to note that not even at this stage of the revolution did the separatists come up with a convincing indictment of Spanish rule in the colony as a justification for independence. The declaration of independence if anything highlights once more to what extent the revolution was fundamentally the product of the events of the preceding three years.[78] Freed from the constraints of the fiction of loyalty to Ferdinand, which had tied the tongues of radical propagandists since 19 April, Roscio and Isnardi, who wrote the document, still managed to come up with a remarkably vague justificatory litany. Grand references to 300 years of tyrannical abuse, the right of oppressed people to rise against their conquerors and to mythic Spanish medieval compacts failed to hide the lack of substantive or substantiated criticism of Spanish colonial rule. The one concrete and indisputable set of reasons offered for the break was a rehash of the cumulative negative effects of the imperial crisis begun in 1808.

Epilogue

Moderates whatever their colour, gave way to the forces of extremism across the next ten years (1811–21) of the history of the province. The old ruling elite of Caracas, and for that matter most of the province's white population, seem to have tried to stay out of the conflict that escalated around them in the years after July 1811. When this was not possible, as was often the case, they accommodated to whichever royalist or republican currently held the central reins of power. They had plenty of practice in transferring nominal allegiances.[1] The radical rulers of the First Republic (July 1811 – July 1812) gave way to the royalist *caudillo* Domingo Monteverde (July 1812 – August 1813). He, in turn, was ousted by a resurgent Bolívar, who held sway in the province for less than a year (August 1813 – July 1814) before fleeing before another royalist maverick, José Tomás Boves. A combination of Boves, his lieutenants and bureaucratic Spanish officials from other provinces then governed Caracas for a period of nine months (July 1814 – April 1815) until the arrival of an expeditionary army from Spain under the leadership of Field Marshall Pablo Morillo. He and his aides ruled the province under a curious mixture of military occupation and partial restoration of the colonial order until mid-1821 when Bolívar finally liberated the province and Venezuela.

If anything, the multiple changes of government increased the determination of the population of Caracas to remain on the sidelines. It is probably often noticed but seldom remarked that every successful military effort to supplant the central authority in Caracas, from 1812 on, was mobilized outside the province or at best in its regional peripheries. Domingo Monteverde invaded from Coro; Bolívar from New Granada; Boves from the Llanos; Morillo from Spain; and Bolívar again from New Granada. Furthermore, each time the foreign incursion was made, the presiding government crumbled in a matter of a few months. In other words there was no groundswell of popular sentiment or support inside the province which either insurgents or governments could draw on throughout the independence wars. This was true even of the last phase of the struggle, when the issues of the conflict had become over-whelmingly clear, and when there were finally two reasonably organized, legitimized antagonists facing each other.

More specifically, a glance at the leadership ranks of the contending sides across the 1810s reveals that few of the pre-1810 elite were directly involved with either side. Earlier I observed that the radical, now republican, faction contained a high proportion of individuals from the middle sectors of white society and from areas outside the province. If anything the latter group's preponderance increased as the 1810s progressed: in the political sphere the *granadinos* Leopoldo Zea and Francisco Santander and the *trujillanos* Mendoza and Briceño came to the fore; in the military sphere Bolívar came to depend on Mariño, Sucre, Monagas, Arismendi and Piar from the eastern provinces, Páez from the Llanos and Urdaneta from Maracaibo. The situation was scarcely different on the royalist side, where a procession of military men headed the various royalist governments between 1812 and 1821, and paid little heed to the surviving civilian colonial authorities and representatives of the *caraqueño* elite. Men like Monteverde, Boves and Morales were little better than renegades; yet even when the colonial order was to some extent restored after 1815 under Morillo, military men continued to be the supreme authority in the province, with the old ruling elite barely in evidence.

Accommodation and neutrality did not always save the lives and properties of the uncommitted majority; indeed they suffered from the ravages of the independence wars more than the population of any other major colony. A high and undoubtedly exaggerated contemporary esti-mate of the loss of life during the worst years of conflict (1811–15) is roughly 80,000, or just under one fifth of the province's 420,000 inhabitants in 1810.[2] At least 10,000 deaths may have resulted from the effects of a major earthquake in March 1812, but many more perished in the wars and from the pestilence and hunger which followed in their wake. Whatever the final tally, it is clear that a disproportion-ately large number of *caraqueños* died in connection with the civil and social conflicts occasioned by the struggle for independence.

The extraordinary bloodshed of the independence wars would appear to contradict the central argument of this study: that late-colonial Caracas was a relatively stable society with few simmering social or poli-tical tensions. There is no contradiction however: in accounting for the war dead we would do well to remember that the incidence of violence varied considerably between 1811 and 1821. Comparatively speaking not many lives were lost before 1813. Beginning in June 1813, however, the *Libertador* Simón Bolívar, entering from New Granada, launched his war to the death against all Spaniards; and in 1814 the royalist Tomás Boves countered with his indiscriminate slaughter of creoles. This recrudescence of the conflict extended to the battlefield, and across 1814 thousands of lives were lost in battles where no quarter was given. The bloodshed, in other words, was not really the result of the *caraqueño* population's political commitment to one or the other side of the struggle for independence but rather of the deliberate, extremist policies of two rival *caudillos*, who commanded little support from the mass of the white population.

Why did Boves and Bolívar act as they did? In Bolívar's case the reasoning which impelled him was rather straightforward. Commanding little support inside Caracas, he hoped that by isolating the Spanish contingent of the white population, he would create a sense of difference so great between creoles and Europeans that the former would abandon their neutrality and come to identify their future with the republic. He was ruthless in his pursuit of this goal across 1813 and 1814, and it is seldom realized just how systematic he was in implementing his reign of terror. If it is remembered that there were only 7,000–8,000 Spaniards in the province, the dimensions of what he achieved assume horrifying proportions. In the process of overthrowing Monteverde in the summer of 1813, Bolívar himself spoke of how he 'advanced . . . through the cities and *pueblos* of Tocuyito, Valencia, . . . Maracay, Turmero, San Mateo and La Victoria, where all Europeans . . ., almost without exception, were shot'.[3] Once Bolívar arrived in the city of Caracas in August 1813, small groups of Spaniards were put to death on one pretext or another.[4] Those who were not executed in the first few months were thrown into prison and had their goods confiscated. The reason given for their arrest in the official documentation was chilling in its simplicity: 'por ser Español Europeo' or 'por ser oriundos de canarias'.[5] Finally, in February 1814, Bolívar had the over-1,000 Spanish prisoners he was still holding murdered in cold blood.[6]

It is significant that Bolívar's bid to radicalize creole opinion failed, and it failed miserably. The one effect he could be sure his policy had, was negative: the extreme radicalization of the surviving royalist Spanish community. Those that could fled the province, while the others melted into the Llanos of the interior. It was there that the alliance between white royalists and *pardo* plainsmen was formed to overthrow the Second Republic, and very nearly the fabric of white society as well.

The violence perpetrated by Boves' *pardo* hordes across 1814 had a much more intricate genesis and motivation than that practised by the republicans. Perhaps in reaction to this complexity, the Boves phenomenon has been subjected to a wide assortment of interpretations focusing on everything from Boves' charismatic leadership, to the inducements with which he may have bought the loyalty of the *pardos*; to the royalist reaction to Bolívar's war to the death; to the role played by the exploding resentments of the mass of free-coloureds, and indeed of black slaves, against the creole aristocracy.[7] What is seldom remarked, however, is that the politicization, for that is what it was, of the *castas* had its origins in the lack of support for the royalist cause among the white population, and that such support as did exist fell under the direction of extremists willing to countenance any measure to reinstall Spanish authority. What made these royalists different from the republican leaders who suffered from the same lack of popular appeal, was that the royalists did not flinch from involving the free-coloureds in the conflict which developed.

Boves and his *pardo* army were the logical culmination of the indiscriminate counter-revolutionary tactics which had been employed since 1808. The process of involving the free-coloureds in the political divisions of the white caste began when Captain-General Casas and the Regent of the Audiencia, Joaquín Mosquera, in an effort to mobilize support for their position, hit upon the device of portraying the *junta* proposal of 24 November 1808 by Caracas notables as a manoeuvre to install an oligarchic tyranny over the province and other castes.[8] Casas and Mosquera apparently struck a responsive chord among urban *pardos* who had witnessed the white elite oppose the few legal gains made by the free-coloureds. This inclination of the *pardos*, and also of black slaves, to identify their wellbeing with the Crown was further exploited in 1810–11. José Francisco Heredia, a lawyer of the Audiencia, one of the most important civilian royalists in Caracas between 1812 and 1817, and also, incidentally perhaps, the most astute contemporary observer of the revolution, described how amoral this exploitation was. He is worth quoting at length:

'. . . to restore the [royalist] government the leaders only used the atrocious method of an internecine reaction . . . which they wished for or sought by whatever means possible. Sr Cortabarria in some of his papers [applauded] the faithful *gente de color*, and in Coro and Maracaibo any news of . . . uprisings, even those of slaves, was greeted with enthusiasm . . . as being for the good cause . . . if Venezuela becomes another Algiers of *zambos* and blacks, we owe it undoubtedly to the seeds sown in this first period, and to the celebrity accorded the revolts, robberies and deaths which took place, in the name of Ferdinand VII.'[9] Furthermore, royalist guerillas incited 'mortal hatred between whites and *pardos* . . . so that it became proverbial among extremist Europeans that *pardos* were loyal, while white creoles were revolutionaries whom it was necessary to finish off [kill]'.[10]

It is not to be supposed that the republicans did not attempt a kind of co-optation themselves, but it was executed in a more orderly fashion and ultimately had less appeal. The abolition of legal racial distinctions in the republican constitution of 1811, though far from being the half-measure many historians have supposed, certainly did not have much impact when coupled with the formalization of the Ordenanza de los Llanos, which finally established the long-sought white goal of a pass-system for the inhabitants of the Llanos.[11] The royalist agitators in contrast, and benefiting from the flexibility accorded those out of power, offered the opportunity, especially to rural *pardos* and slaves, to get back at their white masters through pillage and murder in the name of Ferdinand VII. These visceral enticements were accompanied by vague promises of a total reform of the caste system once the colonial order was restored. In June 1812 the royalist effort was rewarded with a major *pardo* and slave uprising in the Tuy valleys east of Caracas.[12] The spectre of race war helped induce the republicans to surrender to Monteverde in the following month.[13]

Once aroused, the *castas* were not easily tamed. Politicized by appeals from both sides, drafted into the contending armies, their hopes aroused by promises of reform and witnessing the collapse of the social order, the *castas* became ever more directly involved in the struggle across 1813–14.

Boves therefore emerged as the formidable leader and scourge he was, in an environment which was tailor-made for what he had in mind: terrorizing the creole population into submission. With a handful of Europeans and thousands of *pardos* he launched his extermination campaign with its well-known results. By the time Boves died in December 1814, and coincidental with the reappearance of legitimized royalist authorities, the anti-white hatred of the *castas* which he had so effectively marshalled was threatening to turn on the surviving European portion of the white caste. Officials as varied as the acting Captain-General, Juan Cagigal, the interim Regent Heredia, the Audiencia lawyer Javier Ucelay, Archbishop Coll y Prat, the newly-arrived Field Marshall Morillo and the ex-Commandant of Coro, José Cevallos, all expressed alarm about the influences the race war unleashed by the extremist royalists had had on the racial balance in the colony. [14] They need not have concerned themselves unduly. With Boves dead and other royalist radicals seemingly in tow, the unscrupulous exhortations to the free-coloureds ceased and the impetus went out of the race conflict. By late 1815, with peace temporarily restored, with the colonial government back in place and with the 19,000-man army Boves had built up successfully disbanded, the threat to white society from the *pardos* receded, without any significant concessions being made to the latter.

The arrival of Morillo and the Expeditionary Army in 1815 signalled an end to the violence and devastation of the 1813–14 period, and for the next five years something like the reinstitutionalization of government occurred. A peace of sorts was maintained in the central areas of the province, as was normality in day-to-day life. The economy began to recover from the effects of the previous five years and by 1819 may have been reaching two thirds of its 1810 production levels. [15] A *de facto* free trade was allowed. [16] The Audiencia, the Consulado and the Intendancy were re-established. All the same, the new regime found it as difficult to gain the adherence of the inhabitants as its predecessors had. Morillo, as he retreated in 1820 before the final republican offensive, complained: 'there is not a single inhabitant who is thinking of following the government of the nation, some because they oppose it [us], and the majority out of expediency'. [17] This expediency was well learned and well justified: in June 1821 Simón Bolívar re-entered the city of Caracas, this time for good.

Appendix A

Geographical distribution of haciendas and *hatos* in Caracas 1785–1787

Region	Partido	Cacao	Sugar	Indigo	Livestock
Coast	Coro	7	?	—	95
	La Guaira	218	22	—	—
	Puerto Cabello	86	1	—	—
Coastal Range	Caracas City	—	—	—	—
	Guarenas	213	46	6	—
	Nirgua	103	20	2	13
	Ocumare del Tuy	100	7	24	—
	Petare	1	13	2	—
	Valencia	46	25	15	—
	La Victoria	13	51	121	—
Segovia Highlands	Barquisimeto	129	51	7	3
	Carora	8	?	—	25
	Rio Tocuyo	10	1	—	11
	San Felipe	152	4	13	—
	El Tocuyo	—	68	1	6
Llanos	Araure	22	—	10	65
	Calabozo	—	—	—	116
	Guanare	10	3	3	53
	San Carlos	—	1	—	135
	San Rafael de Orituco	15	10	—	20
	Valle de la Pascua	—	30	—	—
Llanos/ Coastal Range	San Sebastián	11	30	16	138
	Santa Maria de Ipire	—	—	—	183
Total		1144	436	220	863

Sources: Estado General de la Población y Producciones de . . . Venezuela formado por D. José de Castro y Aráoz . . . (15 June 1787), A.A., Ar. 6 salon 115, *passim.* The sugar-plantation totals for Coro and Carora do not appear in the copy of the *Estado* I have, although the total number of plantations does. The geographical distribution of the *partidos* is done in accordance with the regions delineated by John V. Lombardi, *People and Places in Colonial Venezuela* (Bloomington, Indiana, 1976), and described in chapter 1 of this study.

Appendix B

Consulado Membership

One of the lists I used to determine the membership of the Consulado actually pre-dates its creation in 1793. This is the preliminary list drawn up by Intendant Saavedra in 1786, with the names of worthy individuals who might be called upon to form a Guild. The other lists are for 1805–6, or well into the Consulado's short life. Space limitations do not permit the reproduction of these lists, but they are easily accessible in printed and secondary works. For 1786 and 1806 see Federico Brito Figueroa, *La Estructura Económica de Venezuela Colonial*, 2nd ed. (Caracas, 1978), pp. 247–8 and 436–7. For merchants in 1805 see Idelfonso Leal (ed.), *Documentos del Real Consulado de Caracas* (Caracas, 1964), pp. 33–6. The only addition from original sources is the list of *hacendados* for 1805. See A.G.I., Caracas 803, memorial by *junta* of agriculturalists dated 11 March 1805, included in a despatch by Arce to the Crown on the province's finances, 9 April 1805.

What follows below is a catalogue of the wills I have found pertaining to members of the Consulado. They are classified under the headings of *Hacendados*, *Comerciantes* and *Mercaderes*, with further subdivisions into those names included in the 1786 list and those from the 1805–6 lists. I have also distinguished between individuals for whom I have a personal will, and those for whom information is only indirectly available through the will of a relative. The reference number following the names is to the Bibliographical Appendix. Under *Comerciante* I have further identified national origin, the locally-married immigrants and merchants with agricultural properties. I have attempted to keep overlap to a minimum by not listing twice names which appear in both the 1786 and the 1805–6 lists.

(1) **Hacendados**

    (a)   *1786 (Personal wills)*:   F. Ascanio (Conde de la Granja, Bibl. App. 25a); F. Blanco y Mixares (34h); G. Blanco y Plaza (34m); D. Blanco y Ponte (34r); J. D. Blanco y Rengifo (34w); J. Cocho e Iriarte (372); L. Escalona (75b); J. Escorihuela (76); M. Monserrate (157a); D. Moreno (163a); J. Pacheco (Conde de San Xavier, 182c); F. Pacheco (182b); F. Palacios y Sojo (186g); J. Palacios y Sojo (181i); J. I. Plaza y Liendo (201e); S. Ponte (203f); M. Ribas (436); S. Toro (Marqués del Toro, 250a); M. F. Tovar (252e); M. Tovar y Blanco (Conde de Tovar, 252i); J. Vegas (259); and V. Verois (262).

    (b)   *1786 (wills of relatives)*:   J. Aristiguieta (94d); M. Aristiguieta (19a); and F. Mijares (Marqués de Mijares, 155a).

    (c)   *1805–6 (personal wills)*:   J. M. Alonso Gil (6b); J. Anza (270); A. Arnal (22); J. Ascanio (25f); B. Blandain (35); L. Blanco y Blanco (34b); J. Blanco y Liendo (34g); R. Blanco y Plaza (34q); G. Blanco Uribe (34y); G. Bolivar (36b); B. Butrageño (279); J. M. Echezuría (287b); J. T. Espinosa (79e); J. E. Gonzales (302); T. Hernández Sanabria (113); M. Herrera (114c); V. Ibarra (116a); L. López Méndez (131h); B. Machillanda (140a); J. V. Machillanda (140b); S. Mier y Terán (326); M. Monasterios (156h); J. Montenegro (158); J. J. Mora (161); J. I. Moreno (163b); J. M. Muro (166b); C. Palacios (186c);

T. Paz del Castillo (428); L. Ponte y Mixares (203c); M. Rada (207a); A. Rengifo Pimentel (214b); J. F. Ribas (216a); V. Ribas (216c); M. Sanz (235); J. R. Sabas Berdu (341); F. Toro (fourth Marqués del Toro, 250b); F. Tovar y Tovar (252v); D. Tovar (252l); and A. M. Urbina (254a).

(d) *1805–6 (wills of relatives)*: M. Berrotaran (32e); A. and M. Blanco y Blanco (34b); N. Blanco y Monasterios (34g); J. V. Bolivar Jr (36e); E. Buroz (252t); L. and P. Clemente y Francia (282); D. Domínguez de la Mota (384); F. Espejo (77); G. Ibarra (103f); M. and C. Machado (138f); F. Madrís (143h); P. M. Martínez de Porras (149); M. Montilla (476); F. Palacios (186g); J. I. and J. F. Palacios (186h); C. and E. Ponte (34j, 190 and 203a); and S. Vega (259).

(2) **Comerciantes**

(The wills marked with asterisks are of those immigrants who married creoles.)

(a) *1786 (personal wills)*: *Creoles* I. Gedler (94a); L. López Méndez (131h). *Peninsulares* J. J. Anza (270)*; J. Castilloveittia (281)*; M. Clemente y Francia (282)*; J. M. Echezuría (287b)*; A. Egaña (288)*; J. Iriarte (306)*; F. Llaguno (316)*; J. I. Michelena (324)*; D. Zulueta (351)*. *Canarios* F. Monteverde (423)*.

(b) *1786 (wills of relatives)*: *Peninsular* B. Magan de Pazos (38b)*.

(c) *1805–6 (personal wills)*: *Creoles* I. López Méndez (131f); J. F. Santana (234); M. Tovar y Ponte (2520). *Peninsulares* P. Aguerrevere (266); S. Cordova (284)*; J. E. Echezuría (287a)*; P. Echezuría (287c); J. J. Echenique (286)*; J. V. Galguera (294)*; J. M. Lizarraga (313); V. Linares (312)*; J. Lander (310b)*; F. Martínez de Abia (320); S. Mayora (321); P. Navas (332). *Canarios* F. Baez de Orta (357); A. Carballo (336); A. Hernández de Orta (407); F. Key Muñoz (461a); D. A. Pérez (430).

(d) *1805–6 (wills of relatives)*: *Creoles* J. Melo Navarrete (420a); V. Sarria (81a). *Canario* M. Sopranis (231)*.

(e) *Owners of agrarian properties*: *1786* Anza, Castilloveittia, Clemente y Francia, J. M. Echezuría, Egaña, L. López Méndez and Zulueta; *1805–6* Carballo, J. E. and P. Echezuría, Echenique, Key Muñoz, Lánder, Lizarraga, Linares, I. López Méndez, Llamosas, Martínez de Abia, D. A. Pérez, Sopranis and Tovar y Ponte.

(3) **Mercaderes**

1786 E. Nuñes (R.P., Escribanías, Aramburu, ff. 130–2); A. Martínez de Orihuela (418); P. Pérez Velásquez (434c); M. Santana (453); L. Seijas (454); and M. Vargas (257).

Notes

Note on sources

In researching this study I made extensive use of the notarial records of the city of Caracas. While they proved extremely illuminating as a source of information on the economy and society of late-colonial Caracas, the sheer bulk of the data they contained threatened to make them almost unusable by turning the notes to this work into a second text. I am referring in particular to a sample of wills for 782 persons collected from the notarial books for the late-colonial and early-republican periods. In order to incorporate the sample and the information it contained, I have had to reclassify the references to sources by forming a Bibliographical Appendix wherein the wills are recatalogued according to a straightforward numbering system. The original sources, as well as the names and castes of the given individuals, are contained within the listing.

Source abbreviations

Archives:

A.A.   Archivo de la Academia Nacional de la Historia (Caracas)
A.G.I.   Archivo General de Indias (Seville)
A.G.N.   Archivo General de la Nación (Caracas)
Bibl. App. Bibliographical Appendix
P.R.O.   Public Records Office (London)
R.P.   Archivo del Registro Principal del Distrito Federal (Caracas)

Journals:

B.A.N.H. Boletín de la Academia Nacional de la Historia
H.A.H.R. Hispanic American Historical Review
J.L.A.S. Journal of Latin American Studies
Anuario Anuario del Instituto de Antropologia e Historia

Introduction

1 For facsimiles of these decrees see *Real Cédula de Intendencia de Ejército y Real Hacienda Diciembre 8 de 1776*, estudio prelim. G. Morazzini de Perez Enciso (Caracas, 1976), and *La Capitanía-General de Venezuela 1777–8 de Septiembre 1977*, estudio prelim. A. Arellano Moreno (Caracas, 1977).

2 A seventh province, Barinas, was created in 1786. See Guillermo Morón, *A History of Venezuela* (New York, 1963), p. 65.
3 For a succinct summary of Venezuela's institutional development see Morón, *History of Venezuela*, pp. 63–8.
4 A. G. I., Caracas 513, trade statistics for 1795 included in memorial by the syndic of the Real Consulado of Caracas, 20 February 1796.
5 For cacao see Miguel Izard, 'La Venezuela del Cafe Vista por los Viajeros del Siglo XIX', *Boletín Histórico*, XX (1969), 189. For indigo and coffee see François Depons, *Travels in South America during the years 1801, 1802, 1803 and 1804* ... (London, 1807), I, 407, 426.
6 The calculation is by A. von Humboldt, quoted, along with less reliable estimates, in Miguel Izard, *El Miedo a la Revolución: La Lucha por la Libertad en Venezuela (1777–1830)* (Madrid, 1979), pp. 175–6.
7 Morón, *History of Venezuela*, pp. 79–84.
8 For a history of this trade see Eduardo Arcila Farías, *Comercio entre Venezuela y México en los Siglos XVII y XVIII* (Mexico, 1950).
9 The history of the company is covered in Roland D. Hussey, *The Caracas Company 1728–1784: A Study in the History of Spanish Monopolistic Trade* (Cambridge, Mass., 1934).
10 Antonio García-Baquero González, *Cádiz y el Atlántico 1717–1778: el Comercio Colonial Espanol Bajo el Monopolio Gaditano* (Seville, 1976), I, 338, 349.

1 The caste society

1 John V. Lombardi, *People and Places in Colonial Venezuela* (Bloomington, Indiana, 1976).
2 *Estado General de la Población y Producciones de* ... *Venezuela formado por D. José de Castro y Aráoz* ... (15 June 1787), A.A., Ar. 6 salon 115.
3 For a good contemporary example of the application of *pardos* see A.G.I., Caracas 180, report by the Caracas City Council to the Crown, 28 November 1796, contained in despatch of the Council on the proposed revocation of the royal decree of 10 February 1795. For a review of the ambiguities of racial terms as applied to free-coloureds see Lombardi, *People and Places*, pp. 43–4.
4 Most of the following discussion is taken from Lombardi, *ibid.* pp. 9–22, 69–75 and 132–3.
5 A full account of the distribution of production of each crop is given in chapter 3.
6 For a full description of livestock production see chapter 3.
7 The number of cacao and sugar-cane plantations is given in *Estado General de 1787*, pp. 20–2. On livestock see A.G.N., Real Hacienda, Libros de Contabilidad: 2360 Barquisimeto 1787–8 and (?) El Tocuyo 1786. For a partial history of the region see Ermila Troconis de Veracoechea, *Historia de El Tocuyo Colonial: periodo historico 1545–1810* (Caracas, 1977).
8 Lombardi, *People and Places*, pp. 52–65. The population figures for the individual urban centres in order of mention, with the exception of Caracas, are taken respectively from Lombardi, pp. 226, 205, 201, 225, 211, 186, 195, 178–9, 196–7, 212, 210, 200. For the city of Caracas see *Gazeta de Caracas*, 21 May 1817, in *Gazeta de Caracas* (Paris, 1939), VI, 1027.
9 For a list of towns founded between the early 1500s and late 1700s see *Atlas de Venezuela* (Caracas, 1971), p. 197.

10 Alexander von Humboldt, *Personal Narrative of Travels to the Equinoctal Regions of America during the years 1799–1804* (London, 1852), I, 398. *Canarios* in all probability far outnumbered *peninsulares*. See Poudenx and Mayer's observation in *Tres Testigos Europeos de la Primera República 1808–1814: Semple, Delpech, Poudenx y Mayer* (Caracas, 1974), p. 105.

11 A.G.I., Caracas 180, Guevara Vasconcelos to Crown, 13 July 1801.

12 François Depons, *Travels in South America during the years 1801, 1802, 1803 and 1804* . . . (London, 1807), I, 112.

13 A.G.I., Caracas 939–40, *Expedientes sobre licencias de embarque*, 1787–1801 and 1802–20. About 80 licences granted between 1789 and 1810 are included in the collection.

14 A.G.I., Caracas 59, Guillelmi to Crown, 24 June 1791; A.G.I., Caracas 101, Guevara Vasconcelos to Crown, 23 December 1802.

15 See A.G.I., Caracas 469, and report by Matías Fortunato Costa, 30 July 1787 and A.G.I., Caracas 381, reports dated 26 November 1796 and 23 December 1802.

16 A.G.I., Caracas 99, list of refugee arrivals in despatch by Guevara Vasconcelos to Minister of War, 10 August 1801.

17 For 1793 see A.G.I., Caracas 505, León to Crown, 11 December 1793. For 1797 see A.G.I., Caracas 169, López Quintana to Jovellanos, 16 September 1798. On their continued presence over the years see Humboldt, *Personal Narrative*, II, 57; Elias Pino Iturrieta, *La Mentalidad Venezolana de la Emancipación 1810–1812* (Caracas, 1971), p. 37; and J. J. Dauxion-Lavaysse, *Viaje a las Islas de Trinidad, Tobago y Margarita y a Diversas Partes de Venezuela en la América-Meridional* (Caracas, 1967), p. 244.

18 For the locally married selection, see the asterisked wills in Bibl. App., under *Peninsulares* and *Canarios*.

19 In 1806 there were about 30 to 35 senior treasury and political officials in Caracas. See the contemporary account of the Provincial Treasury, José Limonta, *Libro de la Razón General de la Real Hacienda del Departamento de Caracas*, estudio prelim. M. Briceño Perozo (Caracas, 1962), pp. 227, 259. In 1787 middle-level employees of both branches together numbered 354. See *Estado General de 1787*, p. 29.

20 The figure of 600 is from Depons, *Travels in South America*, I, 269–7.

21 *Semanario de Caracas*, 16 December 1810, in *Semanario de Caracas* (Caracas, 1959), p. 52.

22 See chapter 4.

23 On the nationality of the captains-general of Venezuela betwen 1777 and 1810 see Luis A. Sucre, *Gobernadores y Capitanes Generales de Venezuela*, 2nd ed. (Caracas, 1964), pp. 288–317. The origins of the intendants Francisco Saavedra, Esteban Fernández de León, Vicente Basadre and Dionisio Franco are given respectively in: Ángel López Cantos, *Don Francisco de Saavedra, Segundo Intendente de Caracas* (Seville, 1973), p. 1; Mario Briceño Iragorry, *Casa León y su Tiempo: Aventura de un Anti-Héroe* (Caracas, 1946), p. 13; A.G.I., Caracas 41, request by Basadre to return to Spain, 1808–9, in collection of papers on official appointments to the province 1803–9; *Gazeta de Caracas*, 24 July 1816, in *Gazeta de Caracas*, VI, 669. León and Franco were also directors of the tobacco monopoly at earlier stages in their career. The brigadier commander of the captaincy-general armed forces in 1800, Juan Manuel Cagigal, was a Spaniard. See his memoirs, Juan M. Cagigal, *Memorias del Mariscal de Campo Don Juan Manuel de Cagigal Sobre la Revolución de Venezuela* (Caracas, 1960). On the European origins of various treasury officials see M. Briceño Perozo, estudio

prelim. to Limonta, *Libro de la Razón General*, pp. xxiii–xxv. On the Audiencia lawyers see p. 33. In addition, see the wills of Captain-General Carbonell and Regent (of the Audiencia) López Quintana. Bibl. App. 280 and 315.

24 The service records of ninety-eight colonial officials can be found in A.G.I., Caracas 54, *Hojas de Servicios 1784–1821*.

25 *Ibid.* 26 January 1810.

26 *Ibid.* Garate, December 1809.

27 *Ibid. passim.* Among senior treasury officials there are the cases of J. Emasável, J. Yarza, F. Sojo, L. Sata y Subira and J. Alustiza, who by 1810 had all served a minimum of eighteen years in the province.

28 For León see Briceño Iragorry, *Casa León*, pp. 14–15. For Franco's appointment to the monopoly see A.G.I., Caracas 766, royal confirmation at Aranjuez, 27 March 1802. On his promotion to Intendant see A.G.I., Caracas 42, royal confirmation at Cádiz, 1 August 1812. On his marriage and son see Bibl. App. 292.

29 See chapter 5.

30 *Ibid.*

31 See chapter 6.

32 Bibl. App: *Caraqueño Creoles*, 3, 10, 19d, 25b, 30b, 32c, 38a, 50, 51, 53a, 55, 66, 72b, 79b, 81c, 83, 84, 89a, 92, 98, 99, 107, 114d, 116b, 119c, 127, 128, 131g, 131j, 137, 140b, 153, 156f, 156h, 159, 163b, 165b, 170, 178, 183, 186e, 192, 195, 198a, 207a, 236, 239, 244, 245, 252p, 252q and 464; *Peninsulares* 265, 290, 300, 319 and 334.

33 Mary Watters, *A History of the Church in Venezuela 1810–1930* (Chapel Hill, N.C., 1933), p. 39.

34 On the Audiencia lawyers see Mark Burkholder and D. Chandler, *From Impotence to Authority: the Spanish Crown and the American Audiencias, 1687–1808* (Columbia, 1977), Appendix V (no page-numbers). For an 1802 list of sixty-one member-lawyers of the Caracas Colegio de Abogados see A.G.I., Caracas 47, despatch on case of execution of will of J. Escorihuela, Council of Indies, 2 April 1803.

35 A.G.I., Caracas 27, report on the Aragua valleys contained in *reservada* by Saavedra on Mancebo case, 4 September 1790.

36 A.G.I., Caracas 101, Guevara Vasconcelos to Ministry of Justice, 23 December 1802.

37 For the purposes of this study no distinction will be made between the different components of the free-coloured caste, unless otherwise specified, and the terms *castas*, *pardos* and 'free-coloured' will be used interchangeably.

38 For a general discussion of the status of free-coloureds in Spanish colonial society see Leslie B. Rout Jr, *The African Experience in Spanish America: 1502 to the present day* (Cambridge, 1976), pp. 126–61. On the application of the restrictions in Venezuela see James King, 'A Royalist View of the Colored Castes in the Venezuelan War of Independence', *H.A.H.R.*, XXXIII (1953), 531–3.

39 A.G.I., Caracas 513, memorial on state of the province by V. Linares, 20 February 1796, in 1802 despatch on issue of new maritime duties.

40 A.G.I., Caracas 180, report by the Caracas City Council to the Crown, 28 November 1796, in despatch of the Cabildo on the royal decree of 10 February 1795, 1796–8.

41 A.G.I., Caracas 168, memorial by D. Gédler, 16 November 1788.

42 A.G.I., Caracas 15, memorial by M. Tovar and A. Ibarra, 13 May 1794, in despatch on formation of patrol squadrons for the Llanos, Council of the Indies, 26 August 1797.

43 *Estado General de 1787*, pp. 3–4.

44 For 1721 see Pedro Olavarriaga, *Instrucción General y Particular del Estado Presente de la Provincia de Venezuela en los Años de 1720 y 1721* (Caracas, 1965), pp. 270–5. For 1745 see Federico Brito Figueroa, *La Estructura Económica de Venezuela Colonial*, 2nd ed. (Caracas, 1978), pp. 319–21.

45 See Bibl. App. Sample listed under free-coloureds.

46 Bibl. App. 482, 484, 490, 496, 506, 516, 519, 521, 523 and 524.

47 Bibl. App. 516.

48 Bibl. App. 524.

49 Bibl. App. 485a–b.

50 Bibl. App. 507.

51 Bibl. App. 514.

52 Bibl. App. 487 and 504.

53 J. Kinsbruner, 'The Pulperos of Caracas and San Juan during the first half of the nineteenth century', *Latin American Research Review*, XIII (1978), 68–9.

54 A.G.N., Real Hacienda, Libros de Contabilidad 2360: Barquisimeto 1787–8.

55 *Ibid.*, Libros de Contabilidad 1924: La Victoria 1803–4. On use of 'don' see p. 219.

56 Bibl. App. 506.

57 For an example of a *pardo* overseer see Bibl. App. 496. On the question of slave and free-coloured *mayordomos* in Coro see Idelfonso Leal (ed.), *Documentos del Real Consulado de Caracas* (Caracas, 1964), pp. 217–26.

58 Eduardo Arcila Farías *et al.*, *Estudio de Caracas* (Caracas, 1967), II, 1,008.

59 The major studies of slavery in Venezuela are by Miguel Acosta Saignes, *Vida de los Esclavos Negros en Venezuela* (Caracas, 1967), and John V. Lombardi, *The Decline and Abolition of Negro Slavery in Venezuela 1820–1854* (Westport, Conn., 1971).

60 A.G.I., Caracas 513, memorial on state of the province by V. Linares, 20 February 1796, in an 1802 dispatch on the issue of new maritime duties.

61 Troconis de Veracoechea, *Historia de El Tocuyo Colonial*, pp. 254–66.

62 Brito Figueroa, *Estructura Económica*, pp. 317–28.

63 The number of slaves cannot be given any more exactly because of the often imprecise disclosures made by their owners. For the wills of the sample see Bibl. App.:

Caraqueño Creoles: 1(a, b), 2b, 8, 9, 10, 13, 18b, 22, 24, 25a, 30a, 31, 32e, 34(d, k, m, n, r, t, w, x, y), 36(c, e), 37, 44–6, 51, 52b, 53a, 54–5, 65b, 66, 74, 77–8, 79(a, c, e), 80, 81b, 82, 83, 87, 89a, 95, 103(a, b), 107, 110–12, 114c, 115, 116d, 118, 119(a, b), 121–2, 124–6, 130, 131(f, h), 133, 134c, 137, 138(b, f), 140b, 141–2, 143(c, e, f, h), 147, 153–4, 155b, 156(e, f), 157c, 160a, 162, 163(a, b), 165b, 168, 171, 178, 180, 182(c, f), 184, 186(b, c, e, g, i), 188, 189, 194–5, 197b, 200, 201(e, f), 203c, 204, 207d, 208, 210, 212, 214b, 216e, 224, 230, 247c, 250a, 252a, 254a, 257–9, and 262.

Peninsulares: 268, 271, 273, 277, 279, 281–2, 287a, 291, 293, 295, 298–302, 312, 319–20, 322, 330–1, 334, 339–41 and 344–5.

Canarios: 356–7, 359, 363, 365–70, 374–5, 378, 380a, 382–3, 388–90, 393, 397–8, 400(a, b), 404, 407–9, 411–12, 414, 418, 420–1, 424–5, 427, 429–30, 434c, 436, 438, 445, 447, 449, 452, 454–5, 457–8 and 462.

Other White: 474, 476, 479 and 481.

Free-Coloureds: 484, 485(a, b), 487, 488b, 490, 493–4, 496, 498, 504, 513, 516, 521, 522 and 524.

Caste Unknown: 544.

64 For a chart of slave imports across the eighteenth century, see Brito Figueroa, *Estructura Económica*, pp. 123–4.

65 On the need for more slaves see A.G.I., Caracas 501, memorial by Diego Moreno *et al.*, 18 August 1787, in despatch by Saavedra on measures to aid indigo production, 23 November 1787; and A.G.I., Caracas 917, despatch on the need to import black slaves, Emparán and Basadre to Ministry of the Treasury, 10 January 1809.

66 On Coro see pp. 124–5.

67 The best-known are the Barry contracts of the mid-1780s, which resulted in roughly 4,000 slaves being brought into the province. See Acosta Saignes, *Vida de los Esclavos*, pp. 45–56. In 1809 Captain-General Emparán and Intendant Basadre pointed out how the slave-trade had been disrupted because of the wars with the major supplier. See A.G.I. 917 (n. 65).

68 On slave imports into Havana see Jorge I. Domínquez, *Insurrection or Loyalty: the Breakdown of the Spanish American Empire* (Cambridge, Mass., 1980), pp. 30–1.

69 *Estado General de 1787*, p. 29. Tributary Indians paid the poll-tax, which had been levied on *indígenas* in one form or another since the sixteenth century. See Troconis de Veracoechea, *Historia del Tocuyo Colonial*, pp. 91–2. Who exactly the *libres* were, is not clear.

70 Eduardo Arcila Farías, *Economía Colonial de Venezuela*, 2nd ed. (Caracas, 1973), II, 259–64.

71 Brito Figueroa, *Estructura Económica*, pp. 165–72. On the experiences of Indians in the El Tocuyo and La Guaira municipalities in the late eighteenth century, see Troconis de Veracoechea, *Historia de El Tocuyo Colonial*, pp. 138–40, and the same author's *La Tenencia de la Tierra en el Litoral Central de Venezuela* (Caracas, 1979), pp. 95–6, 118–21.

72 A.G.I., Caracas 36, report by F. Machado, 15 July 1778.

73 A.G.I., Caracas 27, memorial by F. Carvajal, 15 December 1796.

74 A.G.I., Caracas 478, Saavedra to Gálvez, 25 October 1783.

75 See p. 81.

76 *Ibid.*

77 On the wages of agricultural labourers, see p. 49.

78 A.G.I., Caracas 769, memorial by V. Emparán, 10 February 1794, in despatch on protest by Cumaná against the tobacco monopoly.

79 The same set of documents reveal an economy based on a variety of cash crops including cacao, cotton, indigo and coffee, grown by over 200 planters, as well as on livestock production and a lively, if small-scale, coastal trade. See A.G.I., Caracas 769, *passim*.

80 *Estado General de 1787*, p. 3.

81 The 289 wills are taken from the larger sample of 808 referred to in the Bibl. App. I have tried as far as possible to eliminate any overcount by not including haciendas and *hatos* mentioned in more than one will. The wills mentioning haciendas and *hatos* are the following:

Caraqueño Creoles: 1(a, b), 2b, 6b, 7, 8, 9, 10, 13, 17, 18b, 19(a, d), 22, 23(a–c), 24, 25(a, d, e), 29, 30a, 31, 32e, 33, 34(b, d, f, g, h, j, l, m, n, o, s, t, w, x, y, z), 35, 36(a–e), 37, 42b, 43, 45–6, 48b, 52b, 53a, 54–6, 64, 65b, 67a, 68–9, 71, 76, 77, 78, 79(c–e), 81c, 82–3, 85, 87, 88(a, b), 89a, 90, 94(b–d), 98–100, 112, 114(b, c, e), 115, 116f, 117a, 119a, 120–2, 126, 130, 131(a, b, f, h, j), 134(b, c), 138(b, c, f, g), 139d, 140(a–b), 142, 143(c, h), 147–9, 152b, 154, 155(a, b, e, f),

156(b, c, h), 157c, 160a, 161–2, 163b, 165(a–c), 168, 170–1, 172(a, c), 173–4, 176, 180, 182(a, c, d), 183–4, 186(a, b, c, g, h, i), 188–9, 195, 198a, 199c, 201(a, c, e, f), 203(b–d), 204, 206, 207(a, d), 209, 214b, 216(b–e), 217–19, 221, 224–5, 228, 229b, 230, 235–7, 243(a, b), 249, 250a, 252(a, e, h, i, p, u), 254a, 257, 259, 261–2 and 264.
Peninsulares: 270, 276, 277, 279, 281–2, 286, 287(a, b), 288, 291, 297–302, 310b, 312, 317, 320, 326, 329, 334, 341–2, 345, 348, 351 and 377.
Canarios: 353, 356, 359, 365–9, 372, 380b, 381–2, 384, 388, 390, 393–4, 400(a, b), 405, 408, 409, 414, 418, 423–4, 428–31, 436, 441, 443, 445, 449 and 451.
Other White: 468, 471, 474–6 and 481.
Free-Coloureds: 484, 490, 516, 521 and 524.
Caste Unknown: 530, 537, 544, 547 and 552.

82 Brito Figueroa, *Estructura Económica*, p. 177.

83 Many of the institutions of Caracas have been studied extensively in their structural aspects. What follows is an interpretation of their role.

For the town councils, see Joaquín Gabaldón Marqués, 'El Municipio, Raiz de la República', *El Movimiento Emancipador de Híspano-américa* (Caracas, 1961), II, 333–460. For a less sanguine review, see Julio Febres Cordero, 'El Municipio Colonial, y su Régimen Político Anti-Democrático', *Memoria del Segundo Congreso Venezolano de la Historia* (Caracas, 1975), I, 287–310. On the Audiencia, see Demetrio Ramos Pérez, 'El Presidente de la Real Audiencia de Caracas en su fase inicial', *ibid.*, II, 465–98. On the Consulado, see Manuel Nuñes Días, *El Real Consulado de Caracas 1793–1810* (Caracas, 1971). On the structure of the military before 1810, see Lucio Mijares Pérez, 'La Organización de las Milicias Venezolanas en la Segunda Mitad del Siglo XVIII', *Memoria del Tercer Congreso Venezolano de la Historia* (Caracas, 1979), II, 259–82, and Santiago G. Suarez, *Las Instituciones Militares Venezolanas del Periodo Hispánico en los Archivos* (Caracas, 1969). The standard study of the Church is the aforementioned Watters, *Church in Venezuela*.

84 For an exhaustive example of the activities of the Caracas City Council see *Actas del Cabildo de Caracas 1810–1811* (Caracas, 1971), I, *passim*. Even as the province slid into revolution the Cabildo still found plenty of time for mundane issues.

85 A particularly illustrative example of the issue of attendance is provided by the absence of three of Caracas City's twelve councillors on the day one of the most noteworthy documents produced by the Cabildo was signed. This was the famous protest against the 1795 royal decree of dispensation. See A.G.I., Caracas 180, despatch on royal decree of 10 February 1795. Also see chapters 5 and 6.

86 On the question of water-rights see Depons, *Travels in South America*, I, 384–5. For a full record of criminal and civil cases see A.G.I., Caracas 170, certification of criminal and civil cases judged between 1799 and 1802, 29 April 1803.

87 For a record of the tribunal see Mercedes M. Alvarez, *El Tribunal del Real Consulado de Caracas* (Caracas, 1967), *passim*.

88 In a general meeting of 27 March 1806, for example, half of the merchant members did not turn up. Leal (ed.), *Documents*, pp. 69–71.

89 See chapter 5.

90 The calculation is made from Lombardi, *People and Places*, pp. 442–67.

91 *Ibid.*, pp. 451, 461 and 444.

92 Depons, *Travels in South America*, I, 360–4.

93 Watters, *Church in Venezuela*, p. 36.

94 A.G.N., Negocios Eclesiásticos XXVIII, despatch on amount and collection of Church subsidy to the war effort, 1800–(?), ff. 4–6 (no date on actual list but it is presented in connection with the request from the Council of Indies, 27 April 1795). The total *diezmo* for Caracas was given as 207,000 pesos.

95 A.G.I., Caracas 950, *diezmo* account book for 1802.

96 A.G.N., Negocios Eclesiásticos, *ibid.*, ff. 208–12.

97 *Ibid.*, ff. 156–9.. The *cofradía* was that of Nuestra Señora de Candelaria.

98 See chapter 6.

99 The estimate is arrived at by totalling the *censos* held by 8 of the 18 vicarages of the province of Caracas, including the capital. The figure for the 8 is just over 1,100,000 pesos. Even allowing that the remaining vicarages had *censos* equalling or surpassing the latter sum, the combined total would still be in the range of the estimate. As it is, considering that institutions in Caracas City held 866,070 pesos of the catalogued *censos*, it is very unlikely that even the combined wealth of the 10 missing, smaller vicarages would have equalled the 1,100,000 pesos figure. For the latter see A.G.N., Negocios Eclesiásticos, *ibid.* ff. 85–363. My 2,500,000 pesos estimate is almost half the provincial figure given in Brito Figueroa, *Estructura Económica*, pp. 260–3.

2 The export economy 1777–1809

1 On the pre-1777 economy of Caracas see Eduardo Arcila Farías, *Economía Colonial de Venezuela*, 2nd ed. (Caracas, 1973), I, 43–336. For a revisionist review of the province's first phase of growth see R. Ferry, 'Encomienda, African Slavery, and Agriculture in Seventeenth-Century Caracas', *H.A.H.R.*, 61 (1981), 609–35.

2 In 1721 production was estimated to be 67,123 fanegas a year. By the 1760s, 60,000–70,000 fas. were being exported a year in addition to the more than 34,000 fas. consumed annually inside the province. For the first two figures see Arcila Farías, *ibid.*, I, 231, 320–1. On internal consumption see José L. Cisneros, *Descripción Exacta de la Provincia de Venezuela 1764* (Caracas, 1950), p. 48. One contemporary estimate of total production in 1775 goes as high as 133,920 fas. per year. See A. Marón, 'Relación Histórico – Geográfica de la Provincia de Venezuela, año de 1775', in Antonio Arellano Moreno (ed.), *Documentos para la Historia Económica en la Epoca Colonial: Viajes e Informes* (Caracas, 1970), p. 429.

3 See Table 3b, p. 36.

4 See Table 4, p. 41.

5 In the early 1790s the surplus currency generated by tax revenues was turned over to local merchants and planters in return for promissory notes payable in Spain. See p. 64. After 1796 the surplus declined in the face of the mounting fiscal difficulties of the province. See p. 144. Tobacco exports dwindled even as production increased, suggesting that internal consumption of the crop rose apace. See pp. 57–9.

6 Full statistics for 1796–1800 are also available but they are for a period when provincial exports were at half their usual level, in the face of a particularly destructive war with Britain. Table 4 uses these figures, more usefully, in connection with the changing markets of the province.

7 For a good analysis of the appearance of the new crops see M. Izard, 'La Agricultura Venezolana en una Época de Transición: 1777–1830', *Boletín Histórico*, XXVIII (1972), 81–96.

8 On the application of imperial free trade to Caracas see Arcila Farías, *Economía Colonial*, II, 59–68.

9 Izard, 'Agricultura Venezolana', p. 86.

10 The competition was from cheaper cacao from Ecuador. See Arcila Farías, *Comercio entre Venezuela y México en los Siglos XVII y XVIII* (Mexico, 1950), pp. 249–78.

11 For Intendant Abalos's famous condemnation in 1780 of the Caracas Company see Arcila Farías, *Economía Colonial*, II, 24–9.

12 For more on the New Spain trade see chapters 4 and 6. On cacao prices see Table 3b.

13 Between 70,000 and 90,000 fas. in years when trade was not negatively affected by wars. See Table 3a.

14 On the aid given to indigo farmers see Izard, 'Agricultura Venezolana', pp. 89–90. Also see p. 113 of this study. By 1792 Venezuela as a whole was supplying 45% of Spain's indigo imports. See Miguel Izard, *El Miedo a la Revolución: La Lucha por la Libertad en Venezuela (1777–1830)* (Madrid, 1979), p. 93.

15 See p. 113.

16 Contraband trade with the foreign Caribbean was pronounced before 1777. See Arcila Farías, *Economía Colonial*, I, 323–4.

17 On the regulations governing imperial trade after 1777 see *ibid*. II, 59–68. On the structure of *caraqueño* commerce see chapter 4 of this study.

18 A summary of the terms of this decree can be found in Humberto Tandrón, *El Real Consulado de Caracas y el Comercio Exterior de Venezuela* (Caracas, 1976), p. 67.

19 The importance of the British in the slave-trade has already been referred to. For the participation of Danish, American, French and Dutch ships in *caraqueño* trade there is plenty of incidental evidence, but an 1806 register of ships leaving the province's ports puts the question beyond doubt. See A.G.I., Caracas 899, Register of neutral commerce for 1806. Of 42 ships listed 19 were American, 15 Danish, 5 French, 2 Dutch and 1 Swedish.

20 On the various decrees see the contemporary review of regulations governing the province's trade with foreign colonies (1777–1809), José Limonta, *Libro de la Razón General de la Real Hacienda del Departamento de Caracas*, estudio prelim. M. Briceño Perozo (Caracas, 1962), pp. 318–39. On the suspension of 1803–5 see pp. 140–2 of this study.

21 A similar claim for Havana is made by Jorge I. Domínguez, *Insurrection or Loyalty: the Breakdown of the Spanish American Empire* (Cambridge, Mass., 1980), p. 105. The phases of free trade in Caracas will be examined in greater detail in chapter 6.

22 A.G.I., Caracas 478, Saavedra to Gálvez, 25 October 1783.

23 Arcila Farías, *Economía Colonial*, I, 157.

24 Spain's ability to bounce back from war-induced depression is highlighted in Javier Cuenca Esteban, 'Statistics of Spain's Colonial Trade 1792–1820: Consular Duties, Cargo Inventories, and Balances of Trade', *H.A.H.R.*, LXI (1981), 412–14.

25 A.G.I., Caracas 513, memorial on maritime duties, Linares, 20 February 1796. His estimate was an insignificant 50,000 pesos a year. He is backed up by Intendant Saavedra's reference in 1783 to the 'much diminished' contraband. See A.G.I., Caracas 478, Saavedra to Gálvez, 25 October 1783.

26 See pp. 140–2.

27 Between 1791 and 1795 an average of 47% of imports from Spain were of non-Spanish origin. See A.G.I., Caracas 117, account of ships entering La Guaira from Spain and the Canary Islands 1791–5, Eyarálar etc., 3 October 1799.

28 An interesting review by the Spanish Court of a memorial by the Intendant of

Havana strongly suggests import-smuggling was also a serious problem at the Spanish end of imperial trade: 'the ships . . . from Cádiz [to the colonies] [do not] register half . . . of the goods [they carry], among them English and French [cloths] which are [disguised] with the [trademarks] of Spanish factories'. See A.G.I., Caracas 24, Aranjuez, 27 June 1778.

3 Agriculture

1 *Estado General la Población y Producciones de . . . Venezuela formado por D. José de Castro y Aráoz* . . . (15 June 1787), A.A., Ar. 6 salon 115.
2 A.G.I., Caracas 822, opinion by León on petition by the indigo planters of Aragua, 14 August 1809, 15 January 1810.
3 Space does not allow for an analysis of the sample but it is interesting to note that among the owners of these haciendas were Juan Vicente Bolivar Sr, Fernando Blanco y Mixares, Martin Herrera, Jose Ignacio Moreno and Marcos Ribas. As we shall see in chapter 6, all of these men were among the very wealthiest in the province. Bolivar had two sugar-cane haciendas founded on 38½ fas or on less than 80 hectares or 200 acres. Blanco had three cacao plantations on 139 fas, including fallow land. Herrera's 5,000 fas for one hacienda growing coffee and cacao was the exception which proved the rule. Only the Marques del Toro's 'Mocundo' plantation, about which more later, may have equalled or surpassed Herrera's in size. For Bolivar, Blanco, Herrera and Toro see Bibl. App. 8, 21, 24, 34(n, t), 56, 94d, 117a, 122, 140a, 143h, 156h, 163b, 206, 219, 252p, 262, 291, 334, 367, 436 and 516. Also see R.P., Escribanías: *1790*, Aramburu 335–42 and Armas 110–16; *1791*, Mota 298–303; *1792*, Castrillo ff. 202–8; *1794*, Aramburu 62–7; *1795*, Castrillo ff. 124–9 and ff. 339–45; *1796*, Aramburu ff. 201–16; *1797*, Castrillo ff. 152–6; *1800*, Abad ff. 40–66; *1802*, Cobian ff. 60–4 and 116–18 and Tirado ff. 326–34; *1803*, Texera ff. 15–24; *1804*, Aramburu ff. 330–1 and Tirado ff. 319–20; *1805*, Ascanio ff. 180–2 and Aramburu ff. 105–7; *1814*, Escrituras de Real Hacienda ff. 7–8.
4 François Depons, *Travels in South America during the years 1801, 1802, 1803 and 1804; containing a description of the captain-generalship of Caracas . . .* (London, 1807), I, 488.
5 A.G.I., Caracas 374, despatch on case of F. Figueredo against Tovar, Crown to Saavedra, 24 May 1787.
6 Bibl. App. 122.
7 Alexander von Humboldt, *Personal Narrative of Travels for the Equinoctial Regions of America during the years 1799–1804* (London, 1852), I, 504.
8 A.G.I., Caracas 766, Franco to Soler on the need to import Virginia tobacco, 10 February 1804.
9 A.G.I., Caracas 773, despatch by León on the state of the tobacco monopoly, 17 February 1787.
10 Quoted in Miguel Izard, 'La Venezuela del Café Vista por los Viajeros del Siglo XIX', *Boletín Histórico*, XX (1969), 193.
11 A.G.I., Caracas 501, memorial by indigo planters, 26 May 1787, in report on indigo crisis by Saavedra, 23 November 1787.
12 A.G.I., Caracas 27, report on the Aragua valleys contained in the *reservada* by Saavedra on the Mancebo case, 4 September 1790.
13 A.G.I., Caracas 168, memorial by J. Blanco y Plaza, 18 August 1788.

14 They are listed as *arrendamientos* in the notarial books of Caracas City. See R.P., Escribanías: *1786*, Aramburu ff. 301–2, 316–17 and Castrillo ff. 70–1, 156; *1804*, Tirado(?) f. 170; *1805*, Texera ff. 199–202 and Ascanio f. 158; *1806*, Ascanio ff. 124–5 and Tirado ff. 238–9; *1807*, Ascanio ff. 6, 52–3 and León y Urbina f. 264; *1808*, Ascanio ff. 179–80, 192–4, 250–3 and 265–7.

15 This estimate was given by hard-pressed indigo planters in 1787 during a crisis of over-production, so it may be high. See A.G.I., Caracas 501, memorial by indigo planters, 26 May 1787. For a lower estimate of 4–5 ps. a month plus food see Humboldt, *Personal Narrative*, I, 505.

16 See Appendix A., p. 175.

17 Pedro Olavarriaga, *Instrucción General y Particular del Estado Presente de la Provincia de Venezuela en los Años de 1720 y 1721* (Caracas, 1965), pp. 221–87.

18 Idelfonso Leal (ed.), *Documentos del Real Consulado de Caracas* (Caracas, 1964), pp. 192–216.

19 For the Depons and Chacón estimates see Miguel Izard, 'La Agricultura Venezolana en una Época de Transición: 1777–1830', *Boletín Histórico*, XXVIII (1972), 104–5.

20 For the references for the sample as a whole, see below:
    Bibliographical Appendix: 2b, 7–8, 17, 19d, 24, 32e, 34(h, m, n, t, y), 36(b, e), 37, 45–6, 53a, 55–6, 64, 68, 76, 79c, 82, 83, 89a, 92, 94b, 100, 103a, 114c, 119a, 121–2, 131h, 138(e, f), 140(a, b), 143(c, h), 147, 155b, 156h, 157c, 162, 163b, 165b, 171, 174, 182(c, d), 184, 186(g, i), 195, 198a, 201e, 203(b, d), 206, 207d, 214b, 215, 216c, 219, 235–6, 243a, 247c, 249, 250a, 252(a, i, p), 254a, 259, 262, 276, 282, 286, 287(a, b), 288, 291, 298–9, 301, 312, 334, 345, 351, 356, 359, 367, 369, 382, 409, 424, 429, 436, 441, 449, 462, 490, 516, 530 and 535.
    R.P., Escribanías: *1783*, Aramburu ff. 46–57; *1790*, Aramburu ff. 335–42 and Amitesarove ff. 198–211; *1791*, Aramburu ff. 159–60, Castrillo ff. 101–4, Mota ff. 298–303 and Ponce ff. 443–67; *1792*, Aramburu ff. 262–72, Castrillo ff. 125–8 and Mota ff. 88–106; *1794*, Aramburu ff. 62–7 and Tirado ff. 45–53; *1795*, Castrillo ff. 124–9; *1796*, Aramburu ff. 201–16; *1798*, Tirado ff. 312–17; *1800*, Abad ff. 17–33 and 40–66; *1801*, Mota ff. 9–15 and 51–6; *1802*, Barcenas ff. 161–6, Cobian ff. 60–4, 116–18, 150–8 and Tirado ff. 326–34; *1803*, Aramburu (see under 'Reconocimiento' by Miguel Aristiguieta), Cires ff. 117–21 and 141–2 and Tirado ff. 87–9, 284–9 and 409–12; *1804*, Aramburu ff. 330–1, Armas ff. 67–74, Cires 12–14, Hernández 14–16 and 51–2 and Tirado ff. 319–20; *1805*, Ascanio ff. 180–2 and Cobian 229–35 and 237–9; *1806*, Ascanio ff. 49–55, Ravelo ff. 118–23, Santana ff. 91–2 and Texera ff. 43–51; *1815*, Leon y Urbina ff. 26–30; *1820*, Texera, ff. 1–3, 123–6, 179–80 and 277–84.
    A.G.I., Caracas 15, decision on the title of succession for Conde de la Granja, Council of Indies, 18 April 1796; Caracas 384, despatch on case of ex-Treasurer of Tithes, Pedro Gallego, 1801.
    A.G.N., Diversos LX, Survey of the valley of Patanemo, 10 January 1785, ff. 116–17.

21 Augustin Codazzi, *Obras Escogidas* (Caracas, 1960), I, 132.

22 For Codazzi's estimate, made in 1840, see *ibid.* I, 130. For Depons's and Chacón's estimates see Izard, 'Agricultura Venezolana', pp. 104–5.

23 *Bibliographical Appendix*: 34(m, n, t), 131h, 140(a, b), 143h, 235, 250a, 259, 262, 291, 409 and 516. See also R.P., Escribanías, 1815; León y Urbina, ff. 76–84. The average value of this group of plantations is about 23,000 ps., which compares

favourably with the 20,600 ps. average value of 104 haciendas of the wider selection (including the above 26) for which monetary value is given or for which the latter can be estimated.

24 The accounts were located in the inventories and partitions of the wills of J. Hernández Sanabia (carried out in 1780) and of Miguel José Sanz (1829). See Bibl. App. 409 and 235. The accounts for the Sanabia plantations are dated 1766–8, for the Sanz hacienda January 1821–August 1826.

25 The figures are the following: for the two Sanabia haciendas combined, 4,415 ps. in production costs, 16,803 ps. in the gross value of the crop and 79,935 ps. in the total value of the two haciendas. For the Sanz plantation the respective figures are 2,790 ps., 9,442 ps., and 21,377 ps. (Figures are rounded to the nearest peso.)

26 See Appendix A, p. 175.

27 A.G.I., Caracas 501, memorial by indigo planters 2 July 1787, in a report on the indigo crisis by Saavedra, 23 November 1787.

28 A.G.I., Caracas 501, memorial by Moreno and Palacios, 18 August 1787. They were not exaggerating: as we shall later see, as many as two thirds of indigo planters temporarily ceased production in the crisis of 1797–1801.

29 There were complaints about the rental of land in the petitions of 1787, the aforementioned memorial of 1809 (see p. 47) and in 1804. For the latter see A.G.I., Caracas 104, memorial by Guevara Vasconcelos to the Ministry of Justice on a petition by A. Arbide for trade concessions, 10 March 1804.

30 For haciendas growing indigo exclusively see Bibl. App. 341, 36e, 149, 171, 174, 291, 342 and 476. For mixed plantations see 140a, 163b, 259 and 264.

31 See respectively Bibl. App. 291, 174 and 36e.

32 A.G.I., Caracas 501, memorial by indigo planters, 26 May 1787.

33 See Table 3b, pp. 36–7.

34 For a summary of coffee's beginnings in Caracas see Izard, 'Agricultura Venezolana', pp. 92–5.

35 A.G.I., Caracas 517, memorial by coffee planters of November 1802 included in a deposition by Arce on their petition, 4 August 1803.

36 The information is contained in his will. See Bibl. App. 408.

37 Codazzi, *Obras Escogidas*, I, 146.

38 For the number of slaves (2) needed to cultivate 1 fa of coffee see the 1784 estimate by Chacón in Izard, 'Agricultura Venezolana', p. 105.

39 For the sample see Bibl. App. 6b, 21, 30a, 83, 131f, 140(a, b), 163b, 182c, 216b, 385, 398, 408 and 430. See also R.P., Escribanías: *1792*, Aramburu ff. 262–72; *1801*, Mota ff. 9–15; *1802*, Tirado ff. 47–51; *1803*, Tirado ff. 122–9; *1804*, Besares 96–104, Cires ff. 91–6 and Hernandez ff. 1–6; *1805*, Aramburu ff. 78–80; *1806*, Tirado ff. 294–9; *1808*, Tirado ff. 104–5; *1815*, Texera ff. 134–9; *1819*, Alcaya ff. 52–5; *1820*, Texera ff. 155–7 and 285–6. Also see A.G.I., Caracas 15 and 384, cited in p. 188, n. 20.

40 For San Xavier see Bibl. App. 182c. For Moreno see '*arrendamiento*' in R.P., Escribanías 1808, Tirado ff. 104–5. For Alzuru see '*reconocimiento*' in Escribanías 1804, Besares ff. 96–104.

41 Bibl. App. 131f.

42 A.G.I., Caracas 15, papers on granting the title of succession to F. Ascanio, Council of the Indies, 18 April 1796. Assuming a yield of about ¾ kilogram (1½ lbs.)/tree at a favourable price of 12 ps./qq., his estimate would have been an

operating profit on a gross of 3,240 ps. For a yield estimate see Codazzi, *Obras Escogidas*, I, 146. For price see Table 3b, pp. 36–7.

43 At about ¾ kilogram (1 ½ lbs.)/tree, a total of over 4,500 qq., out of total exports of 60,000 qq.

44 Bibl. App. 131f.

45 A. Marón, 'Relación Histórico-Geográfica de la Provincia de Venezuela, año de 1775', in Antonio Arellano Moreno (ed.), *Documentos para la Historia Económica en la Epoca Colonial: Viajes e Informes* (Caracas, 1970), p. 454. The figure, to put it into perspective, was the equivalent of over a fifth of the value of provincial exports in 1795.

46 *Ibid.* 429–30. On the legalization of *aguardiente* production in 1784 see Angel López Cantos, *Don Francisco de Saavedra, Segundo Intendente de Caracas* (Seville, 1973), pp. 108–10.

47 The aforementioned surveys of 1775 and 1787.

48 For the regional distribution of the 1787 haciendas see Appendix A, p. 175.

49 For the sample see Bibl. 1a, 9, 24, 25a, 30a, 32e, 34y, 36e, 65b, 79c, 81c, 117a, 134c, 138(f, g), 143h, 155f, 156b, 163b, 168, 180, 186i, 201f, 203c, 207d, 217, 219, 243a, 250a, 262, 264, 320, 400b, 414, 445 and 516. Also see R.P., Escribanías: *1783*, Aramburu ff. 46–57; *1790*, Armas ff. 79–81 and Ponce ff. 334–45; *1791*, Ponce ff. 316–25 and 443–67; *1792*, Barcenas ff. 145 and 342–4, Castrillo ff. 202–8, Mota ff. 215–26 and Texera ff. 6–16; *1794*, Aramburu ff. 197–212; *1795*, Castrillo ff. 124–9 and Mota ff. 213–16; *1800*, Abad ff. 40–66; *1802*, Armas ff. 36–8, Cobian ff. 45–53 and Tirado ff. 30–3; *1803*, Texera ff. 15–24; *1804*, Besares ff. 30–46, Hernández ff. 210–13, 201–11 and 479–85; *1806*, Ascanio ff. 49–55 and Tirado ff. 64–7 and 146–7; *1807*, Santana ff. 307–12 and Tirado ff. 186–9; *1815*, Texera ff. 134–9; *1816*, Castrillo ff. 1–2 and 12, León y Urbina ff. 64–5 and Tirado ff. 154–7; *1820*, León y Urbina ff. 111–17.

50 Bibl. App. 36e, 117a, 143h, 186i, 219, 250a and 262.

51 'Mocundo', owned by the Toro family, is the largest plantation I have found in the notarial archives, with a total value of 115,337 ps., 5 rs. in 1800. The profit estimate is by Humboldt. See latter's *Personal Narrative*, II, 17–18.

52 The two merchants were Fernando Key Muñoz, who in 1802 rented an hacienda belonging to a Tovar, and Juan Bautista de Echezuría who in 1790 rented two plantations from the Gédler family. See respectively R.P., Escribanías 1802, Armas and Escribanías 1790, Armas ff. 79–81.

53 A.G.I., Caracas 19, accounts of Junta de Secuestros, Duarte, 8 December 1819. The following examples are taken from document no. 2 contained in the above, entitled 'Account of haciendas which have been or are being rented' 25 June 1819.

54 For the institutional history of the monopoly see Eduardo Arcila Farías, *Historia de un Monopolio: el Estanco de Tabaco en Venezuela 1779–1833* (Caracas, 1977).

55 Olavarriaga, *Instrucción General*, p. 290.

56 A.G.I., Caracas 767, examination of proposal for a poll-tax on smokers, J. Fernández, 9 (?) 1779.

57 A.G.I., Caracas 766, despatch by Franco to Soler on need to import Virginia tobacco, 10 February 1804.

58 A.G.I., Caracas 493, account of tobacco monopoly receipts, expenditures and profits 1779–1809, Sierra, 10 October 1816.

59 On the political battle over the creation of the monopoly see chapter 6.

60 The retailers were estimated to number 3,000–4,000 in 1783. See López Cantos, *Don Francisco de Saavedra*, p. 82.

61 A.G.I., Caracas 766, table of planters in Guaruto and Orituco 1791–1804 in a despatch by Franco to Soler on the need to import Virginia tobacco, 10 February 1804.

62 A.G.I., Caracas 779, memorial by tobacco planters, 2 October 1809.

63 A.G.I., Caracas 771, accounts for the monopoly for 1809. In Guaruto 285,682 ps. were outstanding, in Orituco 33,053 ps.

64 A.G.I., Caracas 773, memorial by León on state of tobacco monopoly, 17 February 1787.

65 A.G.I., Caracas 766, despatch by Franco to Soler, 10 February 1804.

66 *Ibid.*

67 *Ibid.*

68 A.G.N., Libros de la Renta de Tabaco 315, account book of labourers of Guaruto for 1818.

69 In the city of Caracas alone, livestock produce for local consumption regularly paid about 20% of the total 5% sales-tax collected on all commercial transactions. See A.G.N., Real Hacienda, Libros de Contabilidad 1243: Caracas, September–December 1806.

70 *Estado General de 1787*, p. 29.

71 *Relaciones Geográficas de Venezuela*, A.A., Ar. 6 salon 212 ff. 36–8. The survey is dated 1761 with no signature. The estimate is in arrobas: 12 arrobas 5 lbs. per inhabitant. Humboldt in the 1800s estimated that the city of Caracas alone consumed 40,000 head a year. See his *Personal Narrative*, III, 102–3.

72 *Ibid.*

73 *Estado General de la Nueva Provincia de Barinas . . . formada por Don Fernando Miyares . . . Noviembre, 1787*, A.A., Ar. 6 salon 116.

74 See Appendix A, p. 175.

75 A.G.I., Caracas 168, petition by Marqués del Toro and other ranchers, 9 October 1789.

76 For the sample see Bibl. App. 34m, 67b, 110, 115, 139d, 143h, 160a, 163b, 171, 196, 218, 230, 252u, 258 and 455. Also see R.P., Escribanías: *1783*, Aramburu ff. 46–57; *1801*, Castrillo ff. 221–2; *1805*, Cobian ff. 170–80; *1807*, Peoli ff. 86–7.

77 For the sample see Bib. App. 25e, 34(m, n), 114(b, c), 115, 139d, 140a, 156h, 160a, 163b, 171, 221, 233, 258, 279 and 516. See also R.P., Escribanías: *1786*, Rio ff. 28–31 and Texera ff. 122–2; *1805*, Cobian ff. 170–80; *1806*, Aramburu ff. 45–8, Ascanio ff. 49–55 and Santana ff. 67–8; *1807*, Peoli ff. 86–7. Also see A.G.I., Caracas 374, despatch on the case of F. Figueredo against Tovar, the Crown to Saavedra, 24 May 1787.

78 Federico Brito Figueroa, *La Estructura Económica de Venezuela Colonial*, 2nd ed. (Caracas, 1978), pull-out between pp. 192 and 193.

79 A.G.I., Caracas 181, memorial on reasons for scarcity of meat in Cumaná, Manuel Rubio, 1808 (no other date).

80 *Semanario de Caracas*, 10 February 1811, in *Semanario de Caracas* (Caracas, 1959), p. 119.

81 *Ibid.*, p. 143.

4 Commerce

1 A.G.I., Caracas 478, Saavedra to Gálvez, 25 October 1782.

2 Of 5,000 ship-tons allowed for the commerce between Spain and Caracas, 1,500 were reserved for company ships. See A.G.I., Caracas 503, despatch on a concession to José María Tovar to take a ship to Spain, 31 May 1793. The company's privileges were more a political issue than an economic one, and they are examined in connection with the politics of the province. See chapter 6.

3 A.G.I., Caracas 501, memorial by the indigo planters of Maracay, Arbide etc, 23 November 1787.

4 A.G.I., Caracas 501, memorial by D. Moreno and F. Palacios, 18 August 1787.

5 A.G.I., Caracas 898–9, *Duplicados de Registros de Buques de la Guaira*, 1795–6 and 1796–1806.

6 The total of cacao loaded onto the 41 ships was about 77,870 fas.

7 The traders were Muñoz-Orea (5.9%), T. Ascarate (4.5%), J. B. Oruesagasti (3.9%), the Filipinas Company (3.8%) and J. E. Echezuría (2.9%).

8 A total of 575,814 lbs. of indigo were exported on the 41 ships.

9 They are Segura y Grasi (5.9%), López Méndez (5.7%), V. Galguera (4.3%) and J.M. Jauregui (3.6%).

10 In the case of cacao it was 29 merchants carrying about 25% of the total. In the case of indigo it was 30 carrying about 23%.

11 A.G.I., Caracas 898–9, *Duplicados de Registros.* A few large firms seem to have dominated the trade at the Spanish end, including those of M. Altuna in Santander and those of Irigoyen, Bonechen, Muñoz-López, Iriarte, Irribarren and Gough in Cádiz, among a handful of others.

12 This is certainly what is implied by Intendant León's comment in 1801 that 'when [a] planter carries out the commercialization of his crops at his own risk, he enjoys the classification of *verdadero comerciante*'. See A.G.I., Caracas 512, abstract of the report of León on the regulations governing land and maritime sales-taxes, 13 July 1801.

13 More detailed definitions and analysis of the terms *comerciante, mercander, pulpero* and *bodeguero* can be found in Mercedes M. Alvarez, *Comercio y Comerciantes, y sus proyecciones en la Independencia Venezolana* (Caracas, 1963), pp. 48–54. For an example of a *bodeguero* exporting, see Bibl. App. 457. Bartolomé Soyomayor, who owned a clothes store and a *pulpería* of foodstuffs, in 1814 sent 37 zurrones of indigo to one merchant in Cádiz and was awaiting payment of 943 ps. from another in the same port.

14 Escurra and Pedro Martín and Juan Iriarte appear on Saavedra's 1786 list of suggested members for a future Consulado. Aguerrevere, Alzualde, Argos, Arrizurieta, Baraciarte, Bolet, Echenique, Galguera, García Jove, Goicoechea, Larrain, Lizzarraga, López Méndez, Martínez Avia, Mayora, Mintegui, Muñoz-Orea, Segura y Grasi, Yllas and Zulueta appear on the 1805–6 membership lists. For sources see Appendix B, pp. 176–7.

15 On agents purchasing directly from the production areas see A.G.N., Real Hacienda, Libros de Contabilidad 1936 and 1954; sales-tax account books for Maracay, 1789–90 and 1804–5, *passim.* Maracay, as we have seen, was the centre of indigo production. Thus, for example, on 21 October 1790 M. Garay paid tax on 600 pounds of indigo he had bought for the Filipinas Company. The same month, J. Gómez paid tax on 800 pounds he had bought for Martín Iriarte, another major wholesaler.

16 A.G.N., Real Hacienda, Libros de Contabilidad 2430 and 1291–2: sales-tax account books for Caracas 1786 (January–February) and 1819. There are literally hundreds of examples of *hacendados* selling their various crops to wholesale and retail merchants in the city. In January 1786 alone, members of the elite Toro, Ascanio, Mixares, Rada, Urbina, Blanco, Ribas, Aristiguieta and Berrotarán families were engaged in selling their crops. For more on these families see chapter 5.

17 A.G.I., Caracas 512, abstract of report by León, 13 July 1801.

18 See, for example, the case of the captain of the brigantine *Consolación*, M. Marien, who had 1,040 fas. of cacao aboard in his name or better than 1% of the 1795–6 total of 77,807 fas. See A.G.I., Caracas 899, copy of the registers of 5 September 1796.

19 A.G.I., Caracas 898–9, *Duplicados de Registros, passim*.

20 Two of the ships were consigned to Segura y Grasi: the frigates *Gertrudis* and *Nuestra Señora del Pilar*. See respectively A.G.I., Caracas 898, copy of the register of 6 and 26 November 1795, and Caracas 899, copy of the register of 11 June 1795. The brigantine *Jesus, María y José* was consigned to S. Eduardo. See Caracas 899, copy of register of 8 June 1795.

21 A.G.I., Caracas 899, registers of the neutral commerce for 1806, Arce to Soler, 16 May 1806, *passim*.

22 Estimates of individual trader's investments are arrived at by using the local prices for the exported commodities. Thus Segura y Grasi, with about 8,991 fas. of cacao at 18 ps./fa., 34,235 lbs. of indigo at 1½ ps./lb., 1,170 q. of cotton at 20 ps./q., 680 hides at 1 ps. each and 1,293 qq. of coffee at 12 ps./q. would have invested 252,786½ ps. in his purchases.

23 A.G.I., Caracas 501, memorial by D. Moreno and F. Palacios, 18 August 1787. On another occasion, Intendant Saavedra described Pedro Martín and Juan Iriarte as 'the merchants with most credit and capital in [this province]'. A.G.I., Caracas 478, Saavedra to Gálvez, 4 April 1784.

24 For Iriartes see *ibid*. For Escorihuela see A.G.I., Caracas 503, report by León on Veracruz trade, 26 April 1793.

25 The estimated value of the goods they purchased in 1795–6 is about 107,000 ps. For the 80,000 ps. figure see Bibl. App. 463. For the date the company was founded see R.P., Escribanías 1812, Texera ff. 22–9, declaration and separation of company.

26 R.P., Escribanías 1809, Aramburu ff. 95–7, registration of company formed by Camacho brothers.

27 Captain-General Carbonell, in response to a request by merchants that they should be exempted from militia service, observed that only those whose '*caudal de manejo* is over 50,000 pesos' should be granted the privilege, otherwise there would be an avalanche of petitions. See A.G.I., Caracas 94, Carbonell to Alanga, 13 November 1793. A study of merchants in Buenos Aires uses the same figure as a dividing line. See Susan M. Socolow, *The Merchants of Buenos Aires 1778–1810: Family and Commerce* (Cambridge, 1978), p. 54.

28 Of six import–export companies formed between 1800 and 1804 none was capitalized at more than 24,000 ps. See R.P., Escribanías *1800*: Cobian ff. 52–4 and Barcenas ff. 210–12; Escribanías *1803*: Aramburu 334–5; Escribanías *1804*: Aramburu ff. 35–7, 158–9 and Barcenas ff. 63–5.

29 A.G.I., Caracas 479, report by Saavedra on request by Francia for trade concessions, 16 March 1785.

30 For Manuel Felipe Tovar see A.G.I., Caracas 503, despatch on the concession to José María Tovar to take a ship to Spain, 31 May 1793. For the others see A.G.I., Caracas 483, report on the petition by two *hacendados* that the trade with Veracruz should be widened, Saavedra, 31 March 1787.

31 R.P., Escribanías 1794(?), Barcenas ff. 175–6, sale of a ship by M. Tovar to M. Pérez of Tenerife.

32 R.P., Escribanías 1801, Cires ff. 124–5, sale of a frigate by B. Vilar to S. Villalonga.

33 R.P., Escribanías 1804(?), Hernández ff. 404–5, sale of a brigantine by F. Rosado to J. Ibarra.

34 A.G.I., Caracas 490, Basadre to Saavedra, 16 December 1809.

35 A.G.I., Caracas 491, abstract of report by Basadre to Saavedra, 7 February 1810.

36 See chapter 6.

37 A.G.I., Caracas 119, abstract of request by Juan Nepomuceno and José Ribas for a concession to import 8,000 blacks, 21 March 1804.

38 A.G.I., Caracas 503, acknowledgement by León of the royal concession, 31 May 1793.

39 Gerónimo Alzualde loaded onto one ship in 1795 consignments for five different firms in Cádiz. Juan Esteban Echezuría on the same ship supplied six commercial houses. See A.G.I., Caracas 898, copy of the register of *La Caraqueña* of 27 June and 21 October 1795.

40 Bibl. App. 316.

41 Angel López Cantos, *Don Francisco de Saavedra, Segundo Intendente de Caracas* (Seville, 1973), pp. 26–33.

42 See Table 3a, p. 36.

43 A.G.I., Caracas 775, collection of documents on the transfer of tobacco funds, León, 22 November 1791. For more on the political handling of the question see chapter 6.

44 A.G.I., Caracas 771, *Cuentas Generales de la Venta de Tabacos en Caracas 1787 a 1809, passim.*

45 On the classification of these surnames as ones of *hacendado* families see chapter 5.

46 R.P., Escribanías 1802, Cires ff. 87–97, record of the dissolution of the company.

47 Bibl. App. 351.

48 The sales-tax books of towns near Caracas City contain numerous examples of *vecinos* from the Llanos passing through selling cattle *en route* for Caracas. Drivers from Tinaco, San Carlos, El Pao and Nutrias bound for the Aragua valleys all paid sales-taxes in Valencia in November 1787. See A.G.N., Real Hacienda, Libros de Contabilidad 1799: Valencia 1787–8.

49 In 1808 the provincial total was 380,524 ps. 7½ rls. See A.G.I., Caracas 491, general account of the treasury of Caracas for 1808, 10 February 1810. In eight months in 1805 the collection in Caracas City was over 80,000 ps. See A.G.N., Real Hacienda, Libros de Contabilidad 1241–2: Caracas, May–December 1805.

50 R.P., Escribanías 1802, Cires ff. 87–97, record of the dissolution of the company.

51 A.G.N., Real Hacienda, Libros de Contabilidad 2360: Barquisimeto 1787–8.

52 *Ibid.*

53 A.G.N., Real Hacienda, Libros de Contabilidad 1924: La Victoria 1803–4.

54 Bibl. App. 293.

55 The number of commercial establishments in the sample's urban units is contained in their sales-tax or *alcabala* books. The projection for the province was done in the

following manner. John V. Lombardi, *People and Places in Colonial Venezuela* (Bloomington, Indiana, 1976), establishes four urban categories for the Bishopric of Caracas: hamlets (less than 500 inhabitants); villages (500–2,000); towns (2,000–4,000); and cities (over 4,000). See pp. 52–9. My selection includes 3 villages (Tacata, Valle de la Pascua and Yare) with an average of just over 3 stores per village; 3 towns (Chaguaramos, Cua and Ocumare del Tuy) with an average of 6 stores per town; 7 provincial cities (Barquisimeto, Calabozo, La Victoria, Maracay, San Carlos, Valencia and Villa de Cura) with an average of just over 36 stores each; and the capital, Caracas, with 285 *bodegas, mercerías* and *pulperías* in 1797. Assuming that the first 3 averages held for the other 89 villages, 50 towns and 19 cities of the province, we arrive at a total of about 1,500 outlets, not including any stores which may have existed in the 21 hamlets and in the municipality of Coro. The latter, as will be remembered, is not factored into Lombardi's calculations. The presence in the sample of such outsize centres as Barquisimeto and San Carlos distorts the average for cities, but the imbalance would probably be more than rectified if Coro were included in the projection. For the sample see A.G.N., Real Hacienda, Libros de Contabilidad: 1415 (Sabana de Ocumare, Yare, Tacata and Cua for 1805–6); 1799 (Valencia 1787–8); 1924 (La Victoria 1803–4); 1936 (Maracay 1789–90); 2116 (Valle de la Pascua 1807–8); 2145 (Villa de Cura 1805–6); 2244 (San Carlos 1787–8); 2362 (Chaguaramos 1804–5); 2363–4 (Barquisimeto 1814 and 1816); 2433 (Caracas January–March 1797); and Calabozo 1805–6, for which there is no volume number.

56 A.G.N., Real Hacienda, Libros de Contabilidad 2433; Caracas January–March 1797.

57 A.G.N., Real Hacienda, Libros de Contabilidad 1799: Valencia 1787–8.

58 For the sample see Bibl. App. 293, 301, 355, 361, 373, 378, 386, 402, 406 and 454. See also R.P., Escribanías: *1790*, Amitesarove ff. 176–7; *1794*, Rio ff. 28–9, 72–3, 94, 205–7; *1795*, Rio ff. 52–3, 102, 152–5, 159–61, 162–3, 214–15, 224–5, 231–4; *1796*, Cobian ff. 29–30, 194–5, 211–12, 215–16, 218–20; *1797*, Aramburu ff. 231–2, 256–8 and 373–5, Barcenas ff. 272–3 and 85–7, Ximenes ff. 4–5; *1798*, Barcenas ff. 145–6 and 154–5, Castrillo ff. 17–18, 50–1 and 125–6; *1799*, Aramburu ff. 87–8, 180–4, 204–6 and 322–3, Castrillo ff. 82, 103 and 118–19, Tirado ff. 119–22 and 467; *1800*, Aramburu ff. 305–7 and 419–20, Texera ff. 177–80, Tirado ff. 202–4; *1801*, Aramburu ff. 113–15 and 122–3, Barcenas ff. 38–40, Mota ff. 64–5 and 118–19, Ravelo/Tirado ff. 152–4; *1802*, Aramburu ff. 176–9, Barcenas ff. 1–2, Cires ff. 122–3; *1803*, Aramburu f. 1, Barcenas ff. 38–9 and 51–2, Cires f. 93, Tirado f. 417; *1804*, Aramburu ff. 40–1, 158–9 and 353–4, Cires ff. 68–9, Hernandez ff. 8–9; *1805*, Ascanio f. 90, Aramburu ff. 208–9 and 232.

59 For gross profit margins of 49% on one year's sales in two *mercerías* see R.P., Escribanías *1795*, Rio ff. 159–61 and ff. 162–3. Calculations by Depons suggest that retailing profits generally were high, in the range of 25%–35%. See François Depons, *Travels in South America during the years 1801, 1802, 1803 and 1804; containing a description of the captain-generalship of Caracas* ... (London, 1807), II, 73–4.

5 Elites

1 Crane Brinton, *The Anatomy of Revolution*, rev. ed. (New York, 1959), p. 53.

2 See Appendix B, pp. 176–7.

3 Mercedes M. Alvarez, *El Tribunal del Real Consulado de Caracas* (Caracas, 1967), II, 256. On the exception made for *mercaderes* who also engaged in commerce, see pp. 88–9 of this study.

4 On New Spain see D. A. Brading, *Miners and Merchants in Bourbon Mexico 1763–1810* (Cambridge, 1971), p. 212.

5 Eduardo Arcila Farías, *Economía Colonial de Venezuela*, 2nd ed. (Caracas, 1973), II, 100.

6 On the origins and genealogies of the families in order of mention with the exception of Pacheco, see Carlos Iturriza Guillén, *Algunas Familias Caraqueñas* (Caracas, 1967), I, 61–5, 79–90, 107–25, 153–6, 159–96, 197–212, 335–66, 373–95, II, 501–16, 525–44, 593–601, 603–29, 643–61, 663–702, 711–21, 723–33, 807–26 and 827–64. For Pacheco see Hector Parra Marqués, *El Doctor Tomás Hernández de Sanabria* (Caracas, 1970), pp. 367–70.

7 On the immigrant origins of the Clemente y Francia, López Méndez, Paz del Castillo, Reverón, Ribas and Vegas families see Iturriza Guillén, *Algunas Familias*, I, 229–38, 271–84, II, 469–74, 631–42, 735–51 and 765–75. On those of Fernández León see Mario Briceño Iragorry, *Casa León y su Tiempo: Aventura de un Anti-Héroe* (Caracas, 1946), p. 13. On Moreno, see Guillermo Lohmann Villena, *Los Americanos en las Ordenes Nobiliarias 1529–1900* (Madrid, 1947), I, 387. On Sanz see Juan S. Canelón, *Miguel José Sanz (1756–1814)* (Caracas, 1958). On the remaining families in order of mention see Bibl. App. 270, 341, 279, 35, 372, 384, 287, 76, 302, 409, 138, 166, 161, 188 and 326.

8 Iturriza Guillén, *Algunas Familias*, I, 271–84, II, 469–74.

9 See Appendix B, pp. 176–7.

10 *Ibid.*

11 The stability of their economic base across time can be gauged by comparing the Consulado lists with the 1721 and 1745 surveys of plantation in Caracas and their owners. The surnames of the pre-1713 families predominate. For the 1721 list see Pedro Olavarriaga, *Instrucción General y Particular del Estado Presente de la Provincia de Venezuela en los Años de 1720 y 1721* (Caracas, 1965), pp. 221–91. For the 1745 survey see 'Padrones de Haciendas de Cacao', *Documentos del Real Consulado*, pp. 192–216.

12 A.G.I., Caracas 477, Abalos to Gálvez, 11 July 1781.

13 *Ibid.* report by León, 11 June 1781.

14 Bibl. App. 250.

15 Bibl. App. 252i.

16 Alexander von Humboldt, *Personal Narrative of Travels to the Equinoctial Regions of America during the years 1799–1804* (London, 1852), I, 504.

17 A.G.I., Caracas 15, Decision by Council of Indies on Ascanio's petition for the title, 18 April 1796.

18 Bibl. App. 182c. See also A.G.I., Caracas 91, Guillelmi to Porlier on house arrest of San Xavier for non-payment of wife support, 29 April 1788.

19 Bibl. App. 114c.

20 Bibl. App. 163b.

21 Bibl. App. 36e.

22 Briceño Iragorry, *Casa León*, pp. 229–30.

23 Bibl. App. 34m, 163a, 116a, 131h, 287b, 140b and 428.

24 Bibl. App. 250a.

25 Bibl. App. 36e

26 Bibl. App. 34t.
27 Bibl. App. 34m.
28 Bibl. App. 19a.
29 Bibl. App. 252i.
30 Bibl. App. 287b, 76, 282 and 436.
31 For Toro and Tovar see Bibl. App. 250a and 252i.
32 A.G.I., Caracas 15, decision by the Council of Indies, 18 April 1796. See also Bibl. App. 25a.
33 Bibl. App. 250a.
34 The notarial records contain numerous records of transactions with the Church. See the following examples from R.P., Escribanías: *1792*, Barcenas f. 145, *reconocimiento* by Juan Montilla; *1794*, Tirado, ff. 37–45, *reconoc.* by María Isabel Gédler; *1803*, Tirado ff. 409–12; and *1804*, Cires ff. 91–6, *reconoc.* by Adrian Blanco.
35 R.P., Escribanías: *1790*, Ponce ff. 334–45, *reconocimiento* by Juan José Machado; *1792*, Mota ff. 88–106, *reconoc.* by María Concepción Palacios; *1795*, Castrillo ff. 339–45, Mota ff. 9–15, *reconoc.* by José María Toro.
36 See, for example, the cases of Vicente Verois, who left debts of 23,661 ps. 2 rls. on 60,712 ps. 5 rls. or about 38%, and of Miguel Sanz, who left about 12,500 ps. of debts on 28,162 ps. of assets, or about 45%. See respectively Bibl. App. 262 and 235.
37 Bibl. App. 163b.
38 Bibl. App. 34t.
39 The history of the nobility titles in Caracas is summarized in Parra Marqués, *El Doctor Tomás Hernández*, pp. 362–74; that of the membership in the military orders in G. Lohmann Villena, *Americanos, passim.*
40 A.G.I., Caracas 15, decision by the Council of Indies, 18 April 1796.
41 A.G.I., Caracas 181, petition by Manual de Urbina for the restoration of his title, supported by interim Captain-General, José Ceballos, 30 September 1815.
42 Of 49 petitions from Caracas for entry into the honorary military orders, 32 were made after 1770.
43 An indication of elite participation in the militias is given in A.G.I., Caracas 91, review of militia units in the Aragua valleys and the city of Caracas, 1786. The Conde de Tovar, the Marqués del Toro, the Marqués de Mijares and members of the Ponte, Ribas, Butrageño, Clemente y Francia, Palacios, Bolívar, Plaza and Buroz families, among others, were represented in the officer corps of the various units.
44 In 1807 several officers of the urban militias requested the same *fuero* rights as regular troops. See A.G.I., Caracas 106, abstract of a report by Casas, 9 November 1807.
45 These petitions were numerous. The captains-general of the province often felt constrained to discourage the Crown from granting the titles, as in the case of Antonio Suárez de Urbina, who wanted to be made a sub-lieutenant over other officers of greater seniority and experience. See A.G.I., Caracas 89, abstract of a report by Guillelmi to Sonora, 11 June 1786.
46 This will become clear in the discussion of politics in the province in the next chapter.
47 For an extremely full listing of the purchase of Cabildo posts across the province see A.G.I., Caracas 51, *passim.* The cost of council posts seems to have been declining towards 1810. In 1779 José Escorihuela paid 1,650 ps. to become a *regidor*. By the early 1800s José María Tovar, Juan Ascanio and Dionisio Palacios were only paying

450 ps. for the same privilege. The above are taken from a summary of *títulos de regidores* etc granted to the city of Caracas since 1752 contained in the above *legajo*.

48 A reform of eligibility rules for Cabildo posts meant that any white person not 'exercising any menial trade' could serve, thus theoretically opening the way for a 'middle-class' takeover of the councils. See A.G.I., Caracas 36, report by Casa Blanca, 16 April 1795.

49 For an accessible summary of the *alcaldes* or mayors of the city between 1777 and 1810 see Luis A. Sucre, *Gobernadores y Capitanes Generales de Venezuela*, 2nd ed. (Caracas, 1964), pp. 288, 291–2, 296, 300, 304, 311 and 313.

50 A.G.N., Diversos LXIII, orders by Guillelmi to all justices of the peace arranging for mourning of the death of Charles III, all dated 25 February 1789. For Blanco, Gédler and Palacios see respectively ff. 358, 369 and 391.

51 A.G.I., Caracas 950, book of *diezmos* for the diocese of Caracas for 1802, ff. 1–5.

52 R.P., Escribanías 1786, Acosta ff. 1–2, *fianza* by Conde de San Xavier.

53 R.P., Escribanías 1803, Aramburu f. 187, *fianza* by J. V. Bolívar.

54 The notary book of Acosta for 1786 has 6 other examples. Other concentrated samples of 7 or more can be found in R.P., Escribanías 1790 and 1794, Escrituras de Real Hacienda, and Escribanías 1809, Quintero.

55 See pp. 47, 127–8.

56 A.G.I., Caracas 180, petition by Cabildo of Nueva Barcelona, 29 February 1796.

57 See Appendix B, pp. 176–7. I have also located the wills of relatives of four more merchants, bringing the sample total up to 36.

58 In Saavedra's 1786 list of 50 *comerciantes* and *mercaderes*, 38 were based in Caracas, 6 in La Guaira and 6 in Puerto Cabello. See Arcila Farías, *Economía Colonial*, II, 100.

59 See Appendix B, p. 177.

60 Leal (ed.), *Documentos*, pp. 47–8.

61 See Appendix B, p. 177, for those married to creoles.

62 Manuel Francia married a Palacios, Juan Iriarte an Aristiguieta, Felipe Llaguno a Garay and Domingo Zulueta an Urbina. See Bibl. App. 282, 306, 316 and 351.

63 The following cases emerge through comparison of the 1786 and 1805–6 Guild lists. See Appendix B, p. 177.

64 For the sample see Appendix B, p. 177.

65 Bibl. App. 287a.

66 Bibl. App. 287b.

67 Bibl. App. 430.

68 Bibl. App. 366, 310b and 316.

69 Bibl. App. 287a.

70 Bibl. App. 291.

71 Bibl. App. 282.

72 Bibl. App. 131f and h.

73 Bibl. App. 295.

74 Bibl. App. 131h.

75 Bibl. App. 430.

76 Bibl. App. 316.

77 Bibl. App. 418.

78 R.P., Escribanías 1809, Quintero (no page-numbers), *fianza* by J. Argos.

79 *Ibid.*

80 R.P., Escribanías 1786, Acosta f. 1, *fianza* by P. M. Iriarte.

81 A.G.I., Caracas 91, review of militia units in the Aragua valleys and the city of Caracas, 1786.

82 A.G.I., Caracas 94, abstract of report by Carbonell to Alange, 13 November 1793.

83 A.G.I., Caracas 94, *ibid*.

84 A.G.I., Caracas 36, despatch on the creation of four *regidor* posts for Europeans, 3 August 1776.

85 A.G.I., Caracas 36, report by Casa Blanca, 16 April 1795.

86 A.G.I., Caracas 51, titles of *regidor* confirmed respectively in order of mention, 8 July 1770, 7 November 1770, 19 August 1778 and 17 July 1779. On their agricultural holdings see respectively Bibl. App. 281, 282, and 288. Escorihuela, as we have seen, was classified as an *hacendado* in 1786.

87 A.G.I., Caracas 36, names of four Europeans proposed as replacements for deceased *regidores*, Casa Valencia, 10 November 1803. On Echezuría's and Key's agrarian interests see Bibl. App. 287a. and R.P., Escribanías 1816, León y Urbina ff. 16–19, *protesta* (deposition) by Key Muñoz.

88 For the 1796 figure see A.G.I., Caracas 513, report by V. Linares of the Consulado on the need for new trade laws, 20 February 1796. For 1802 see A.G.I., Caracas 47, *protesta* by J. Escorihuela on the partition of his father's legacy, 20 September 1802. It includes a complete list of lawyers.

89 Contemporary observers were despairing about the number of law-suits. See A.G.I., Caracas 513, *ibid*. and François Depons, *Travels in South America during the years 1801, 1802, 1803 and 1804; containing a description of the captain-generalship of Caracas . . .* (London, 1807), I, 296–7.

90 Bibl. App. 235.

91 Bibl. App. 161.

92 On the role of the Church during the wars of independence see Mary Watters, *A History of the Church in Venezuela 1810–1930* (Chapel Hill, N.C., 1933), pp. 53–69.

93 In 1815, 78 royal officials were investigated for their collaboration with the republicans. Stephen K. Stoan, *Pablo Morillo and Venezuela 1815–1820* (Columbus, Ohio, 1974), pp. 77–8.

94 Sucre, *Gobernadores y Capitanes*, pp. 288–317.

95 Saavedra and León went on to become senior ministers in Spain after their tenures in Caracas. On Saavedra see Angel López Cantos, *Don Francisco de Saavedra, Segundo Intendente de Caracas*, (Seville, 1973), p. 4. On León see Briceño Iragorry, *Casa León*, p. 125.

96 The best general discussion of the Abalos years is given by Arcila Farías, *Economía Colonial*, II, 11–30.

97 For a detailed study of Saavedra's time in Caracas see López Cantos, *Don Francisco de Saavedra*, *passim*.

98 The beginnings and rise of the León family up to 1810 are traced by Briceño Iragorry, *Casa León*, pp. 5–129.

6 Politics 1777–1808

1 Roland D. Hussey, *The Caracas Company 1728–1784: A Study in the History of Spanish Monopolistic Trade* (Cambridge, Mass., 1934), p. 250.

2 *Ibid*. pp. 238–9, 269–71.

3 A.G.I., Caracas 371, El Pardo, 31 January 1778.

4 Eduardo Arcila Farías, *Economía Colonial de Venezuela*, 2nd ed. (Caracas, 1973), I, 337–9.

5 *Ibid.* I, 150, II, 13–14. See also Miguel Izard, 'Contrabandistas, Comerciantes e Ilustrados', *Boletín Americanista*, XXVIII (1978), 43.

6 Arcila Farías, *Economía Colonial*, I, 150.

7 *Ibid.* II, 20.

8 For the facts of the case see *ibid.* II, 31–9.

9 Izard, 'Contrabandistas', pp. 60–2.

10 The number of *composiciones de tierra* seem to have fallen markedly after the 1750s. See Eduardo Arcila Farías *et al*, 'La Formación de la Propriedad Territorial', *Estudio de Caracas* (Caracas, 1967), II, 941–5.

11 The law is mentioned in the case of a contested land sale by José Mena. A.G.I., Caracas 372, proceedings of case 1777–82.

12 Arcila Farías, *Economía Colonial*, I, 344–5, and Izard 'Contrabandistas', p. 78.

13 Arcila Farías, *Economía Colonial*, II, 21.

14 *Ibid.* I, 340–3; II, 21.

15 *Ibid.* II, 344–5.

16 *Ibid.* II, 21–2; Izard, 'Contrabandistas', p. 80.

17 Although the purchase programme began in late 1779, only 9,000 fas. had been bought by the Treasury by mid-1781. See A.G.I., Caracas 477, Abalos to Gálvez, 9 July 1781.

18 Arcila Farías, *Economía Colonial*, I, 349.

19 *Ibid.* I, 349–50.

20 The Caracas Company alone sent out over 40,000 fas. through Curaçao. A.G.I., Caracas 34, Marqués de Sonora to Francisco Machado, 1 May 1787.

21 Arcila Farías, *Economía Colonnial*, I, 357.

22 *Ibid.* II, 28.

23 *Ibid.* I, 357.

24 Angel López Cantos, *Don Francisco de Saavedra, Segundo Intendente de Caracas* (Seville, 1973), p. 12.

25 Arcila Farías, *Economía Colonial*, II, 25–6.

26 Izard, 'Contrabandistas', p. 67.

27 Arcila Farías, *Economía Colonial*, I, 348.

28 José Limonta, *Libro de la Razón General de la Real Hacienda del Departamento de Caracas*, estudio prelim. M. Briceño Perozo (Caracas, 1962), pp. 50–3, 318–32.

29 A.G.I., Caracas 477, deposition by Toro, 5 June 1781.

30 A.G.I., Caracas 475, Cabildo resolution, 18 June 1781, contained in a deposition on the duties question, 24 September 1781.

31 A.G.I., Caracas 477, Abalos to Gálvez, 23 September 1781.

32 A.G.I., Caracas 477, *ibid.*

33 *Ibid.* See also Izard, 'Contrabandistas', p. 66–7.

34 P.R.O., F.O. 95/7/2, ff. 62–74: Abalos to Floridablanca, 28 September 1781.

35 Mauro Paez-Pumar (ed.), *Las Proclamas de Filadelfia de 1774 y 1775 en la Caracas de 1777* (Caracas, 1973), *passim*.

36 P.R.O., F.O. 95/7/2, f. 293: incomplete and undated letter by J. Cocho de Iriarte.

37 A.G.I., Caracas 477, Abalos to Gálvez, 9 July 1781.

38 A.G.I., Caracas 476, summary of licence dated 7 June 1782 in index of Intendance correspondence with Spain nos. 656–80, 20 June 1782.

39 Izard, 'Contrabandistas', p. 67. See also P.R.O., F.O. 95/7/2, ff. 62–74: Abalos to Floridablanca, 28 September 1781.

40 Arcila Farías, *Economía Colonial*, II, 30.

41 '... poverty [is] almost endemic in the Province; agriculture is very decayed', as were commerce and royal finances. A.G.I., Caracas 478, Saavedra to Gálvez, 25 October 1783.

42 On the distorting effects of the *tonelage* restrictions see A.G.I., Caracas 482, Saavedra to Marqués de Sonora, 11 June 1786.

43 A.G.I., Caracas 478, Saavedra to Gálvez, 28 June 1784.

44 *Ibid.*

45 López Cantos, *Don Francisco de Saavedra*, pp. 134–5.

46 A.G.I., Caracas 772, report on tobacco exports 1779–87, 28 December 1788. The reason was the lack of Spanish transports. A.G.I., Caracas 479, Saavedra to Gálvez, 30 July 1785.

47 Arcila Farías, *Economía Colonial*, II, 60.

48 A.G.I., Caracas 502, Guillelmi to Lerena, 29 September 1790.

49 A.G.I., Caracas 28, report by Guevara Vasconcelos, 25 June 1806.

50 On his direct intercessions on behalf of the trade see López Cantos, *Don Francisco de Saavedra*, pp. 142–4. On the support of individual petitions see A.G.I., Caracas 478, Saavedra to Gálvez, 4 April 1784; and Caracas 478, report on case of José Tovar and Diego Moreno, 31 March 1787.

51 Eduardo Arcila Farías, *Comercio entre Venezuela y México en los Siglos XVII y XVIII* (Mexico, 1950), p. 304.

52 *Ibid.* pp. 175–6.

53 A.G.I., Caracas 484, Alcalde to Lorena, 13 July 1791; Caracas 775, collection of documents on transfer of tobacco funds, León, 22 November 1791.

54 López Cantos, *Don Francisco de Saavedra*, pp. 57–70. For the list of purchasers see Miguel Acosta Saignes, *Vida de los Esclavos Negros en Venezuela* (Caracas, 1967), pp. 356–9.

55 López Cantos, *Don Francisco de Saavedra*, pp. 87–91.

56 At a time when exports were running at less than 300,000 lbs. per year, planters produced a crop of 600,000 lbs. For a good summary of the crisis see López Cantos, *Don Francisco de Saavedra*, pp. 87–91. For greater detail see A.G.I., Caracas 501, report by Saavedra, 23 November 1787. It includes documents on planters' complaints, records of government purchases etc.

57 A.G.I., Caracas 501, report on indigo crisis by Saavedra, 23 November 1787.

58 A.G.I., Caracas 482, Saavedra to Marqués de Sonora, 11 June 1786.

59 A.G.I., Caracas 806, *protesta* by Caracas Cabildo, 14 February 1787.

60 A.G.I., Caracas 507, report by León on Cabildo and Consulado petitions for convoys, 22 December 1796.

61 The company was allowed to carry 2,000 of the 5,000 toneladas permitted to the province. See Hussey, *Caracas Company*, p. 297.

62 A.G.I., Caracas 501, Saavedra to Crown, 23 November 1787.

63 Arcila Farías, *Economía Colonial*, I, 359.

64 *Ibid.* II, 43–4.

65 See p. 64.

66 Arcila Farías, *Economía Colonial*, II, 44.

67 Ernesto Blanco Uribe, 'The Military in Venezuela 1810–1836' (Oxford Univ. M.Litt. thesis, 1981), p. 16.

68 Leslie B. Rout, Jr, *The African Experience in Spanish America: 1502 to the present day* (Cambridge, 1976), p. 156.

69 Blanco Uribe, 'Military in Venezuela', p. 18.

70 *Ibid.*

71 *Ibid.* pp. 18–19. According to Captain-General Guevara Vasconcelos the practice of segregation may have been peculiar to Caracas. He was in favour of 'militias composed of all castes as is the case in other parts of America'. A.G.I., Caracas 180, report on militias by Guevara Vasconcelos, 13 July 1801.

72 Jorge I. Domínguez, *Insurrection or Loyalty: the Breakdown of the Spanish American Empire* (Cambridge, Mass., 1980), p. 79.

73 The *informe* is reproduced in Santos R. Cortés, *El Régimen de las 'Gracias al Sacar' en Venezuela durante el Periodo Hispánico* (Caracas, 1978), II, 91–207.

74 For the complete list see A.G.I., Caracas 180, despatch by the Cabildo on the royal decree of 10 February 1795, 1796–8.

75 Rout, *African Experience*, pp. 156–9 *passim*.

76 *Ibid.* p. 157.

77 *Ibid.* p. 158.

78 A.G.I., Caracas 180, Gremio de Pardos de Caracas to Crown, 9 June 1797.

79 Cortés, *Régimen*, I, 469.

80 In 1795 it cost 500 ps. to be dispensed from the condition of *pardo*, a sum few free-coloureds, or whites, were likely to have had on hand for legal matters. See Rout, *African Experience*, p. 156.

81 1789 Audiencia document quoted in M. Lucena Solmoral, 'El Sistema de Cuadrillas de Ronda para la Seguridad de los Llanos a Fines de Periodo Colonial. Los Antecedentes de las Ordenanzas de Llanos de 1811', in *Memoria del Tercer Congreso Venezolano de la Historia* (Caracas, 1979), II, 194.

82 Acosta Saignes, *Vida de los Esclavos*, p. 249.

83 *Ibid.* p. 266.

84 *Ibid.* p. 270.

85 *Ibid.* p. 271.

86 On the location of *cumbes* in the eighteenth century, see *ibid.* pull-out map between pp. 256 and 257.

87 Lucena Salmoral, 'El sistema de cuadrillas de rondas', p. 207.

88 *Ibid.* p. 194.

89 *Ibid.* pp. 195–9.

90 *Ibid.* pp. 202, 212–15.

91 Acosta Saignes, *Vida de los Esclavos*, p. 314.

92 For examples of slaves appealing against their masters see A.G.I., Caracas 170, deposition of civil and criminal cases tried by the Audiencia of Caracas, 1799–1802.

93 Pedro Olavarriaga, *Instrucción General y Particular del Estado Presente de la Provincia de Venezuela en los Años de 1720 y 1721* (Caracas, 1965), p. 215.

94 Federico Brito Figueroa, *La Estructura Económica de Venezuela Colonial*, 2nd ed. (Caracas, 1978), p. 311.

95 Miguel Izard, *El Miedo a la Revolución: La Lucha por la Libertad en Venezuela (1777–1830)* (Madrid, 1979), p. 55.

96 Antonio Arellano Moreno, *Orígenes de la Economía Venezolana*, 3rd ed. (Caracas, 1974), p. 130.

97 Acosta Saignes, *Vida de los Esclavos*, p. 274.

98 See, for example, Brito Figueroa, *Estructura Económica*, p. 311.

99 The standard study of this revolt, on which all other analyses are based, is Pedro M. Arcaya, *Insurrección de los Negros en la Serranía de Coro* (Caracas, 1949).
100 *Estado General de la Población y Producciones de . . . Venezuela formado por D. José de Castro y Aráoz . . .* (15 June 1787), p. 19.
101 Brito Figueroa, *Estructura Económica*, pp. 330–1.
102 *Estado General de 1787*, pp. 19, 29.
103 A.G.I., Caracas 34, report by the Contador General, 10 October 1784.
104 A.G.I., Caracas 88, abstract of a report by Guillelmi, 27 May 1785.
105 A.G.I., Caracas 36, memorial by the notary F. Mexía, 10 February 1786.
106 A.G.I., Caracas 168, Vidaondo and Malló to Valdez, 28 February 1789.
107 A.G.I., Caracas 529, report by Ayerdi, 23 September 1790.
108 A.G.I., Caracas 180, report by the Ayuntamiento de Caracas, 4 May 1790.
109 A.G.I., Caracas 15, decision by the Council of Indies, 14 June 1797.
110 A.G.I., Caracas 169, memorial by the Audiencia of Caracas, 31 July 1794. See also the protest of the Cabildo of Venezuela against the appointment of a Justice of the Peace. A.G.I., Caracas 15, Council of Indies to the Crown, 15 July 1795.
111 On the removal of S. Mancebo in the 1780s see A.G.I., Caracas 59, Guillelmi to Valdez, 24 November 1787. Also A.G.I., Caracas 27, memorial by Mancebo, 23 November 1787. On the Carvajal case, *ibid.* memorial by F. Carvajal, 15 December 1796. On the 1800s see A.G.I., Caracas 171, a collection of documents on the case of the *tenientes* of Maracay, 5 April 1808.
112 A.G.I., Caracas 503, introduction to accounts of the tobacco monopoly for 1792, León, 18 April 1793.
113 For *temporalidades* see A.G.I., Caracas 59, Guillelmi to Porlier, 30 April 1789, for *bienes de difuntos* see A.G.I., Caracas 503, report by León, 30 June 1793.
114 A.G.I., Caracas 821, case of F. Rueda, 1792–1803.
115 A.G.I., Caracas 113, Guillelmi to Valdes, 17 July 1789.
116 A.G.I., Caracas 59, Guillelmi to Marqués de Sonora, 20 October 1786; A.G.I., Caracas 16;, memorial by the Audiencia of Caracas, 31 July 1794.
117 An especially notorious case involved Rafael Mérida, the future Minister of Justice under Bolívar in 1813–14. See A.G.I., Caracas 36, report on the case of the *escribanía de camara* of Caracas 1767–1817, Texada, 23 August 1817.
118 *Ibid.* report on the case of J. D. Fernández 1795–9, Casa Valencia, 28 February 1799.
119 Antonio's life is the subject of Mario Briceño Iragorry, *Casa León y su Tiempo: Aventura de un Anti-Héroe* (Caracas, 1946).
120 A.G.I., Caracas 27, report by Saavedra on the Mancebo memorial, 4 September 1790.
121 Luis A. Sucre, *Gobernadores y Capitanes Generales de Venezuela*, 2nd ed. (Caracas, 1964), pp. 300–1.
122 The more comprehensive of the criticisms of the León faction is contained in A.G.I., Caracas 15, report by Carbonell to the Council of Indies, 28 January 1796.
123 *Ibid.*
124 *Ibid.*
125 A.G.I., Caracas 799, report by León, 25 July 1793.
126 A.G.I., Caracas 508, report by León, 21 April 1797. See also A.G.I., Caracas 799, report by León, 25 July 1793.
127 A.G.I., Caracas 503, report by León, 22 July 1792. See also A.G.I., Caracas 505, León, 11 December 1793 and A.G.I., Caracas 506, León, 25 June 1794.

128 Humberto Tandrón, *El Real Consulado de Caracas y el Comercio Exterior de Venezuela* (Caracas, 1976), pp. 98–102.

129 A.G.I., Caracas 503, report by León, 25 July 1793.

130 For the 300,000 figure see A.G.I., Caracas 799, report by León, 29 November 1793. In 1792, for example, total tax intake was 1,451,107 ps. 6½ rls. *vs* 1,276,138 ps. 2½ rls. in expenditures. A.G.I., Caracas 505, account of royal taxes for 1792, 28 September 1793.

131 John H. Parry and P. Sherlock, *A Short History of the West Indies*, 3rd ed. (London and Hong Kong, 1978), p. 165.

132 For an account of the province's participation in the Haitian venture see Angel Sanz Tapia, *Los Militares Emigrados y los Prisioneros Franceses en Venezuela durante la Guerra contra la Revolución* (Caracas, 1977).

133 *Ibid.* p. 91.

134 *Ibid.* pp. 77, 79.

135 A.G.I., Caracas 507, abstract of a report by León, 1 November 1795.

136 Sanz Tapia, *Militares Emigrados*, pp. 75–9.

137 A.G.I., Caracas 516, account of the ships from Spain to Caracas 1793–6 and 1797–1800, 4 March 1801, contained in a despatch on the issue of free trade.

138 On the total number of ships see *ibid.* account of the ships from Caracas to Spain 1797–1800, 4 March 1801. On the losses see Tandrón *Real Consulado*, p. 280.

139 *Ibid.* p. 105.

140 A.G.I., Caracas 507, report by León, 22 December 1796.

141 Tandrón, *Real Consulado*, pp. 104–7.

142 *Ibid.* pp. 115–16.

143 The report is reproduced *ibid.* pp. 297–311.

144 A.G.I., Caracas 508, report on the sale of tobacco by León, with documents, 31 March 1798.

145 Tandrón, *Real Consulado*, pp. 122–3.

146 The *hacendado representación* is reproduced *ibid.* pp. 247–93.

147 A.G.I., Caracas 16, decision by the Council of the Indies on the merchant–*hacendado* controversy, 20 July 1799.

148 *Ibid.*

149 Manuel Nuñes Días, *El Real Consulado de Caracas 1793–1810* (Caracas, 1971), p. 278.

150 A.G.I., Caracas 512, report by León on the regulations governing the registration of ships, 27 June 1801.

151 A.G.I., Caracas 16, decision by the Council of the Indies on the merchant–*hacendado* controversy, 20 July 1799.

152 Tandrón, *Real Consulado*, pp. 150–1.

153 *Ibid.* pp. 146–9.

154 *Ibid.* p. 152.

155 A.G.I., Caracas 180, *pedimiento* no. 5, included in the despatch on the issue of free trade collected by the Ayuntamiento of Caracas, 28 May 1801. The documents were gathered by José Llamosas, one of the signers of the 1797 merchant *representación*.

156 *Ibid. pedimiento*, no. 4.

157 *Ibid. pedimiento*, no. 6.

158 Tandrón, *Real Consulado*, p. 154.

159 A.G.I., Caracas 512, report by León on the regulations governing the registration of ships, 27 June 1801.

16 Tandrón, *Real Consulado*, p. 153.

16. A.G.I., Caracas 512, León to Soler, 16 October 1801.

162 Tandrón, *Real Consulado*, p. 157.

163 See p. 14.

164 The following is offered as an interpretation of well-known events. For fuller discussions see Pedro Grases, *La Conspiración de Gual y España y el Ideario de la Independencia* (Caracas, 1949), and Castro F. López, *Juan Picornell y la Conspiración de Gual y España* (Caracas, 1955). A good summary is given in C. Parra Pérez, *Historia de la Primera República de Venezuela*, 2nd ed. (Caracas, 1959), I, 126–47. For an interesting view of Picton's role see V. Naipaul, *The Loss of El Dorado* (London, 1969), pp. 123–54. A modern interpretation of the conspiracy's ideology is Elias Pino Iturrieta, *La Mentalidad Venezolana de la Emancipación 1810–1812* (Caracas, 1971), pp. 64–74.

165 A.G.I., Caracas 169, Quintana to Jovellanos, 16 September 1798.

166 Quoted in Parra Pérez, *Historia de la Primera República*, I, 140.

167 Pino Iturrieta, *Mentalidad Venezolana*, pp. 33–50.

168 Parra Pérez, *Historia de la Prima República*, I, 95–102.

169 Briceño Iragorry, *Casa León*, p. 48.

170 A.G.I., Caracas 16, decision by the Council of the Indies on the merchant–*hacendado* controversy, 20 July 1799.

171 A.G.I., Caracas 822, report by P. González Ortega, 31 December 1808.

172 A.G.I., Caracas 180, report by José Llamosas, syndic of the Caracas Cabildo, 26 May 1801.

173 A.G.I., Caracas 473, Arce to Soler, 4 July 1805.

174 Pio Zabala y Lera, *España bajo los Borbones* (reprinted; Madrid, 1945), p. 239. Another ex-Venezuelan Intendant, Saavedra, was also chosen.

175 A.G.I., Caracas 28, report by Guevara Vasconcelos, 25 June 1806; and A.G.I., Caracas 516, report by Arce, 10 May 1803.

176 A.G.I., Caracas 180, Llamosas to the Crown, 26 May 1801.

177 A.G.I., Caracas 802, report by León, 28 May 1802.

178 A.G.I., Caracas 516, abstract of a report by Arce, 14 July 1803.

179 Antonio García-Baquero González, *Comercio Colonial y Guerras Coloniales: la Decadencia Económica de Cádiz a Raiz de la Emancipación Americana* (Seville, 1972), pp. 165, 170, 174.

180 A.G.I., Caracas 34, report by Casa Valencia, 27 March 1805.

181 A.G.I., Caracas 766, Franco Soler on the reasons for the need to import Virginia tobacco, 10 February 1804.

182 A.G.I., Caracas 516, abstract of a report by Arce, 14 July 1803.

183 The following discussion is based primarily on Jacques A. Barbier, 'Peninsular Finance and Colonial Trade: the Dilemma of Charles IV's Spain', *J.L.A.S.*, XII, 1 (1980), 21–37.

184 *Ibid.* p. 31.

185 Tandrón, *Real Consulado*, pp. 175–6.

186 *Ibid.* p. 215.

187 *Ibid.* pp. 179, 182–3.

188 *Ibid.* pp. 179–80.

189 A.G.I., Caracas 486, Arce to Soler, 18 November 1805.

190 Tandrón, *Real Consulado*, p. 182.
191 A.G.I., Caracas 487, Arce to Soler, 12 March 1806.
192 Tandrón, *Real Consulado*, p. 183.
193 *Ibid.* p. 184.
194 A.G.I., Caracas 488, abstract of a report by Arce, 20 September 1806.
195 Tandrón, *Real Consulado*, p. 185.
196 *Ibid.* p. 196.
197 A.G.I., Caracas 489, report by Arce, 4 April 1808.
198 The story of the flour controversy is told in Tandrón, *Real Consulado*, pp. 186–90.
199 A.G.I., Caracas 518, despatch on the importation of Virginia tobacco, 4 July 1804.
200 A.G.I., Caracas 488, abstract of a report by Arce, 28 November 1806.
201 A.G.I., Caracas 490, Basadre to Saavedra on the agreement by J. Ibarra to supply *tasajo*, 16 December 1809. For the contract on weapons etc. in London see R.P., Escribanías 1809, Quintero, fiat for M. Baraciarte, 15 November 1809. On the taking of *libranzas* see *ibid. passim*.
202 Tandrón, *Real Consulado*, pp. 176–7.
203 A.G.I., Caracas 473, abstract of a report by Arce, 26 September 1805.
204 A.G.I., Caracas 488, abstract of a report by Arce, 2 August 1806.
205 R.P., Escribanías 1808, Aramburu, ff. 176–235, record of *libranzas* issued in Spain against Caracas.
206 A.G.I., Caracas 489, report by Casas and Arce, 27 August 1808.
207 For an account of the invasions see Parra Pérez, *Historia de la Primera República*, I, 231–64.
208 Salvador de Madariaga, *Bolívar* (reprinted; New York, 1969), p. 104.
209 *Ibid.* p. 93.

7 The balance overturned 1808–1810

1 The following discussion of events in Spain is based on Raymond Carr, *Spain 1808–1939* (Oxford, 1966), pp. 38–146; R. Herr, *The Eighteenth Century Revolution in Spain* (Princeton, N.J., 1958), pp. 348–444; and, for a more detailed chronology of events between 1808 and 1810, Pio Zabala y Lera, *España bajo los Borbones* (reprinted; Madrid, 1945), pp. 184–251.
2 Full accounts are given in C. Parra Pérez, *Historia de la Primera República de Venezuela*, 2nd ed. (Caracas, 1959), I, 285–346, and Andrés F. Ponte, *La Revolución de Caracas y sus Próceres* (reprinted; Caracas, 1960), pp. 5–56.
3 Parra Peréz, *Historia de la Primera República*, I, 318.
4 This is the decidedly minor affair which came to be known as the Matos conspiracy of July 1808. For the documents of the case see Vicente Lecuna, 'La conjuración de Matos', *B.A.N.H.*, XIV (1931), 381–440.
5 For the latest interpretation along these lines see Jorge I. Domínguez, *Insurrection or Loyalty: the Breakdown of the Spanish American Empire* (Cambridge, Mass., 1980), pp. 150–1.
6 During the early 1700s, for example. See Luis A. Sucre, *Gobernadores y Capitanes Generales de Venezuela*, 2nd ed. (Caracas, 1964), pp. 195–216, 237–42.
7 For the only complete list of those involved see Ponte, *Revolución de Caracas*, p. 47.
8 For the merchants see Mercedes M. Alvarez, *Comercio y Comerciantes y sus proyecciones*

en la Independencia de Venezuela (Caracas, 1963), p. 130. On the investigation see Ponte, *Revolución de Caracas*, pp. 48–51.

9 Parra Pérez, *Historia de la Primera República*, I, 333.

10 A.G.I., Caracas 822, report by P. González Ortega on events and officials in Caracas, 1786 to the present, 31 December 1808. See also A.G.I., Caracas 171, report by Astiguieta and Martínez de Aragón of the Audiencia, 12 December 1808.

11 López Quintana was actually under investigation. See his self-defence in A.G.I., Caracas 171, report by Quintana, 20 October 1808. On the relationship between Mosquera and Casas see Ponte, *Revolución de Caracas*, pp. 5–6, 49.

12 Parra Pérez, *Historia de la Primera República*, I, 337–40.

13 Ponte, *Revolución de Caracas*, p. 56.

14 Salvador de Madariaga, *Bolívar* (reprinted; New York, 1969), p. 111.

15 On the reputation of Arce see A.G.I., Caracas 822, report by P. González Ortega on events and officials in Caracas, 1786 to the present, 31 December 1808. For character sketches of Emparan see Madariaga, *Bolívar*, pp. 120–1, and Parra Pérez, *Historia de la Primera República*, I, 367–8. On Basadre see Brian R. Hamnett, *Politics and Trade in Southern Mexico 1750–1821* (Cambridge, 1971), p. 115.

16 Humberto Tandrón, *El Real Consulado de Caracas y el Comercio Exterior de Venezuela* (Caracas, 1976), pp. 199–200.

17 *Ibid.* p. 198.

18 On the revival of *libranzas* see A.G.I., Caracas 489, report by Arce, 4 April 1808. On the cases of Bolívar and León see Madariaga, *Bolívar*, p. 125.

19 Carr, *Spain 1808–1939*, pp. 103–4.

20 Tandrón, *Real Consulado*, p. 199.

21 Parra Pérez, *Historia de la Primera República*, I, 366. The case later served as propaganda for the independence cause. See, for example, *Mercurio Venezolano*, January 1811, in *El Mercurio Venezolano* (Caracas, 1960), facsimile edition.

22 On the conflict with the Audiencia, see A.G.I., Caracas 171, report by the Audiencia, 15 December 1809. For disagreements over appointments with the Caracas Town Council see A.G.I., Caracas 181, complaint by López Méndez etc. over the election of a syndic for the Cabildo, 15 January 1810.

23 Tandrón, *Real Consulado*, p. 200.

24 Miguel Izard, *El Miedo a la Revolución: La Lucha por la Libertad en Venezuela (1777–1830)* (Madrid, 1979), p. 139. The author expresses doubt as to what exactly Emparán was charged with. That Urquinaona, a contemporary royalist chronicler, uses the word 'exonerated' in 1810 suggests strongly that it was the latter's handling of the crisis which was investigated. See Pedro Urquinaona y Pardo, 'Relación Documentada del origen y progresos del trastorno de las provincias de Venezuela hasta la exoneración del capitán general Don Domingo Monteverde', *Anuario*, IV–VI (1967–9), I, 156.

25 Madariaga, *Bolívar*, pp. 123–4, and Parra Pérez, *Historia de la Primera República*, I, 369.

26 *Ibid.* I, 378–9.

27 Accounts of the events of 19 April can be found in Parra Pérez, *Historia de la Primera República*, I, 377–401, and Ponte, *Revolución de Caracas*, pp. 97–117.

28 Parra Pérez, *Historia de la Primera República*, I, 389–92, 467–8.

29 This observation will be developed presently.

30 Indeed 'it was because of the prompt and spontaneous co-operation of Spanish

military officers' that the coup of 19 April was successful, according to the royalist Level de Goda. See Andrés Level de Goda 'Memorias', *Anuario*, II, 1161.

31 *Gazeta de Caracas*, 25 May 1810, in *Gazeta de Caracas 1808–1812* (Caracas, 1960), I, facsimile edition.

32 For the events of Coro see Parra Pérez, *Historia de la Primera República*, I, 417–19.

33 Jose Heredia, 'Memorias Sobre las Revoluciones de Venezuela', *Anuario*, I, 542.

34 Peter M. McKinley, 'Themes of Revolutionary Propaganda in Venezuela's First Republic: 1810–1812' (Oxford Univ. B.Phil. thesis, 1977), pp. 39–72.

35 *Gazeta de Caracas*, 21 December 1810, quoted in McKinley, 'Themes of Revolutionary Propaganda', p. 46.

36 Madariaga, *Bolívar*, p. 133.

37 Heredia, 'Memorias sobre las Revoluciones', p. 542.

38 Parra Pérez, *Historia de la Primera República*, I, 392.

39 *Ibid.* I, 390.

40 *Ibid.* I, 435–66.

41 *Ibid.* I, 474–7.

42 For a list of the names see *Ibid.* I, 389.

43 *Ibid.* I, 389–92.

44 As I said earlier, many royal officials served both loyalist and rebel governments in the 1810s. Among this group were José Domingo Duarte and Dionisio Franco, respectively counsellor to the Intendancy and director of the tobacco monopoly in 1810, and both future royalist intendants. *Ibid.* I, 369, 373, 392, and Stephen K. Stoan, *Pablo Morillo and Venezuela, 1815–1820* (Columbus, Ohio, 1974), pp. 148–9.

45 R. Diaz Sanchez, 'Estudio Preliminar', *Libro de Actas del Supremo Congreso de Venezuela 1811–1812* (Caracas, 1959), I, 11–37.

46 See the composition of the Junta de Guerra, *Gazeta de Caracas*, 4 May 1810, in *Gazeta de Caracas 1808–1812*, I, facsimile edition.

47 The two men were related and members of a wealthy clan of the Andean region of the province of Maracaibo. See Carlos Mendoza, *Cristobal Mendoza (1772–1829)* (Caracas, 1957), *passim*. The wealth of at least part of the Briceño family must have been extensive. In 1801 the priest Dr Domingo Briceño left almost 30,000 ps. in charitable donations in his will. See Bibl. App. 467.

48 For a short biography of Miranda's life before 1810 see Salvador de Madariaga, *The Fall of the Spanish American Empire* (London, 1947), pp. 341–72; for his career between 1810 and 1812 see Madariaga, *Bolívar*, pp. 144–79. On Cortes Madariaga see *ibid.* pp. 125–6. On Sanz see Juan S. Canelón, *Miguel José Sanz (1756–1814)* (Caracas, 1958), and p. 94 of this study. On Isnardi see Joaquín Gabaldón Marqués, 'Estudio Preliminar' to Francisco Isnardi, *Proceso Político* (Caracas, 1960), pp. 15–84. On Roscio see Benito R. Losada, *Juan Germán Roscio (1763–1821)* (Caracas, 1953). On Mérida see Madariaga, *Bolívar*, pp. 209–13. On Revenga see Manuel Pérez Vila, *José Rafael Revenga (1786–1852)* (Caracas, 1960). On Peñalver see Alaricio Gómez, *Fernando Peñalver (1765–1832)* (Caracas, 1955). On Bello as secretary see Parra Pérez, *Historia de la Primera República*, I, 370–2.

49 Most notably, the *pardo* Manuel Piar. For a good summary of his significance see John Lynch, *The Spanish American Revolutions 1808–1826* (London, 1973), pp. 210–11.

50 Parra Pérez, *Historia de la Primera República*, I, 387–8.

51 *Ibid.* I, 438.

52 Stoan, *Pablo Morillo*, p. 32.

53 *Ibid.* p. 33.

54 Parra Pérez, *Historia de la Primera República*, I, 485–6.

55 *Ibid.* i, 487.

56 *Ibid.* I, 403–34. The marginal province of Guayana soon changed its mind and declared for the Regency. *Ibid.* I, 416–17.

57 This became obvious when in 1811, during the Constituent Congress, delegates of the various insurgent provinces, and indeed of cities inside Caracas, argued in favour of a federalist constitution and the break-up of the province of Caracas as conditions for union. See the records of the debates in *El Publicista*, 4 July–29 August 1811, in *El Publicista de Venezuela* (Caracas, 1959), facsimile edition. The economic independence of the regional elites is attested to by an extraordinary survey of Cumana in 1793 listing by name all shipowners, *hacendados* and the like in the province in connection with their holdings. Few of the names are traceable to Caracas in any way. A.G.I., Caracas 769, despatch on the abolition of the tobacco monopoly by Governor Emparán of Cumaná, 10 February 1794.

58 This observation is based on the analysis of the *caraqueño* elites carried out in this study.

59 Parra Pérez, *Historia de la Primera República*, I, 474–81.

60 For an account of the campaign see Julio Febres Cordero, *El Primer Ejército Republicano y la Campaña de Coro* (Caracas, 1973), *passim*.

61 On the history of the society see Parra Pérez, *Historia de la Primera República*, II, 25–32, and Arturo Uslar Pietri, 'Estudio Preliminar', *Testimonios de la Epoca Emancipadora* (Caracas, 1961), pp. vii–xxxvii.

62 Madariaga, *Bolívar*, pp. 152–6.

63 For a history of the press in Caracas up to 1812 see Pedro Grases, *Historia de la Imprenta en Venezuela: hasta el fin de la Primera República (1812)* (Caracas, 1967).

64 J. Godechot, 'La presse française sous la révolution et l'empire', in *Histoire Générale de la Presse Française*, ed. C. Bellanger (Paris, 1969), II, 438.

65 Roscio, Isnardi, Sanz, Salias and Muñoz Tebar edited the various papers. See Parra Pérez, *Historia de la Primera República*, II, 37.

66 McKinley, 'Themes of Revolutionary Propaganda', pp. 46–64.

67 Parra Pérez, *Historia de la Primera República*, II, 31–2.

68 Madariaga, *Bolívar*, p. 154.

69 *Ibid.* pp. 149–56.

70 *Ibid.* p. 152.

71 *Ibid.*

72 Lynch, *Spanish American Revolutions*, p. 239.

73 Parra Pérez, *Historia de la Primera República*, II, 16–18.

74 *Ibid.*

75 *Ibid.*

76 Crane Brinton, *The Anatomy of Revolution*, rev. ed. (New York, 1959), p. 147.

77 Parra Pérez, *Historia de la Primera República*, II, 55–75.

78 See the Declaratoria de Independencia, *El Publicista*, 11 July 1811, *El Publicista de Venezuela*, facsimile edition.

Epilogue

1 For accounts and the chronology of events between 1811 and 1821 see R. McNerney, Jr, *Memorias del General Daniel Florencio O'Leary: Narración* (Austin, Texas,

1970); Vicente Lecuna, *Crónica Razonada de las Guerras de Bolívar*, 2nd ed. (New York, 1960); Salvador de Madariaga, *Bolívar* (reprinted; New York, 1969); G. Masur, *Simón Bolívar* (Albuquerque, N.M., 1948); Stephen K. Stoan, *Pablo Morillo and Venezuela, 1815–1820* (Columbus, Ohio, 1974); and John Lynch, 'Bolivar and the Caudillos', *H.A.H.R.*, LXIII (1983), 3–35.

2 *Gazeta de Caracas*, 21 May 1817, in *Gazeta de Caracas* (Paris, 1939), VI, 1027–34.

3 Madariaga, *Bolívar*, p. 210.

4 *Ibid*. pp. 210–13.

5 R.P., Escribanías 1813, Castrillo and Hernandez, and 1814 Castrillo, *passim*. There are at least 100 examples in the 3 notary books cited.

6 Stoan, *Pablo Morillo*, p. 53. One estimate of the total number of Spaniards killed was 5,000. *Ibid*. p. 73.

7 On Boves see G. Carrera Damas, *Boves, aspectos socio-economicos de la guerra de independencia*, 2nd ed. (reprinted; Caracas, 1972); Laureano Vallenilla Lanz, *Cesarismo Democratico* (reprinted; Caracas, 1961), pp. 81–100; D. Ramos, 'Sobre un aspecto de las tacticas de Boves, *B.A.N.H.*, LI (1968), 69–73; and Jorge I. Domínguez, *Insurrection or Loyalty: the Breakdown of the Spanish American Empire* (Cambridge, Mass., 1980), pp. 177–9.

8 C. Parra Pérez, *Historia de la Primera República de Venezuela*, 2nd ed. (Caracas, 1959), I, 337–43.

9 Jose Heredia, 'Memorias Sobre las Revoluciones de Venezuela', *Anuario*, I, 555.

10 *Ibid*. p. 560.

11 On the social clauses in the constitution of 1811 see Parra Pérez, *Historia de la Primera República*, II, 172. On the Ordenanza de los Llanos see Carrera Damas, *Boves*, pp. 196–207. For a copy of the decree see *Materiales para el Estudio de la Cuestión Agraria en Venezuela (1800–1830)* (Caracas, 1964), I, 65–92.

12 Parra Pérez, *Historia de la Primera República*, II, 343–5.

13 The letters between Miranda and his subordinates between May and July 1812 give a fascinating perspective on the growing anarchy in these months. See *Archivo del General Miranda* (Havana, 1950), XXIV: 'Cartas Referentes a la Campaña de Venezuela', *passim*.

14 For Cagigal and Coll y Prat see Carrera Damas, *Boves*, pp. 31–42, 46–8. On Ucelay, Cevallos and Morillo see Stoan, *Pablo Morillo*, pp. 71–2. For more details on Cevallos's opinions see James King, 'A Royalist View of the Colored Castes in the Venezuelan War of Independence', *H.A.H.R.*, XXXIII (1953), 530–7. For more on Ucelay see A.G.I., Caracas 28, report by J. Ucelay, 2 June 1815.

15 This calculation is made by comparing the *alcabala* receipts for the city of Caracas (an average of 60% of the province's total collection between 1790 and 1799) of the late 1810s with pre-1810 totals. In 1808 the figure was 185,544 ps. 3½ rls. In 1819 it was 113,269 ps. 2½ rls. See respectively A.G.I., Caracas 491, general accounts for 1808, 10 February 1810, and A.G.N., Real Hacienda, Libros de Contabilidad no. 1214, Libro Mayor de Caracas, 1819.

16 Among the ships being allowed into *caraqueño* ports were ones from New York, Curacao, Baltimore, St Thomas and Jamaica. For Puerto Cabello see A.G.N., Real Hacienda, Libros de Contabilidad no, 1777, Entradas, Salidad de Buques, 1817. For La Guaira see A.G.I., Indiferente General 2256, Entradas y Registros, 1817–18.

17 Stoan, *Pablo Morillo*, p. 228. Nominal loyalties never stopped shifting throughout the struggle for independence. Morillo in 1815 had 78 officials of the pre-1810

colonial administration investigated for their collaboration with the republicans, although no indictments were actually handed down and the men continued in their posts. See *ibid.* pp. 77–8. Among the most versatile of the political chameleons of the old guard was Antonio Fernández de León, now Marqués, who held posts in the First Republic, under Monteverde, under Bolívar and even under Boves. See Mario Briceño Iragorry, *Casa León y su Tiempo: Aventura de un Anti-Héroe* (Caracas, 1946), pp. 145–73, 195–6, 200, 205–6. Key Muñoz, Esteban Ponte and Feliciano Palacios, who were involved in the *juntista* regime, lived peacefully under Morillo after 1815. See Parra Pérez, *Historia de la Primera República*, I, 372. Fermin Paul, who signed the declaration of independence, became an auditor under Morillo. See *ibid*, I, 373. Even the Marqués del Toro and his brother Fernando, the military leaders of the First Republic, had sufficiently abandoned the independence cause to seek re-entry to the province after 1815 from their enforced exile in Trinidad. A.G.I., Caracas 385, memorial by Toro brothers, 9 July 1814, and A.G.I., Caracas 386, intercession by Pedro del Toro on behalf of his brothers, 17 May 1816. An 1816 list of *hacendados* and merchants living in royalist Caracas includes the names of many who initially supported the first autonomist movement. See *Gazeta de Caracas*, 4 December 1816, in *Gazeta de Caracas*, VI, 827–8.

Bibliography

A. Manuscript Sources

Archivo General de Indias (Seville)
Audiencia de Caracas: Legajos 14–19, 23–4, 27–9, 32–4, 36, 39–47, 50–4, 59, 86–110, 113–14, 116–19, 168–73, 177, 180–1, 275–80, 346, 364, 371–87, 460, 462–3, 467–9, 473–519, 524–33, 539–40, 569–72, 597, 613, 615–18, 639, 766–80, 789, 791, 795–806, 815–31, 846, 848, 857, 889–90, 895–9, 904–5, 917–18, 921, 939–40, 950.
Indiferente General: Legajos 2,178–80, 2,204–8, 2,253–6.

Archivo de la Academia Nacional de la Historia (Caracas)
Ar. 2, G. 1: 68
Ar. 3, G. 1: 3, 5, 7–12, 14
Ar. 6, G. 1: 30
Ar. 6, Salon: 115, 116, 212

Archivo General de la Nación (Caracas)
Diversos: LX, LXIII, LXVIII, LXX, LXXII
Libros de la Renta de Tabacos: 1, 2, 36, 71, 129, 315, 467, 487, 495–6, 628–9.
Negocios Ecclesiásticos: XXVIII
Real Hacienda, Libros de Contabilidad: 1152, 1178, 1209, 1214–15, 1227, 1241–3, 1283–4, 1286, 1290–2, 1294, 1405, 1415, 1420–2, 1602, 1636, 1667, 1683, 1685, 1776–7, 1781, 1799, 1803, 1872, 1910, 1924, 1936, 1954, 1960, 2017, 2040, 2091, 2116, 2145, 2244, 2246, 2360, 2362–3, 2430, 2433, 2436, 2439, 2443–4, 2447, 2468, 2479.

Archivo del Registro Principal del Distrito Federal (Caracas)
Escribanías: 1781–1820, 1829, 1931.
Protocolos: 1836–41, 1841–3, 1844–6, 1847–52.
Testamentarias

Public Records Office (London)
Foreign Office: 95/7/2

B. Printed Sources

(1) Primary Sources (printed documents and contemporary works)

Actas del Cabildo de Caracas 1810–1811 (Caracas, 1971)

Actas del Cabildo de Caracas 1812–1814 (Caracas, 1972)

Actas del Cabildo de Caracas (Monárquicas) 1810, 1812–1814 (Caracas, 1976)

Archivo del General Miranda (Havana, 1950), vol. XXIV.

Arellano Moreno, Antonio (ed.), *Documentos para la Historia Económica en la Epoca Colonial: Viajes e Informes* (Caracas, 1970)

Cagigal, Juan M., *Memorias del Mariscal de Campo Don Juan Manuel Cagigal Sobre la Revolución de Venezuela* (Caracas, 1960)

La Capitanía – General de Venezuela 1777–8 de Septiembre 1977, estudio prelim. A. Arellano Moreno (Caracas, 1977).

Cisneros, José L., *Descripción Exacta de la Provincia de Venezuela 1764* (Caracas, 1950).

Dauxion-Lavaysse, J. J., *Viaje a las Islas de Trinidad, Tobago y Margarita y a Diversas Partes de Venezuela en la América–Meriodional* (Caracas, 1967).

Depons, François, *Travels in South America during the years 1801, 1802, 1803 and 1804; containing a description of the captain-generalship of Caracas . . .* (2 vols., London, 1807).

García Chuecos, Hector (ed.), *Historia Documental de Venezuela* (Caracas, 1957).

Gazeta de Caracas 1808–1812 (2 vols., Caracas, 1960).

Gazeta de Caracas (6 vols., Paris, 1939).

Heredia, José, 'Memorias Sobre las Revoluciones de Venezuela', *Anuario*, IV–VI (1967–9), I, 517–740.

Humboldt, Alexander von, *Personal Narrative of Travels to the Equinoctal Regions of America during the years 1799–1804* (3 vols., London, 1852).

Leal, Idelfonso (ed.), *Documentos del Real Consulado de Caracas* (Caracas, 1964).

Level de Goda, Andrés, 'Memorias', *Anuario*, II, 1149–459.

Libro de Actas del Supremo Congreso de Venezuela 1811–1812 (2 vols., Caracas, 1960).

Limonta, José, *Libro de la Razón General de la Real Hacienda del Departamento de Caracas*, estudio prelim. M. Briceño Perozo (Caracas, 1962).

Materiales para el Estudio de la Cuestión Agraria en Venezuela (1800–1830) (Caracas, 1964), vol. I.

El Mercurio Venezolano (Caracas, 1960).

McNerney Jr, R. (ed.), *Memorias del General Daniel Florencio O'Leary: Narración* (Austin, Texas, 1970).

Nuñez, Enrique B. (ed.), *Cacao* (Caracas, 1972).

Olavarriaga, Pedro, *Instrucción General y Particular del Estado Presente de la Provincia de Venezuela en los Años de 1720 y 1721* (Caracas, 1965).

Paez-Pumar, Mauro (ed.), *Las Proclamas de Filadelfia de 1774 y 1775 en la Caracas de 1777* (Caracas, 1973).

El Publicista de Venezuela (Caracas, 1959).

Real Cédula de Intendencia de Ejército y Real Hacienda Diciembre 8 de 1776, estudio prelim. G. Morazzini de Pérez Enciso (Caracas, 1976).

Semanario de Caracas (Caracas, 1959).

Testimonios de la Epoca Emancipadora (Caracas, 1961).

Tres Testigos Europeos de la Primera República 1808–1814: Semple, Delpech, Poudenx y Mayer (Caracas, 1974).

Urquinaona y Pardo, Pedro, 'Relación Documentada del origen y progresos del trastorno de las provincias de Venezuela hasta la exoneración del capitán general Don
Domingo Monteverde', *Anuario*, I, 137–360.

(2) Secondary Sources

Acosta Saignes, Miguel, *Vida de los Esclavos Negros en Venezuela* (Caracas, 1967).
Alvarez, Mercedes M., *Comercio y Comerciantes y sus proyecciones en la Independencia de
Venezuela* (Caracas, 1963).
    El Tribunal del Real Consulado de Caracas (2 vols., Caracas, 1967).
Añes, Gonzalo, *El Antiguo Régimen: los Borbones* (Madrid, 1976).
Arcaya, Pedro M. *Insurrección de los Negros en la Serranía de Coro* (Caracas, 1949).
Archer, Christon, 'The Army of New Spain and the Wars of Independence
1790–1821', *H.A.H.R.*, LXI (1981), 705–14.
Arcila Farías, Eduardo, *Comercio entre Venezuela y México en los Siglos XVII y XVIII*
(Mexico, 1950).
    Economía Colonial de Venezuela, 2nd ed. (2 vols., Caracas, 1973).
    Historia de un Monopolio: el Estanco del Tabaco en Venezuela 1779–1833 (Caracas,
1977).
Arcila Farías, Eduardo, *et al.*, *Estudio de Caracas* (Caracas, 1967), vol. II.
Arellano Moreno, Antonio, *Orígenes de la Economía Venezolana*, 3rd ed. (Caracas, 1974).
Baralt, Rafael M., *Resumen de la Historia de Venezuela* (2 vols., Maracaibo, 1960).
Barbier, Jacques A., 'Elites and Cadres in Bourbon Chile', *H.A.H.R.*, LII (1972),
416–35.
    'Peninsular Finance and Colonial Trade: the Dilemma of Charles IV's Spain',
J.L.A.S., XII, 1 (1980), 21–37.
Blanco Uribe, Ernesto, 'The Military in Venezuela 1810–1836' (Oxford Univ. M. Litt.
thesis 1981).
Brading, D. A., *Haciendas and Ranchos in the Mexican Bajio: Leon 1700–1860* (Cam-
bridge, 1978).
    Miners and Merchants in Bourbon Mexico 1763–1810 (Cambridge, 1971).
Briceño Iragorry, Mario, *Casa León y su Tiempo: Aventura de un Anti-Héroe* (Caracas,
1946).
Brinton, Crane, *The Anatomy of Revolution*, rev. ed. (New York, 1959).
Brito Figueroa, Federico, *La Estructura Económica de Venezuela Colonial*, 2nd ed.
(Caracas, 1978).
Burkholder, Mark, and Chandler, D., *From Impotence to Authority: the Spanish Crown and
the American Audiencias, 1687–1808* (Columbia, Miss., 1977).
Canelón, Juan S., *Miguel José Sanz (1756–1814)* (Caracas, 1958).
Carr, Raymond, *Spain 1808–1939* (Oxford, 1966).
Carrera Damas, G., *Boves, aspectos socio-económicos de la guerra de independencia*, 2nd ed.
(reprinted; Caracas, 1972).
Codazzi, Agustín, *Obras Escogidas* (2 vols., Caracas, 1960).
Conniff, Michael, 'Guayaquil through Independence: Urban Development in a
Colonial System', *The Americas* (1977), 384–410.
Cortés, Santos R., *El Régimen de las 'Gracias al Sacar' en Venezuela durante el Periodo His-
pánico* (2 vols., Caracas, 1978).
Cuenca Esteban, Javier, 'Statistics of Spain's Colonial Trade 1792–1820: Consular
Duties, Cargo Inventories, and Balances of Trade', *H.A.H.R.*, LXI (1981),
381–428.

Díaz Sanchez, R., 'Estudio Preliminar', *Libro de Actas del Supremo Congreso de Venezuela 1811–1812* (Caracas, 1960), I, 11–37.

Domínguez, Jorge I., *Insurrection or Loyalty: the Breakdown of the Spanish American Empire* (Cambridge, Mass., 1980).

Febres Cordero, Julio, 'El Municipio Colonial y su Régimen Político Anti-Democrático', *Memoria del Segundo Congreso Venezolano de la Historia* (Caracas, 1975), I, 287–310.

El Primer Ejército Republicano y la Campaña de Coro (Caracas, 1973).

Ferry, Robert J., 'Encomienda, African Slavery and Agriculture in Seventeenth Century Caracas', *H.A.H.R.*, LXI (1981), 609–35.

Fisher, John, 'Imperial "Free Trade" and the Hispanic Economy, 1778–1796', *J.L.A.S.*, XIII (1981), 21–56.

'The Intendant System and the Cabildos of Peru 1784–1810', *H.A.H.R.*, XLIX (1969), 430–53.

Fortoul, José Gil, *Historia Constitucional de Venezuela*, 2nd ed. (reprinted Caracas, 1964), vol. I.

Gabaldón Marqués, Joaquín, 'El Municipio, Raiz de la República', *El Movimiento Emancipador de Hispánoamerica* (Caracas, 1961), II, 333–460.

García-Baquero González, Antonio, *Cádiz y el Atlántico 1717–1778: el Comercio Colonial Español Bajo el Monopolio Gaditano* (2 vols., Seville, 1976).

Comercio Colonial y Guerras Coloniales: la Decadencia Económica de Cádiz a Raiz de la Emancipación Americana (Seville, 1972).

Gibson, Charles, *Spain in America* (New York, 1966).

Gilmore, Robert L. 'The Imperial Crisis, Rebellion and the Viceroy: Nueva Granada in 1809', *H.A.H.R.*, XL (1960), 1–24.

Gómez, Alaricio, *Fernando Peñalver (1765–1832)* (Caracas, 1955).

Grases, Pedro, *La Conspiración de Gual y España y el Ideario de la Independencia* (Caracas, 1949).

Historia de la Imprenta en Venezuela: hasta el fin de la Primera República (1812) (Caracas, 1967).

Griffin, Charles C., *Ensayos Sobre Historia de America* (Caracas, 1969).

Halperin Donghi, Tulio, *Historia Contemporanea de America Latina*, 2nd ed. (Madrid, 1970).

Hamnett, Brian R., 'Mexico's Royalist Coalition: the Response to Revolution 1808–1821', *J.L.A.S.*, XII (1980), 55–86.

Politics and Trade in Southern Mexico 1750–1821 (Cambridge, 1971).

Herr, R. *The Eighteenth Century Revolution in Spain* (Princeton, N.J., 1958).

Humphreys, R.A., and Lynch, J. *The Origins of the Latin American Revolutions 1808–1826* (New York, 1965).

Hussey, Roland D., *The Caracas Company 1728–1784: A Study in the History of Spanish Monopolistic Trade* (Cambridge, Mass., 1934).

Iturriza Guillen, Carlos, *Algunas Familias Caraqueñas* (2 vols., Caracas, 1967).

Izard, Miguel, 'La Agricultura Venezolana en una Época de Transición: 1777–1830', *Boletín Histórico*, XXVIII (1972), 81–145.

'Comercio Libre, Guerras Coloniales y Mercado Americano', in *Agricultura, Comercio Colonial y Crecimiento Económico en la Espan Contemporanea*, ed. J. Nadals and G. Tortella (Barcelona, 1974), 295–321.

'Contrabandistas, Comerciantes e Ilustrados', *Boletín Americanista*, XXVIII (1978), 23–86.

El Miedo a la Revolución: La Lucha por la Libertad en Venezuela (1777–1830) (Madrid, 1979).

'La Venezuela del Cafe Vista por los Viajeros del Siglo XIX', *Boletín Histórico*, XX (1969), 182–225.

Kaufmann, William, *La Política Británica y la Independencia de la América Latina 1804–1828*, Spanish ed. (Caracas, 1963).

King, James, 'A Royalist View of the Colored Castes in the Venezuelan War of Independence', *H.A.H.R.*, XXIII (1953), 526–37.

Klein, Herbert S. 'The Structure of the Hacendado Class in Late Eighteenth Century Alto Peru: The Intendencia de la Paz', *H.A.H.R.*, LX (1980), 191–212.

Ladd, Doris M. *The Mexican Nobility at Independence 1780–1826* (Austin, Texas, 1976).

Leal, Idelfonso, *Historia de la Universidad de Caracas 1721–1827* (Caracas, 1963).

Lecuna, Vicente 'La Conjuración de Matos', *B.A.N.H.*, XIV (1931), 381–440.

Crónica Razonada de las Guerras de Bolívar, 2nd ed. (3 vols., New York, 1960).

Lohmann Villena, Guillermo, *Los Americanos en las Ordenes Nobillarias 1529–1900* (2 vols., Madrid, 1947).

Lombardi, John V., *The Decline and Abolition of Negro Slavery in Venezuela 1820–1854* (Westport, Conn., 1971).

People and Places in Colonial Venezuela (Bloomington, Indiana, 1976).

Venezuela: The Search for Order, The Dream of Progress (Oxford and New York, 1982).

López, Castro F. *Juan Picornell y la Conspiración de Gual y España* (Caracas, 1955).

López Cantos, Angel, *Don Francisco de Saavedra, Segundo Intendente de Caracas* (Seville, 1973).

Losada, Benito R., *Juan Germán Roscio (1763–1821)* (Caracas, 1953).

Lovera, Ildemaro, *Vida de José Angel de Alamo: Historia de un Oligarca* (Caracas, 1965).

Lucena Solmoral, Manuel, 'El Sistema de Cuadrillas de Ronda para la Seguridad de los Llanos a Fines del Periodo Colonial. Los Antecedentes de las Ordenanzas de Llanos de 1811', in *Memoria del Tercer Congreso Venezolano de la Historia* (Caracas, 1979), II, 189–225.

Lynch, John, *The Spanish American Revolutions 1808–1826* (London, 1973).

'Bolivar and the Caudillos', *H.A.H.R.*, LXIII (1983), 3–35.

McFarlane, Anthony, 'Economic and Political Change in the Vice Royalty of New Granada, with special reference to overseas trade, 1739–1810' (Univ. of London Ph.D. thesis, 1977).

McKinley, Peter M., 'Themes of Revolutionary Propaganda in Venezuela's First Republic: 1810–1812' (Oxford Univ. B.Phil. thesis, 1977).

Madariaga, Salvador de, *Bolívar* (reprinted; New York, 1969).

The Fall of the Spanish American Empire (London, 1947).

Masur, G., *Simón Bolívar* (Albuquerque, N.M., 1948).

Mendoza, Carlos, *Cristóbal Mendoza (1772–1829)* (Caracas, 1957).

Mijares Pérez, Lucio, 'La Organización de las Milicias Venezolanas en la Segunda Mitad del Siglo XVIII', *Memoria del Tercer Congreso Venezolano de la Historia* (Caracas, 1979), II, 259–82.

Moore, John P., *The Cabildos in Peru under the Bourbons: a study in the decline and resurgence of local government in the audiencia of Lima 1700–1824* (Durham, N.C., 1966).

Morón, Guillermo, *A History of Venezuela* (New York, 1963).

Nichols, Roy F., 'Trade Relations and the Establishment of the United States Consulates in Spanish America, 1779–1809', *H.A.H.R.*, XIII (1933), 289–313.

Nuñes Días, Manuel, *El Real Consulado de Caracas 1793–1810* (Caracas, 1971).

Parra Marqués, Hector, *El Doctor Tomás Hernández de Sanabria* (Caracas, 1970).

Parra Pérez, C., *Historia de la Primera República de Venezuela*, 2nd ed. (2 vols., Caracas, 1959).

Parry, John H., *The Spanish Seaborne Empire* (New York, 1966).

Parry, John H., and Sherlock, P., *A Short History of the West Indies*, 3rd ed. (London and Hong Kong, 1978).

Pérez Vila, Manuel, *José Rafael Revenga (1786–1852)* (Caracas, 1960).

Pino Iturrieta, Elias, *La Mentalidad Venezolana de la Emancipación 1810–1812* (Caracas, 1971).

Polanco Martínez, Tomás, *Esbozo Sobre la Historia Económica Venezolana* (Madrid, 1960), vol. I: 'La Colonia 1498–1810'.

Ponte, Andrés F., *La Revolución de Caracas y sus Próceres* (reprinted; Caracas, 1960).

Ramos Pérez, Demetrio, 'El Presidente de la Real Audiencia de Caracas en su fase inicial, y su intento de concentración de todos los poderes', *Memoria del Segundo Congreso Venezolano de la Historia* (Caracas, 1975), II, 465–98.

Rout Jr, Leslie B., *The African Experience in Spanish America: 1502 to the present day* (Cambridge, 1976).

Sanz Tapia, Ángel, *Los Militares Emigrados y los Prisioneros Franceses en Venezuela durante la Guerra contra la Revolución* (Caracas, 1977).

Socolow, Susan M., *The Merchants of Buenos Aires 1778–1810: Family and Commerce* (Cambridge, 1978).

Stein, Stanley H. and Barbara, *La Herencia Colonial de América Latina* (Mexico, 1971).

Stoan, Stephen K., *Pablo Morillo and Venezuela, 1815–1820* (Colombus, Ohio, 1974).

Suarez, Santiago G. (ed.), *Las Instituciones Militares Venezolanas del Periodo Hispánico en los Archivos* (Caracas, 1969).

Sucre, Luis A., *Gobernadores y Capitanes Generales de Venezuela*, 2nd ed. (Caracas, 1964).

Tandrón, Humberto, *El Real Consulado de Caracas y el Comercio Exterior de Venezuela* (Caracas, 1976).

Troconis de Veracoechea, Ermila, *La Función Financiera de la Iglesia Colonial Venezolana* (Caracas, 1978).

Historia de El Tocuyo Colonial: periodo histórico 1545–1810 (Caracas, 1977).

La Tenencia de la Tierra en el Litoral Central de Venezuela (Caracas, 1979).

Uslar Pietri, Arturo, 'Estudio Preliminar', *Testimonios de la Epoca Emancipadora* (Caracas, 1961), pp. vii–xxxvii.

Vallenilla Lanz, Laureano, *Cesarismo Democrático* (reprinted; Caracas, 1961).

Waldron, K., 'A Social History of a Primate City: The Case of Caracas 1750–1810' (Indiana Univ. Ph.D. thesis, 1977).

Watters, Mary, *A History of the Church in Venezuela 1810–1930* (Chapel Hill, N.C., 1933).

Woodward, Margaret L., 'The Spanish Army and the Loss of Spanish America 1810–1824', *H.A.H.R.*, XLVIII (1968), 586–607.

Zabala y Lera, Pio, *España bajo los Borbones* (reprinted; Madrid, 1945).

Bibliographical Appendix

There are approximately 2,800 wills for the years 1781–1820 registered in about 250 *Escribanías* volumes for the city of Caracas contained in the archive of the Registro Principal del Distrito Federal. Of these wills, I researched 728. In tracking down the elites of the colonial province, I also delved into notarial volumes beyond my period (collected after 1830 under the title of *Protocolos*), and into a section of the archive known as *Testamentarias* which contains wills, usually in individual volumes, over whose resolution there was some legal problem necessitating extra paper-work. An additional 80 wills of my total sample of 808 were found in the preceding sources.

In indexing the wills of the 782 persons of the sample, I have grouped the references into three headings: name, year and notarial source. In the case of *Escribanías*, it is the notary's name which is listed; in the case of *Testamentarias* and *Protocolos*, the title of the volume. All references are to one volume rather than a series. In the case of the *Escribanías* sources, I decided that, although page numbers were usually available for the will, indicating the volume by the name of the notary in charge of it was sufficient reference, in that almost all notaries placed indexes in their books.

The wills are grouped under six general headings: *Caraqueño Creoles*, *Peninsulares*, *Canarios*, *Other White* (that is whites with origins from places other than the province, Spain and the Canaries), *Free-Coloureds* and *Caste Unknown*. Within the separate categories I have highlighted different characteristics. Among whites of all descriptions I have included official titles where applicable, including those of nobility, Doctor (Dr) and Licenciado (Lic.) (both university titles), Presbitero (Pro: priest), Obispo (bishop), Captain-General and Regente (Regent of the Audiencia). Among *Peninsulares* and *Canarios* I have marked the wills of immigrants who married locally with an asterisk after the surname. In the case of *Free-Coloureds* and *Caste Unknown* I have listed legal status where it can be determined.

The individuals of the total sample are numbered consecutively from start to finish but under each of the six general headings they are listed alphabetically according to surname. Where applicable, members of the same extended family have been grouped under the same number, with a subdivision marked by letters. In the latter cases nuclear family groups are not singled out, nor are generational differences: the listings are simply alphabetical. On occasion, the relation of individuals with the same surname is questionable, but not doubtful enough to dismiss altogether the possibilities of a connection. I have catalogued these cases as members of the same extended family but with a (?) preceding the surname(s) in question.

Two of the wills under *Caraqueño Creoles*, 36e and 207b, were found in sources other than the ones discussed above, so 'source' in their cases is marked with an asterisk. Will

36e can be found in V. Lecuna, 'Los Bolívar y Ponte,' *B.A.N.H.*, XXXVI (1953), 373–445; will 207b can be located in A.A., Ar. 2, G 1–68.

The classification of 45 wills under *Free-Coloureds* requires some justification. Only 22 of the wills are of individuals who designated themselves as *pardo*, *moreno* and *negro libre*. Nevertheless I feel secure about the caste identity of the others for a number of reasons. First, none of the individuals involved used the title 'don' or 'doña' before their names. This is a controversial rule of measure and must be justified. By the eighteenth century 'don' in many colonies had lost a sense of exclusiveness, and was used as a matter of course by whites to distinguish themselves from the coloured masses around them. It was very clearly no longer restricted in practice to government officials, clerics, or people of noble lineage and/or wealth. A 1777 debate on the subject in Madrid recognized this irreversible trend (see Santos R. Cortés, *El Régimen de las 'Gracias al Sacar' en Venezuela durante el Periodo Hispanico* (Caracas, 1978), I, 257–9). Supportive and more specific evidence of this reality is provided in the notarial records, where whites of clearly humble origins used the sobriquet everywhere. The prevalence of the 'don' in the 2,800 wills or so contained in the books for 1780 to 1820, and its application to whites of every condition imaginable, strongly suggests that the relatively few exceptions were not white.

Other means of determining the colour of the small category of non-'dons' strengthen the classification. With the exception of the wealthy few among this group of wills, the occupations given were such as to harmonize with the general image of those performed by the *castas*. Some were artisans, some were small plot-holders, some owned no more than very modest houses. A more useful index was also provided by the parentage and marital patterns of the 23 individuals I have chosen to categorize as free-coloureds. Seventeen were illegitimate. Those that married, married non-'dons' and spouses who themselves were illegitimate. Another standard was established by what we know of late-colonial history. Thus, among the wills are included two of the famous Bejarano family, which tried to buy their way out of the colour bar in the 1790s (458a–b). Three others of the wills are of captains of militias of *pardos* who also happened to be wealthy men (489, 519, 524). But neither wealth nor military title earned them the right to use 'don', even in their own wills. What is more, two married illegitimate spouses (519, 524). Perhaps the most striking case is that of Gervasio de Ponte, the illegitimate son of a scion of an old Caracas family, who married a white woman but whose children – and indeed he himself – could not use 'don' with their names (516).

Caraqueño Creoles

	Name	Year	Source
1a	Acevedo, Ana	1783	Nebot
b	Acevedo, Atanacio	1804	(?) Aramburu
c	(?) Acevedo, Josefa	1839	*Testas*, 1836–41
2a	Acevedo Leal, Jose Feliciano (Dr)	1811	Texera
b	Acevedo Leal, Jose Julian	1806	Texera
3	Acosta, Manuel (Pro)	1788	Izaguirre
4	Aguado, Gertrudis	1799	Texera
5	Alfaro, Ana Tomasa	1790	Armas

6a	Alonso Gil, Francisco	1791	Castrillo
b	Alonso Gil, Jose Manuel	1814	Castrillo
b	Alonso Gil, Jose Manuel	1814	Castrillo
c	Alonso Gil, Margarita	1789	Ponce
7	Alvarado Serrano, Miguel	1784, 1792	Texera
8	Alvarenga, Nicolas	1788	Texera
9	Alvares, Fernando	1799	Testas, A
10	Alvares Avila, Francisco (Pro)	1804	Texera
11	Alvares Lugo, Jose	1805	Hernandez
12	Ancheta, Jose	1784	Aramburu
13	Angulo, Francisca	1784	Aramburu
14	Anzola, Nicolas	1847	*Protocs.*, 1847–52
15	Araujo, Josefa	1806	Ravelo
16	Aresti y Reyna, Josefa	1809	Texera
17	Arguinsones, Francisca	1803	Tirado
18a	Arias Liendo, Maria Isabel	1785	Armas
b	Arias Mendoza, Maria Isabel	1812	Leon y Urbina
19a	Aristiguieta, Miguel	1782	Texera
b	Aristiguieta, Teresa	1786	Rio
c	Aristiguieta, Maria Begoña	1803	Hernandez
d	Aristiguieta, Juan Felix (Pro)	1784	Fernandez
e	Aristiguieta, Leandro	1805	Tirado
20	Armas, Marcos	1807	Texera
21	Armas Montiel, Antonio	1811	Tirado
22	Arnal Ascarate, Agustin (Dr)	1815	Castrillo
23a	Arrechedera, Maria Concepcion	1784	Aramburu
b	Arrechedera, Juana	1802	Barcenas
c	Arrechedera, Luisa	1805	Tirado
24	Arvelo, Luis	1794	Rio
25a	Ascanio, Fernando (Conde de la Granja)	1814	Ximenes
b	Ascanio, Hermoso, Vicente (Pro)	1785	Aramburu
c	Ascanio Herrera, Maria Isabel	1782	Armas
d	Ascanio Herrera, Maria Manuela	1796	Barcenas
e	Ascanio Oviedo, Margarita	1813	Castrillo
f	Ascanio Rada, Juan	1844	*Protocs.*, 1844–6
26	Ascanio, Justa Lorenza	1793	Barcenas
27	Ascanio, Maria Bacilia	1813	Ascanio
28	Ascanio Arvelo, Gregorio	1814	Ascanio-Sabogal
29	Avilan, Miguel	1793	Mota
30a	Barreto, Antonio	1800	*Testas*, B, C
b	Barreto, Carlos (Pro)	1784	Armas
31	Bello, Jose Francisco	1804	Texera
32a	Berrotaran, Ana Catarina	1793	Armas
b	Berrotaran, Angel Maria	1840	*Testas*, 1836–41
c	Berrotaran, Domingo (Pro)	1792	Texera
d	Berrotaran, Maria Trinidad	1806	Ascanio
e	Berrotaran Tovar, Miguel (Marques)	1777–8	*Testas*, B
e	Berrotaran Tovar, Miguel (Marques)	1777–8	*Testas*, B
33a	Betancourt, Josefa	1785	Texera-Nebot

b	(?) Betancourt, Maria	1806	Ravelo
34a	Blanco y Blanco, Josefa	1809	Ascanio
b	Blanco y Blanco, Luis	1808	Ravelo
c	Blanco y Blanco, Joaquin	1805	Tirado
d	Blanco y Blanco, Maria Concepcion	1810	Ascanio
e	Blanco y Herrera, Maria Isabel	1803	Texera
f	Blanco y Herrera, Nicolas	1795	Barcenas
g	Blanco y Liendo, Jose Maria	1818	Zumeta
h	Blanco y Mixares, Fernando	1805	Texera
i	Blanco y Monasterios, Adriana	1895	Tirado
j	Blanco y Monasterios, Luisa	1784	Texera
k	Blanco y Monasterios, Pedro	1787	Eleizalde
l	Blanco y Plaza, Francisco	1789	Aramburu
m	Blanco y Plaza, Geronimo	1798	*Testas*, B
n	Blanco y Plaza, Jose Eugenio	1808	*Testas*, B
o	Blanco y Plaza, Mateo	1791	Aramburu
p	Blanco y Plaza, Petronila	1813	Ximenes
q	Blanco y Plaza, Rafael	1848	*Protocs.*, 1847–52
r	Blanco y Ponte, Diego	1793	Aramburu
s	Blanco y Ponte, Ignacio	1795	Aramburu
t	Blanco y Ponte, Pedro	1768	*Testas*, B
u	Blanco y Ponte, Manuela	1798	Aramburu
v	Blanco y Ponte, Maria Natividad	1784	Fernandez
w	Blanco y Rengifo, Jose Domingo (Dr)	1807	Aramburu
x	Blanco y Rengifo, Fernando	1792	Ponce
y	Blanco de Uribe, Gabriel	1806	Ascanio
z	Blanco de Uribe, Luisa	1783	Texera
35	Blandin, Bartolome	1837	*Testas*, 1836–41
36a	Bolivar y Arias, Domingo	1797	Tirado
b	Bolivar y Arias, Gabriel	1799	Armas
c	Bolivar y Arias, Juan	1789	*Testas*, B
d	Bolivar y Ponte, Josefa	1782	Fernandez
e	Bolivar y Ponte, Juan Vicente	1792	*
37	Bolivar, Ana Teresa (espósita)	1794	Texera
38a	Borges Mendes, Jose (Pro)	1788	Texera
b	Borges Mendes, Francisca	1794	Texera
39	Bosques, Maria Manuela	1793	Barcenas
40	Bravo, Maria Catalina	1805	Texera
41	Caravallo, Ana Rita	1790	Texera
42a	Carballo, Concepcion	1806	Tirado
b	Carballo, Juana Maria	1829	Ochoa
42	Carballo Fernandez, Jose	1798	Texera
44	Cardoso, Antonio	1784	Castrillo
45	Carlomagno, Antolina	1788	Armas
46	Carreno, Filiberto	1805	Tirado
47	Casares, Juana	1785	Nebot
48a	Castilloveittia, Angela Maria	1836	*Testas*, 1836–41
b	Castilloveittia, Juan Bautista	1807	Texera
c	Castilloveittia, Manuel	1840	*Testas*, 1836–41

49	Castro, Ana Maria	1818	Texera
		1810	Ravelo
50	Castro, Juan Jose (Pro)	1792	Texera
51	Cazorla, Luis Jose (Pro)	1812	Tirado
52a	Cedillo, Nicolas	1784	Texera
b	Cedillo, Rafaela	1818	Zumeta
53a	Cedillo, Domingo (Pro)	1783	Texera
b	Cedillo, Isabel	1784	Armas
54	Cerezo, Francisco Jose	1798	Tirado
55	Chavett, Carlos (Pro)	1783–4	Texera
56	Cienfuegos, Josefa Leonarda	1783	Castrillo
57	Colon y Madriz, Juliana	1807	Hernandez
58	Correa, Juana Maria	1784	Aramburu
59a	Dacosta y Romero, Josefa	1818	Hernandez
b	Dacosta y Romero, Maria Francisca	1787	Rio
60	Dias, Andres	1785	Nebot
61	Dias, Francisca	1786	Texera
62	Dias, Francisco	1788	Armas
63	Dias, Josefa	1792	Castrillo
64	Dias, Juan	1787	Eizaguirre
65a	Dias Acevedo, Paula	1785	Rio
b	Dias Acevedo, Victoria	1784	Rio
66	Dias Argote, Domingo (Pro)	1811	Leon y Urbina
67a	Dias Avila, Francisco	1782	Armas
b	Dias Avila, Juan	1788	Texera
c	Dias Avila, Maria Josefa	1792	Castrillo
68	Dias Hernandez, Merced	1802	Aramburu
69	Dias Montero, Maria del Carmen	1816	Pardo
70	Dias Padron, Francisco	1806	Tirado
71	Dominguez, Maria Encarnacion	1814	Hernandez
72a	Echeverria, Diego Manuel	1791	Castrillo
b	Echeverria, Juan Vicente (Pro)	1804	Armas
73	Echezuria, Pablo	1831	Zumeta
74	Eizaguirre, Maria Josefa	1806	Texera
75a	Escalona Arguinsones, Rosa Rosalia	1818	Munoz
b	Escalona Mixares, Luis	1812	Cires
76	Escorihuela, Jose Vicente (Dr)	1809	Viana
77	Espejo, Juan Jose	1806	Aramburu
78	Espinosa Diaz, Maria Candelaria	1813	Leon y Urbina
79a	Espinosa de Monteros, Jose Fernando	1783, 1786	Texera
b	Espinosa de Monteros, Jose Teodoro (Pro)	1813	Ascanio
c	Espinosa de Monteros, Hilario	1785	Texera-Nebot
d	Espinosa de Monteros, Jose Candelario	1816	Leon y Urbina
e	Espinosa de Monteros, Toribio	1820	Leon y Urbina
		1813	Cires
80	Esteves, Salvador	1789	Ponce
81a	Esteves, Gertrudis	1838	*Testas*, 1836–41
b	Esteves, Maria Antonia	1809	Texera
c	Esteves, Rafael (Pro)	1791	*Testas*, E

82	Faxardo, Josefa	1790	Barcenas
83	Fernandez Feo, Manuel (Pro)	1811	Ascanio
84	Fernandez Fuenmayor, Francisco (Pro)	1811	Texera
85	Fernandez Garavan, Francisca	1783	Aramburu
86	Franco, Jesus Maria	1820	Leon y Urbina
87	Freites, Maria Concepcion	1789	Texera
88a	Frias, Buenaventura	1784	Nebot
b	Frias, Maria	1820	Albor
89a	Galindo, Jaime (Pro)	1783	Fernandez
b	Galindo, Maria Manuela	1807	Texera
c	Galindo, Maria Sebastiana	1788	Aramburu
90	Garcia Bellow, Francisco Xavier	1806	Cobian
91	Garcia Bello, Francisco Xavier	1806	Cobian
92	Garcia Castillo, Juan (Pro)	1786	Texera
93	Garcia de Noda, Maria Teresa	1789	Texera
94a	Gedler e Inciarte, Ignacio	1789	Eizaguirre
b	Gedler y Ponte, Maria Eusebia	1805	Cobian
c	Gedler y Ponte, Pedro Francisco	1788	Rio
d	Gedler, Maria Teresa	1802	Hernandez
95	Gomes Rus, Domingo (Lic.)	1806	Santana
96	Gonzalez Betancourt, Margarita	1783	Aramburu
97	Gonzalez Echegaray, Juana Ines	1801	Mota-Cires
98	Gonzalez Nunes, Juan Lorenzo (Pro)	1812	Hernandez
99	Gonzalez Ortega, Juan (Pro)	1806	Texera
100	Gonzalez Perez, Angela	1785	Texera-Nebot
101	Gonzalez Poleo, Jose	1809	Ascanio
102	Gonzalez Rodriguez Canejo, Maria	1781	Terrero
103a	Hermoso de Mendoza, Domingo	1794	Texera
b	Hermoso de Mendoza, Francisco	1793	Barcenas
c	Hermoso de Mendoza, Maria Manuela	1818	Texera
d	Hermoso de Mendoza, Petronila	1806	Texera
104	Hernandez, Antonio	1785	Aramburu
105	Hernandez, Clara Maria	1818	Texera
106	Hernandez, Francisca	1818	Zumeta
107	Hernandez Calixto, Antonio (Pro)	1807	Texera
108	Hernandez Faxardo, Jose Antonio	1786	Rio
109	Hernandez Gonzalez, Francisco	1789	Amitesarove
110	Hernandez Martinez, Cecilia	1805	Ascanio
111	Hernandez Matieta, Maria Manuela	1806	Ascanio
112	Hernandez Montanez, Margarita	1814	Ascanio-Sabogal
113	Hernandez Sanabia, Tomas (Dr)	1781	Aramburu
114a	Herrera y Liendo, Isabel	1789	Ponce
b	Herrera y Mesones, Maria Nicolasa	1784	Texera
c	Herrera y Rada, Martin Eugenio	1826	*Testas*, H
d	Herrera y Rada, Miguel Ignacio (Pro)	1804	Texera
115	Hurtado, Juan Dionisio	1804	Aramburu
116a	Ibarra y Galindo, Vicente	1840	*Testas*, B
b	Ibarra y Herrera, Francisco (Arzobispo)	1806	Texera
c	Ibarra y Herrera, Manuela	1789	Texera

d	Ibarra y Herrera, Petronila	1806	Texera
e	Ibarra e Ibarra, Ana Josefa	1790	Barcenas
f	Ibarra y Ibarra, Gabriel	1783	Texera
117a	Isturris, Martin	1825	*Testas*, I
b	Isturris, Pedro Jose	1810	Tirado
c	Isturris, Rafaela	1810	Tirado
118	Iturriaga, Manuela Jacinta	1807	Peoli
119a	(?) Landaeta y Landaeta, Diego	1810	Tirado
b	Landaeta y Landaeta, Eligio (Lic.)	1804	Cires
c	Landaeta y Landaeta, Francisco (Pro)	1806	Ascanio
120	Landaeta y Rubio, Maria Teresa	1807	Texera
121	Laya y Alcala, Josefa	1814	Leon y Urbina
122	Leon Garcia, Nicolas	1784	Aramburu
		1790	Barcenas
123	Leon Padron, Juana Rosalia	1806	Aramburu
		1813	Castrillo
124	Leon y Puncel, Maria Josefa	1785	Rio
125	Letra, Bartolome	1785	Aramburu
126	Liendo y Blanco, Clara	1782	Terrero
127	Liendo y Ochoa, Sebastian (Pro)	1784	Aramburu
128	Lindo, Gabriel (Pro)	1823	*Testas*, L
129	Linares, Jose	1785	Aramburu
130	Lopes de Lugo, Barbara	1811	Tirado
131a	Lopes Mendez Gonzales, Catalina	1818	Texera
b	Lopes Mendez Gonzales, Juana	1807	(?) Ascanio
c	Lopes Mendez Nuñez, Dionisio	1784	Nebot
d	Lopes Mendez Nuñez, Francisca	1818	Texera
e	Lopes Mendez Nuñez, Isabel	1784	Nebot
f	Lopes Mendez Nuñez, Isidoro	1813	Ascanio
g	Lopes Mendez Nuñez, Jose (Pro)	1784	Nebot
h	Lopes Mendez Nuñez, Luis	1815	*Testas*, R
i	Lopes Mendez Nuñez, Maria Josefa	1784	Nebot
j	Lopes Mendez Nuñez, Silvestre (Pro)	1815	Texera
132	Lopes Rivera, Maria Antonia	1784	Nebot
133	Lopes de Vega, Francisco	1783	Aramburu
134a	Loreto de Silva y Blanco, Ines	1788	Aramburu
b	Loreto de Silva y Blanco, Maria Ana	1809	Tirado
c	Loreto de Silva y Blanco, Luis	1813	Castrillo
135	Losada, Tomas	1805	Ravelo
136	Lovera, Josefa Maria	1807	Texera
		1812	Leon y Urbina
137	Lugo, Jose Vitalde (Pro)	1813	Correa
138a	Machado Caravallo, Juana Luisa	1806	Texera
b	Machado Hernandez, Josefa	1802	Aramburu
c	Machado Hernandez, Maria Isabel	1791	Armas
d	Machado Nuñes, Fernando	1837	*Testas*, 1836–41
e	Machado Nuñes, Juan Jose	1842	*Protocs.*, 1841–3
f	Machado Perez, Jose Bernardo	1800	Mota
		1782	Terrero

g	Machado Perez, Jose Laureano	1799	Tirado
139a	Machado Machado, Jose German	1811	Castrillo
b	Machado Machado, Maria Francisca	1805	Texera
c	Machado Machado, Maria Luisa	1800	Texera
d	Machado Rodriguez, Jose Francisco	1792	Texera
140a	Machillanda, Bernabe	1819	*Testas*, M
b	Machillanda, Jose Vicente (Pro)	1816	*Testas*, M
141	Madera, Francisca Dionisia	1784, 1786	Aramburu
142	Madera, Maria Atocha	1785	Nebot
143a	Madriz Ascanio, Agustin	1802	Cobian
b	Madriz Ascanio, Felipe	1802	Cobian
c	Madriz Ascanio, Maria Josefa	1805	Texera
d	Madriz Ascanio, Rosalia	1814	Ximenes
		1820	Texera
e	Madriz Liendo, Francisca	1786	Eleizalde
f	Madriz Liendo, Isabel	1783	Nebot
g	Madriz Muñoz, Francisco	1786	Texera
h	Madriz y Vasquez, Andres	1774	*Testas*, B
144a	Maestre de la Mota, Juan Julian	1781	Aramburu
b	Maestre de la Mota, Domingo	1801	Mota
145	Malpica, Miguel Ignacio	1804	Armas
146	Marinas, Marina	1787	Armas
		1790	Armas
147	Marrero, Josefa Micaela	1803	Aramburu
148	Marrero Izquierdo, Domingo	1810	Tirado
149	Martinez de Porras, Pedro	1781	Texera
150	Matos, Micaela	1842	*Protocs.*, 1841–3
151a	Mendes Quiñones, Apolonia	1785	Rio
b	Mendes Quiñones, Catalina	1806	Aramburu
c	Mendes Quiñones, Maria Soledad	1791	Rio
152a	Mendoza Carrasquer, Maria Geronima	1812	Ximenes
b	Mendoza Carrasquer, Rosalia	1793	Aramburu
153	Mendoza y Castro, Jose (Pro)	1804	Basares
154	Merida, Maria Magdalena	1803	Texera
155a	Mixares de Solorzano y Ascanio, Francisco (Marques)	1765	*Testas*, M
b	Mixares y Ascanio, Juan	1765	*Testas*, M
c	Mixares y Ascanio, Pedro	1788	Eleizalde
d	Mixares y Mixares, Maria Candelaria	1807	Aramburu
e	Mixares y Ponte, Juan Jacinto	1793	Aramburu
f	Mixares y Tovar, Juan Francisco	1793	Aramburu
156a	Monasterios y Blanco, Adriana	1804	Aramburu
b	Monasterios y Blanco, Juan Felix	1788	Eleizalde
c	Monasterios y Blanco, Miguel	1804	Aramburu
d	Monasterios y Blanco, Pedro	1798	Barcenas
e	Monasterios y Cedillo, Maria Josefa	1814	Castrillo
f	Monasterios y Oviedo, Carlos (Pro)	1788	Aramburu
g	Monasterios y Oviedo, Ines	1789	Aramburu
h	Monasterios y Oviedo, Mateo (Pro)	1816	Garcia y Saume

157a	Monserrate Ibarra, Manuel	1820	Texera
b	Monserrate Urbina, Teresa	1795	Armas
c	Monserrate Urbina, Vicente	1798	Tirado
158	Montenegro, Jose Cayetano (Dr)	1820	Texera
159	Montero Bolaños, Jacobo (Pro)	1789	Texera
160a	Montes de Oca, Agustin	1799	Castrillo
b	Montes de Oca, Gertrudis	1806	Texera
161	Mora, Juan Jose (Lic.)	1809	Ascanio
162	Morales, Santiago	1813	Ximenes
163a	Moreno Martinez de Porras, Diego	1797	Aramburu
b	Moreno y Porras, Jose Ignacio (Pro)	1808	*Testas*, M
164a	Mosquera, Andres (Lic.)	1818	Hernandez
b	Mosquera, Domingo (Lic.?)	1809	Texera
165a	Muñoz, Ana Maria	1815	Ximenes
b	(?) Muñoz Aguado, Miguel (Pro)	1785	Aramburu
c	(?) Muñoz Chavert, Maria Matilde	1820	Texera
d	(?) Muñoz Ortis, Maria Antonia	1839	*Testas*, 1836–41
166a	Muro y Francia, Ramon	1849	*Protocs.*, 1847–52
b	(?) Muro y Monasterios, Jose (Lic.)	1839	*Testas*, 1836–41
167	Narvarte Pimentel, Dominga	1806	Texera
168	Nieves Fernandez, Ana Maria	1814	Ximenes
169	Nieves Reyes, Juan Antonio	1801	Texera
170	Nieves Urra, Francisco (Pro)	1820	Hernandez
171	Nuñes, Maria Rafaela	1790	Armas
172a	Obelmexias y Rengifo, Diego	1813	Hernandez
b	Obelmexias y Rengifo, Geronima	1837	*Testas*, 1836–41
c	Obelmexias y Rengifo, Maria Petronila	1818	Garcia y Saume
173	Ochoa, Bernardo	1786	Aramburu
174	Ochoa, Luisa Josefa	1793	Texero
175	Ojeda, Maria Manuela	1793	Barcenas
176	Olivera, Juana Maria	1788	Aramburu
177	Oliveros, Pedro Nicolas	1785	Aramburu
178	Orellana, Juan Jose (Pro)	1805	Texera
179	Oropeza, Geronimo (Lic.)	1788	Texera
180	Osio, Jose Antonio (Dr)	1794	Aramburu
181	Otamendi, Jose Ramon	1799	Barcenas
182a	Pacheco y Toro, Antonio	1797	Aramburu
b	Pacheco y Toro, Felix	1788	Rio
c	Pacheco y Toro, Jose Antonio (3rd Conde de San Xavier)	1809	Texera
d	Pacheco y Tovar, Jose Antonio (1st Conde)	1774	*Testas*, P
e	Pacheco y Tovar, Maria de Jesus	1809	Texera
f	Pacheco y Villegas, Maria Petronila	1806	Texera
g	Pacheco y Villegas, Rosalia	1784	Texera
183	Padilla, Pedro (Pro)	1784	Castrillo
184	Padron Diaz, Maria Candelaria	1805	Hernandez
185a	Padron Hernandez, Angela	1804	Texera
b	Padron Hernandez, Juana Antonia	1814	Ascanio-Sabogal
186a	Palacios y Aristiguieta, Antonio	1808	Aramburu

b	Palacios y Aristiguieta, Domingo	1804	Texera
c	Palacios y Blanco, Carlos	1805	Ascanio
d	Palacios y Blanco, Maria Concepcion	1792	Aramburu
e	Palacios y Blanco, Pedro (Pro)	1799	Texera
f	Palacios y Obelmexias, Juan	1811	Leon y Urbina
g	Palacios y Sojo, Feliciano	1794	Aramburu
h	Palacios y Sojo, Francisco	1785	Texera-Nebot
i	Palacios y Sojo, Juan	1791	*Testas*, S
187	Paul, Francisca	1839	*Testas*, 1836–41
188	Paz del Castillo, Juan Bautista	1827	*Testas*, P
189	Pelaez y Hurtado, Francisco	1836	*Testas*, 1836–41
190	Pelaez de Ponte, Carmen	1840	*Testas*, 1836–41
191	Peña, Maria Josefa	1807	Ascanio
192	Perez, Manuel Trinidad (Pro)	1785	Aramburu
193	Perez Espina, Francisco	1806	Ravelo
194	Perez Garcia, Juan Cristobal	1784	Armas
195	Perez Mexias, Vicente (Pro)	1792	Castrillo
196	Perez Moreno, Domingo	1784	Aramburu
197a	Perez Velasquez, Manuel	1799	Texera
b	Perez Velasquez, Marcos	1788	Texera
198a	Pimentel Mota, Francisco (Pro)	1812	Leon y Urbina
b	Pimentel Mota, Maria Josefa	1806	Tirado
199a	Piñango Aguado, Maria Manuela	1788	Castrillo
b	Piñango Alonso Gil, Alonso	1783	Texera
c	Piñango Gil, Juana	1785	Aramburu
200	Piron y Oliva, Luisa	1808	Ascanio
201a	Plaza y Blanco, Josefa	1792	Texera
b	Plaza y Blanco, Juana	1787	Texera
c	Plaza y Blanco, Manuel	1791	Aramburu
d	Plaza y Bolivar, Jose Antonio	1804	Besares
e	Plaza y Liendo, Jose Ignacio	1786	Armas
f	Plaza y Tovar, Maria	1786	Texera
202	Poleo, Pedro Jose	1788	Fernandez
203a	Ponte y Blanco, Antonia	1812	Cires
b	Ponte y Mixares, Clara	1810	Ascanio
c	Ponte y Mixares, Lorenzo	1812	Ascanio
d	Ponte y Mixares, Miguel	1798	Texera
e	Ponte y Mixares, Maria Manuela	1814	Ximenes
f	Ponte y Mixares, Santiago	1784	Texera
204	Pozo del Sucre, Serafina	1799	Aramburu
205	Prim, Ramon	1838	*Testas*, 1836–41
206	Quintero Lima, Gonzalo	1812	Leon y Urbina
207a	Rada y Mendoza, Manuel (Pro)	1788	Eleizalde
b	Rada y Mendoza, Maria Luisa	1827	*
c	Rada y Soto, Paula	1781	Castrillo
d	Rada y Olloa, Manuela	1805	Texera
208	Ramirez, Ana Feliciana	1781	Eleizalde
209	Ramirez y Sotomayor, Andres	1793	Aramburu
210	Ramos, Gregoria	1788	Texera

211	Ravelo y Arriaga, Manuel Jacinto	1811	Ravelo
212	Ravelo Gonzalez, Antonia	1806	Ascanio
213a	Ravelo Hernandez, Francisco	1786	Rio
b	Ravelo Hernandez, Bernarda	1786	Texera
214a	Rengifo Pimentel, Maria Luisa	1784	Armas
b	Rengifo Pimentel, Antonio	1807	Aramburu
215	Reyes, Ana	1781	Marrero
216a	Ribas Herrera, Jose Felix	1803	Castro
b	Ribas Herrera, Marcos (Pro)	1812	Tirado
		1818	Texera
c	Ribas Herrera, Valentin	1825	*Testas*, P, R
d	Ribas Pacheco, Luis Jose	1818	Textera
e	Ribas Pacheco, Maria Ignacia	1813	Castrillo
217	Rios, Manuel de los	1818	Munoz
218	Rodriguez, Jose Patricio	1802	Cires
219	Rodriguez Tosta, Maria	1825	*Testas*, R
220	Roldan, Concepcion	1806	Ravelo
221	Rom, Pio	1813	Ascanio
222	Romero Arnau, Felipe (Lic.)	1800	Aramburu
223	Romero Blanco, Maria Manuela	1785	Castrillo
224	Romero Fuentes, Matco	1814	Urbina
225	Rosa, Maria Magdalena	1810	Tirado
226a	Roth, Ana Maria	1793	Barcenas
b	Roth, Maria del Rosario	1793	Barcenas
227a	Salas, Josefa	1785	Aramburu
b	Salas, Maria Petronila	1785	Aramburu
228	Sanchez Arevalo, Juan (Lic.)	1820	Leon y Urbina
229a	Sanchez y Bolivar, Isabel	1784	Texera
b	Sanchez y Bolivar, Juana Ines	1803	Tirado
		1807	Texera
c	Sanchez y Bolivar, Rosa Maria	1786	Texera
230	Sanoja, Jose	1808	*Testas*, S
231	Sanoja Galeno, Margarita	1838	*Testas*, 1836–41
232	Santaellas Peraza, Margarita	1785	Aramburu
233	Santaellas Timudo, Juan Jose	1783	Rio
234	Santana, Jose Ventura	(?)	*Testas*, 1836–41, ff. 109–11
235	Sanz, Miguel Jose (Lic.)	1829	*Testas*, S.
236	Seixas y Romero, Vicente (Pro)	1794	Barcenas
237	Septien y Meñaca, Isabel	1818	Texera
238	Serrada, Clara	1806	Ascanio
239	Sierra, Juan Jose (Pro)	1800	Texera
240	Sistiaga, Juana	1814	Hernandez
241	Sosa, Josefa Lorenza	1811	Ascanio
242	Suarez Aguado, Jose Miguel	1790	Armas
243a	Suarez de Urbina, Manuel	1785	Rio
b	Suarez de Urbina, Juan Jose	1796	Armas
244	Sulstaiza, Juan Jose (Pro)	1786	Rio
245	Tadino, Sebastian (Pro)	1788	Texera

246a	Terrero, Jose Maria	1783	Terrero
b	Terrero, Ana Maria Cayetano and Ma. Anta.	1785	Castrillo
247a	Texera, Antonio Juan	1812	Leon y Urbina
b	Texera, Francisco Remigio	1805	Ascanio
c	Texera, Francisco Vicente	1805	Ascanio
248	Tirado, Geronimo	1805	Tirado
249	Toledo, Maria Marcelina	1805	Ascanio
250a	Toro, Sebastian (3rd Marques)	1827	*Testas*, P, T
b	Toro, Francisco (4th Marques)	1831	Zumeta
251	Torres, Margarita	1814	Tirado
252a	Tovar y Bañes, Martin	1783	Texera
b	Tovar y Blanco, Diego	1843	*Protocs.*, 1841–3
c	Tovar y Blanco, Francisco	1813	Ximenes
d	Tovar y Blanco, Luisa	1786	Aramburu
e	Tovar y Blanco, Manuel Felipe	1795	Texera
f	Tovar y Blanco, Maria Guia	1789	Aramburu
g	Tovar y Blanco, Maria Isabel	1805/1818	Texera
h	Tovar y Blanco, Maria Manuela	1806, 1820	Texera
i	Tovar y Blanco, Martin (Conde)	1807	Cires
j	Tovar y Blanco, Miguel Ignacio	1829	Ochoa
k	Tovar y Ponte, Catalina	1843	*Protocs.*, 1841–3
l	Tovar y Ponte, Domingo	1808	Ascanio
m	Tovar y Ponte, Maria Altagracia	1810	Tirado
n	Tovar y Ponte, Maria de Jesus	1796	Mota
o	Tovar y Ponte, Martin Antonio	1843	*Protocs.*, 1841–3
p	Tovar y Prado, Francisco (Pro)	1794	Texera
q	Tovar Ramires, Andres (Pro)	1810	Ravelo
r	Tovar Ramires, Ines	1809	Texera
s	Tovar Ramires, Isabel	1808	Aramburu
t	Tovar Ramires, Josefa	1849	*Protocs.*
u	Tovar Ramires, Martin	1810	Ascanio
v	Tovar y Tovar, Francisco	1813	Ximenes
253	Travieso Gonzalez, Tomasa	1809	Aramburu
254a	Urbina, Andres Manuel	1806	Ravelo
b	Urbina, Francisca	1816	Texera
c	Urbina, Josefa Antonia	1809, 1811	Texera
255	Urra, Rosalia	1783	Fernandez
256	Valdes, Francisco	1806	Ascanio
257	Vargas Arvel, Miguel	1820	Munoz
258	Vargas Machuca, Carlos	1792	Texera
259	Vegas de Vertodano, Juan	1797	*Testas*, V
260	Velasquez, Juana	1808	Castrillo
261	Velasquez y Rodriguez, Margarita	1784	Nebot
262	Verois Rengifo, Vicente	1798	*Testas*, V
263	Ximenes, Rosalia	1781	Fernandez
264	Zuloaga, Santiago (Dr)	1805	Hernandez

Peninsulares

Name	Year	Source
265	Aguado Castejon, Francisco (Pro)	1786	Rio
266	Aguerrevere, Pedro	1792	Texera
267	Alvarado, Alvaro	1789	Aramburu
268	Amenavar, Jose Antonio*	1784	Texera
269	Andueza, Juan	1806	Ravelo
270	Anza, Jose*	1806	Texera
271	Aragon, Manuel	1788	Amitesarove
272	Aramburu, Gabriel	1814	Urbina
273	Argain, Juan*	1788	Eleizalde
274	Arrieta, Francisco	1783	Aramburu
275	Arrieta, Joaquin	1806	Ascanio
276	Bengoechea, Jacobo*	1797	Armas
277	Berastegui, Juan	1800	Cobian, *Testas*, B, C ·
278	Burgillos, Juan*	1789	Texera
279	Butrageno, Bernardo	1794	Aramburu
280	Carbonell, Pedro (Captain-General)	1804	(?) Aramburu
281	Castilloveittia, Joaquin*	1799	Texera
282	Clemente Francia, Manuel*	1800	Aramburu
283	Cobian, Pedro	1806	Cobian
284	Cordova, Sebastian*	1814	Ximenes
285	Diaz Saraiva, Julian (Lic.)	1797	Texera
286	Echenique, Juan*	1811	Tirado
287a	Echezuria, Juan Bautista*	1802	Aramburu
		1816	*Testas*, E
b	Echezuria, Juan Miguel*	1816	*Testas*, E
c	Echezuria, Pedro	1813	Correa-Cires
288	Egaña, Antonio*	1793	Armas
289	Eguino, Juan	1784	Eleizalde
290	Fernandez de Leon, Lorenzo (Pro)	1788	Eleizalde
291	Francia, Felipe*	1785	Texera-Nebot
292	Franco, Jesus	1820	Leon y Urbina
293	Franco, Manuel*	1806	Ascanio
294	Galguera, Jose Vicente*	1823	*Testas*, G, L
295	Gamo, Pedro	1784	Rio
296	Garate, Domingo*	1788, 1820	Texera
297	Garcia, Francisco*	1798	Barcenas
298	Garcia Roa, Francisco*	1805	Aramburu
299	Garcia, Manuel	1783	Nebot
300	Garcia, Pablo (Pro)	1790	Ponce
301	Gayoso Aldao, Benito*	1788	Rio
302	Gonzalez, Jose de Elias*	1808	Aramburu
303	Goycoechea, Juan*	1800	Barcenas
304	Goyeneche, Juan Pedro	1798	Aramburu
305	Heredia, Felix	1800	Aramburu

306	Iriarte, Juan*	1804	Texera
307	Irrivaren, Diego	1806	Aramburu
308	Iturbe, Manuel	1809	Viana
309	Iturriza, Juan Bautista	1806	Texera
310a	Lander Achotte, Pedro*	1800	Tirado
b	(?) Lander Agueda, Juan Jose*	1817	Texera
311	Lecumberri, Juan Ignacio*	1786	Eleizalde
312	Linares, Vicente	1808	Castrillo
313	Lizarraga, Jose Manuel	1849	*Protocs.*, 1847–52
314	Lopez Loaysa, Joaquin	1786	Rio
315	Lopez Quintana, Antonio (Regente)	1809	Viana
316	Llaguno, Felipe*	1789	Aramburu
317	Llamosas, Jose*	1816	Castrillo
318	Llobet, Ramon*	1789	Cobian
319	Marti, Mariano (Obispo)	1792	Aramburu
320	Martinez Abia, Felix	1813	Ascanio
321	Mayora, Simon	1794	Texera
322	Mayz, Felipe	1807	Ravelo
323	Mendiburu, Jose Joaquin*	1788	Texera
324	Michelena, Jose Ignacio*	1794	Texera
325	Michelena, Jose Xavier	1808	Ravelo
326	Mier y Teran, Sebastian	1782	Fernandez
327	Mintegui, Juan Jose	1802	*Testas*, M.
328	Monzon, Ramon	1800	Barcenas
329	Mota y March, Antonio*	1801	Tirado
330	Muñoz, Antonio*	1809	Texera
331	Navas, Gervasio*	1798	*Testas*, N
332	Navas, Pedro	1817	Garcia y Saume
333	Nuñes Villavicencio, Jacinto	1793	Mota
334	Palomo Burgillos, Sebastian (Pro)	1805	Hernandez
335	Pedrosa, Juan Nepomuceno	1798	Aramburu
336	Perez de la Hoz, Manuel*	1808	Aramburu
337	Pinero, Juan	1806	Ravelo
338	Olayola, Miguel	1803	Aramburu
339	Oruesagasti, Juan Bautista	1799	Texera
340	Recalde, Francisco	1794	Aramburu
341	Sabas Berdu, Jose Ramon*	1800	Tirado
342	Sagarsasu, Pedro*	1804	Aramburu
343	Saldarriaga, Juan Tomas*	1840	*Testas*, 1836–41
344	Sanza, Antonio*	1801	Texera
345	Septien Meñaca, Juan Alonso*	1818	Texera
346	Soria Retortillo, Manuel	1803	Hernandez
347	Ugarte, Gregorio	1794	Aramburu
348	Vaamonde, Pedro*	1792	Texera
349	Zarandia, Juan Bautista	1782	Armas
350	Zulueta, Juan Antonio	1817	Texera
351	Zulueta, Domingo*	1831	*Testas*, Z

	Name	Year	Source
352	Alfonso, Antonio	1806	Aramburu
353	Alman, Vicente	1805	Ascanio
354	Almeyda, Antonio	1786	Aramburu
355	Amaral, Francisco*	1807	Ravelo
356	Asensio, Jose*	1785	Aramburu
357	Baez de Orta, Francisco*	1812	Cires
358	Bello, Angela	1785	Castrillo
359	Bello, Juan Jorge*	1818	Tirado
		1813–14	Tirado
360	Bello, Juan Pedro*	1805–7	Texera
361	Betancour, Domingo	1781	Texera
362	Borges, Manuel	1786	Texera
363	Bueno, Juan*	1807	Peoli
364	Cabrera, Juan	1806	Ravelo
365	Cano, Juan	1809	Ascanio
366	Carballo, Antonio	1817	Texera
367	Carballo, Marcos Melchor*	1808	Castrillo
368	Cartaya, Juan*	1791	Aramburu
369	Casas, Francisco*	1790	Barcenas
370	Castro Quintero, Francisco*	1812, 1814	Ximenes
371	Cevallos, Juan	1784	Nebot
372	Cocho de Iriarte, Jose*	1795	Texera
373	Correa, Pedro	1807	Aramburu
374	Crespo, Antonio*	1806	Texera
375	Delgado, Andres	1789	Eizaguirre
376	Delgado, Antonio Felipe	1789	Eizaguirre
377	Delgado, Francisco*	1793	Mota
378	Delgado, Juan*	1807	Ascanio
379	Delgado Correa, Francisca	1805	Aramburu
380a	Delgado Marrero, Francisco	1805	Ascanio
b	Delgado Marrero, Juan*	1818	Munoz
381	Diaz, Juan*	1781	Castrillo
382	Diaz de Avila, Juan*	1803	Aramburu
383	Diaz Navarro, Antonio*	1818	Urbina
		1834	*Testas*, D
384	Dominguez Roxas, Fernando*	1789	Amitesarove
385	Espindola, Juan Jose*	1809	Ascanio
386	Faxardo, Juan Martin	1784	Nebot
387	Febres Espinosa, Nicolas	1785	Aramburu
388	Fee, Antonio Tadeo	1793	Rio
389	Fernandez Truxillo, Juan*	1789	Amitesarove
390	Fierro Santa Cruz, Jose*	1789–90	Texera
391	Galvan, Juan Nepomuceno	1806	Ravelo
392	Garcia, Antonio	1820	Hernandez

393	Garcia, Sebastian*	1786	Texera
394	Gomes, Marcos*	1813	Leon y Urbina
395	Gonzalez, Bartolome*	1781	Rio
396	Gonzalez, Juan*	1807	Ravelo
397	Gonzalez, Juan*	1807	Ravelo
398	Gonzalez, Manuel*	1809	Ravelo
399	Gonzalez, Simon	1809	Aramburu
400a	Gonzalez Casares, Rita	1813	Ascanio
b	(?) Gonzalez Clavo, Matias*	1785	Texera
		1792	Texera
c	(?) Gonzalez Clavo, Melchor	1784	Rio
401	Gonzalez Grillo, Antonio	1786	Nebot
402	Gonzalez Regalado, Jose	1804	Aramburu
403	Gonzalez Truxillo, Juan*	1814	Castrillo
404	Guardia, Jose (Lic.)*	1786	Texera
405	Hernandez, Maria Soledad*	1801	Tirado
406	Hernandez Orta, Francisco	1806–7	Texera
407	Hernandez Orta, Antonio*	1792	Mota
408	Hernandez Quintero, Juan*	1805	Ascanio
409	Hernandez Sanabia, Jose*	1780	*Testas*, H
410	Hernandez Valentin, Tomas	1784	Aramburu
411	Leon, Francisco	1784	Aramburu
		1807	Texera
412	Lopes, Bernadino*	1785	Aramburu
413	Lopez, Pragedes*	1849	*Protocs.*, 1847–52
414	Macias, Domingo*	1813	Ximenes
415	Martel, Agustin	1783	Aramburu
416	Martinez, Mateo*	1806	Aramburu
417	Martinez Dramas, Jose Antonio*	1819	Munoz
418	Martinez Orihuela, Antonio	1794	Texera
419	Medina, Domingo*	1785	Aramburu
420a	Melo Navarrete, Miguel	1786	Nebot
b	Melo Navarrete, Margarita	1801	Castrillo
421	Mena, Jose Alonso*	1805	Aramburu
422	Mendez, Jose Sebastian*	1783	Fernandez
423	Monteverde Molina, Fernando*	1837	*Testas*, 1836–41
424	Morales, Sebastiana	1789	Ponce
425	Orta, Antonio*	1784	Rio
426	Padron, Marcos	1806	Santana
427	Padron, Sebastian*	1799	Texera
428	Paz del Castillo, Tomas*	1809	Texera
429	Perera, Andres	1800	Aramburu
430	Peres, Domingo Alejandro	1819	Garcia Saume
431	Peres, Jose*	1809	Texera
432	Peres, Salvador*	1812	Ascanio
433	Peres, Vicente*	1807	Peoli
434a	Peres Velasquez, Bartolome	1788, 1793	Texera
b	Peres Velasquez, Domingo	1806	Texera
c	Peres Velasquez, Pedro*	1794	Castrillo

435	Reyes Castaneda, Jose*	1806	Santana
436	Ribas, Marcos*	1793	Aramburu
437	Rodriguez, Francisco	1783	Aramburu
438	Rodriguez, Jose	1794	Aramburu
439	Rodriguez, Jose Sebastian*	1805	Cobian
440	Rodriguez, Jose Vicente	1805	Ascanio
441	Rodriguez, Juan Antonio*	1786	Texera
442	Rodriguez, Lazaro*	1800	Cobian
443	Rodriguez Garcia, Bartolome*	1805	Aramburu
444	Rodriguez Grillo, Juan*	1785	Armas
445	Rodriguez Izquierdo, Salvador	1815	Castrillo
446	Rodriguez Lopes, Jose	1785	Aramburu
447	Rodriguez Mireles, Francisco	1791	Ponce
448	Rodriguez Toledo, Antonio	1786	Santana
449	Rodriguez Vera, Antonio*	1808	*Testas*, R
450	Rosa, Francisco	1809	Ascanio
451	Ruis, Josefa Maria	1787	Castrillo
452	Santana, Jose Gabriel*	1805	Tirado
453	Santana, Marcos*	1792	Aramburu
454	Seijas, Lucas Francisco*	1781	Aramburu
		1798	*Testas*, S
455	Sierra, Juan Jose*	1786	Castrillo
456	Sosa, Salvador	1805	Ascanio
457	Sotomayor, Bartolome*	1815	Castrillo
458	Suarez Alvarado, Juan*	1785	Aramburu
459	Timudo, Francisco	1799	Aramburu
460	Yllaga, Antonio	1786	Nebot
461a	Key Muñoz, Fernando*	1844	*Protocs.*, 1844–6
b	Muñoz, Tomas*	1796	Texera
462	Medina, Geronimo*	1788	Texera
463	Orea, Gonzalo Maria	1817	Texera

Other White

	Name	Origin	Year	Source
464	Antunes, Nicolas	Maracaibo	1819	*Testas*, A
465	Barbara, Manuel	Portugal	1783	Rio
466	Barry, Eduardo	Ireland	1793	Aramburu
467	Briceno, Domingo (Pro)	Truxillo	1801	Armas
468	Doarzan, Carlos	France	1789	Aramburu
469	Duran, Francisco	Ceuta	1809	Aramburu
470	Fransini, Santiago	France	1789	Amitesarove
471	Gascue, Pablo	Santo Domingo	1847	*Protocs.*, 1847–52
472	Lamb, Jaime	U.K.	1818	Hernandez

473	Mancebo, Juan Jose	Cuba	1809	Texera
474	Mendez, Rafael	Barinas	1803	Barcenas
475	Montilla, Jose Santos	Barinas	1803	Barcenas
476	Montilla Briceno, Juan	Truxillo	1803	Tirado
477	Palacios, Ramon	Barinas	1849	*Protocs.*, 1847–52
478	Romero, Jose Gaspar	Maracaibo	1815	Urbina
479	Sanchez, Teresa	Santo Domingo	1806	Cobian
480	Socarras, Francisco (Lic.)	Cuba	1804	Texera
481	Villalonga, Antonio	Mallorca	1789	Texera

Free-Coloureds

	Name	Origin	Year	Source
482	Alvarez, Juan	*moreno*	1781	Aramburu
483	Arias, Petronila	*hijo natural*	1789	Ponce
484	Aristiguieta, Asuncion	*hijo natural*	1818	Texera
485a	Bejarano, Jose Gabriel	*hijo natural*	1802	Cobian
b	Bejarano, Maria Gracia		1797	Texera
486	Blanco, Maria Petronila	*hijo natural*	1806	Ravelo
487	Bolivar, Maria Apolonia	*parda*	1806	Texera
488a	Castro, Juan Jose	*hijo natural*	1812	Texera
b	Castro, Jose Manuel	*hijo natural*	1790	Aramburu
489	Churrion, Baltasar	*pardo*	1786	Nebot
490	Esteves, Juan Tomas	*moreno*	1806	Ascanio
491	Gedler, Rosalia Antonia	*hijo natural*	1811	Ascanio
492	Gedler, Bartola	*hijo natural*	1811	Ascanio
493	Gonzalez, Juana Estefania	*hijo natural*	1784	Nebot
494	Gonzalez, Juana Maria	*hijo natural*	1785	Castrillo
495	Gutierrez, Juana Rosa	*morena*	1788	Texera
496	Herrera y Blanco, Eugenio	*pardo*	1784	Texera
497	Ibarra, Cipriano	*pardo*	1788	Texera
498	Landaeta, Diego Martin	*hijo natural*	1791	Mota
499	Landaeta, Luisa	*morena*	1781	Terrero
500	Landaeta, Manuel	*hijo natural*	1785	Fernandez
501	Landaeta, Maria Candelaria		1794	Texera
502	Landaeta, Maria Matias	*hijo natural*	1784	Nebot
503	Madera, Jose Manuel	son of slave	1809	Tirado
504	Madrid, Petronila	*morena*	1783	Texera
505	Madriz, Maria Antonio	*hijo natural*	1788	Aramburu
506	Mexias, Juan Jose	*pardo*	1789	Amitesarove
507	Mexias Landaeta, Diego	*pardo*	1807	(?) Ascanio
508	Mexias Landaeta, Jose Domingo	*hijo natural*	1791	Mota
509	Mijares Solorzano, Hilaria	*hijo natural*	1789	Amitesarove
510	Motta, Maria Rosaria	*morena*	1786	Castrillo

511	Muñoz, Laureano	*moreno*	1789	Aramburu
512	Palacios y Vera, Francisco	*moreno*	1789	Eizaguirre
513	Piñango, Catalina	*parda*	1785	Aramburu
514	Piñango, Jose Ramon	*hijo natural*	1785	Nebot
515	Ponce, Barbara	*morena*	1789	Aramburu
516	Ponte, Gervasio		1798	Tirado
517	Ponte, Leocadia	*morena*	1784	Castrillo
518	Robles, Gregoria	daughter of slave	1784	Castrillo
519	Sanches, Simon	*hijo natural*	1783	Fernandez
520	Sojo, Maria Rafael	*parda*	1785	Fernandez
521	Solorzano, Maximiano		1807	Aramburu
522	Tablantes, Juana Josefa	*parda*	1789	Texera
523	Toro, Juan Agustin	*moreno*	1791	Castrillo
524	Valle, Juan Tomas del		1805	Hernandez

Caste Unknown

	Name	Origin	Year	Source
525	Aponte, Ines Maria		1806	Tirado
526	Arias, Domingo Antonio		1806	Ascanio
527	Blanco, Jose Marcelino	*hijo natural*	1781	Armas
528	Bolivar, Maria de Nieves	*hijo natural*	1781	Aramburu
529	Calanches, Jacinto		1794	Texera
530	Cienfuegos, Maria Micaela		1808	Ravelo
531	Gallegos, Blas		1806	Ascanio
532a	Gil, Pablo Jose		1801	Aramburu
b	Gil, Pedro Jose		1801	Aramburu
533	Herrera, Angela Maria		1786	Nebot
534	Ledesma, Raimundo		1791	Mota
535	Leon, Pedro Jose		1791	Castrillo
536	Lozano, Domingo		1806	Tirado
537	Machado, Jose Victorio	*hijo natural*	1809	Ravelo
538	Madriz, Josefa		1788	Izaguirre
539	Maria Vicenta	*espósita*	1785	Castrillo
540	Marinas, Juana Petronila	*hijo natural*	1784	Castrillo
541	Monasterios, Pedro		1813	Aramburu
542	Monasterios, Vicente		1806	Santana
543	Morales, Josefa	*hijo natural*	1784	Nebot
555	Olivares, Margarita	*hijo natural*	1789	Eizaguirre
545	Peña, Juan Jacinto		1785	Aramburu
546	Piñango, Francisco Jose		1782	Armas
547	Pino, Ana Antonia	*hijo natural*	1784	Castrillo
548	Ramos, Pedro Ignacio		1781	Texera
549	Renxifo, Mariana	*hijo natural*	1787	Eleizalde

550	Santa, Maria Luisa	1786	Nebot
551	Solorzano, Vicente	1789	Amitesarove
552	Tovar, Maria Petronila	1811	Texera
553	Vera, Jose Tomas	1783	Rio

Index

For further references to people mentioned in this index see pp. 219–37. Spanish terms are explained in the glossary, pp. xi–xiii.

Abalos, J. de (Intendant) 97, 99–107, 139
administration and politics
  (1783–1796) 125–8
agriculture 10–11, 46–62; caste society
  and 19, 22; elites in *see hacendados*;
  equipment 50–1, 53, 55; investment
  in 50, 53, 55, 111; merchants in 88;
  natural disasters 139; size of agricultural
  holdings 46–7, 49, 54, 59, 60–1; *see
  also* cacao; coffee; indigo; livestock;
  profits; sugar; tenants; tobacco
Alamo (in Congress) 166
Alcalde, R. (Intendant) 110
Alzuru, G. 54
America *see* United States
Antilles, trade with 40, 42, 43–4, 100,
  104, 134; *see also* Curaçao
Anza, J. J. de 90, 133, 176, 177
Anza family 80
Aragua valleys: agriculture in 10, 47, 49,
  52, 55, 58; conflict in 126; elites in 87,
  92; exports from 66; slaves in 123
Aramburu, F. 160
Araure (town) 29, 175
Arce (Intendant) 139, 140, 142–4, 154–5
Argentina 147
Argos, J. J. 92, 152
Aristiguieta, M. J. de 79, 82, 132, 176
Aristiguieta family 84, 89
Arteaga, J. M. 71
Ascanio, J. 81, 176
Ascanio family 69, 79, 84, 86, 159
Ascanio y Monasterios, F. (first Conde de la
  Granja) 81, 176
assimilation *see* intermarriage
Audiencia 29, 126–7; abolished 159;
  re-established 174
Aurioles, J. de 86

authority, collapse of 147–56
Ayuntamiento 126, 151; and
  hacendados 85; and trade 92, 130

Baraciarte, M. 131
Barandia, J. J. 86
Barinas (province) 60
Barquisimeto (town) 12, 175; commerce
  in 21, 71, 72
Barreto family 84
Basadre, V. 154
Basque immigrants 17, 80, 89
Bejarano, D. M. 118
Bejarano family 118–19, 219
Bello, A. 161
Berdú family 80
Berrio, E. 159–60
Berrotarán family 79, 84, 177
black people *see* caste society; Indians; *pardos*;
  race question; slaves
Blanco family 53, 69, 79, 84, 86, 176; *see
  also* Tovar y Blanco
Blanco y Blanco family 176, 177
Blanco y Mixares, F. 81, 176; *see also*
  Mixares family
Blanco y Plaza, G. 82, 176
Blanco y Ponte, P. 82, 83, 176; *see also*
  Ponte family
Blandaín family 69, 80, 176
Boconó, Marqués del 84
Bolívar, B. and R. 161
Bolívar, J. V. 81, 86
Bolívar, J. V., Jr 82, 177
Bolívar, M. A. 20
Bolívar, S.: as member of elite 57, 81, 154;
  as radical 160, 161, 164, 165, 169–72,
  174
Bolívar family 52, 69, 79, 152

Boves, J. T.   169, 170–2, 173, 174
Branciforte, Marqués de   141, 143
Briceño, A. H.   160, 170
Brinton, C.   77
Britain: American War of Independence
    and   106; Caracas invasion   144–5;
    Caribbean colonies   40, 130, 135, 143;
    Curaçao conquered   135, 143; Haiti
    attacked   129; slave trade   24; Trinidad
    conquered   130; wars with
    Holland   104, *see also* Spain, wars with
    Britain
Buroz, E.   177
Butrageño family   68, 80, 176

Cabildo, Caracas: and agriculture   128–9;
    and *hacendados*   85–6; *junta*
    suggested   150–1; on *pardos*   19, 117; on
    tax   114; on trade   105, 130
cacao   10, 12, 46, 49–51; exports   36–9,
    42–5, 99, 100, 103, 114
Cagigal, J.   173
Calabozo (town)   72, 175
Camacho family   67, 71
canarios   see Canary Islands, immigrants from
Canary Islands: immigrants from   13–15,
    16, 18, 79, 80, 89, 232–4; trade
    with   39, 41–2
Captaincy-General   93, 96–7, 126; *see also*
    Carbonell; Casas; Emparán; González;
    Guillelmi; Miyares; Unzaga y Amezaga;
    Vasconceles
Caracas (city): agriculture   175; Church
    in   29; commerce in   16, 21, 66, 71–2,
    88–9, 91; elites in   86, 92; elites
    outside   163; massacres in   171;
    population   15–17, 22, 23; Town Council
    see Cabildo
Caracas Company (1728–84)   4–5, 35;
    decline and abolition   63, 65, 99, 107–8;
    and free trade   103–5, 133
Carballo, A.   90, 177
Carbonell, P. (Captain-General)   97, 126,
    128, 131, 137
Caribbean, foreign, trade with   39–45,
    67
Carora (town)   12, 175
Casa León *see* Fernández de León, A.
Casas, J. de (Captain-General)   97, 150–5,
    172
Casas family   84
cash crops *see* agriculture
castas see *pardos*
caste society   9–31; demographics   9–13;
    social characteristics, general   25–8; social

    institutions, role of   28–31; *see also*
    Indians; *pardos*; race question; slaves; whites
Castilloveittia, J.   92, 177
Castro y Aráoz, J. de   9
Cevallos, J.   173
Charles III of Spain   148
Charles IV of Spain   148, 150
Chile   115
Chirinos, J. L.   125
Church   29–31; loans from   83, 141, 144;
    officials   93, 95
class divisions   26–7; *see also* caste society;
    elites
Clemente y Francia, M. de   67, 68, 82, 91,
    92, 177
Clemente y Francia family   80, 84, 159, 177
clerics *see* Church
Coast area: agriculture   49, 175; population
    10–11, 22
Coastal Range area: agriculture   49, 55,
    175; population   11, 12, 13, 22–3, 95,
    119, 122
Cocho e Iriarte *see* Iriarte
Codazzi, A.   50
Código Negro   122, 125
coffee   10, 53–5; exports   36–7, 42, 43,
    45
Coll y Prat, Archbishop   17, 173
Colombia   4
comerciante   see merchants
commerce   63–73; export merchants
    63–70; internal market   70–3; size of
    commercial establishments   72–3; *see also*
    merchants; trade
Congress elected   159, 166
Consulado   29, 126, 174; created   94; flour
    monopoly and   143; free trade and   130,
    155; membership   78, 176–7; *see also*
    merchants, and nacendados
contraband   99, 140; low level of   43–4
copper exports   36
Coro: agriculture   175; attacked   163–4;
    invasions from   169; lack of support for
    coup   157, 162, 164; slave revolt
    in   124–5, 136, 145, 172
Cortabarria, A.   162, 163
Cortés, S. R.   219
cotton exports   36, 37, 42, 43
coup (1810)   156, 158
court *see* Audiencia; Justices of Peace;
    lawyers
credit: loans   83, 141, 144; *see also*
    promissory notes
creoles *see* whites
Cristóbal de León, N.   47

Cumaná 4, 87; agriculture in 61; Church in 29; class in 26–8
Curaçao: British take over 135, 143; trade with 68, 100, 103, 104, 109, 134
Curiepe valley 21
Curimagua region 125
currency: shortage 68, 110; trade 36, 37, 39–40, 45, 69, 108, 110–11

debt *see* credit
demographics 9–13
Denmark 131
Depons, F. 14, 29, 47
Domínguez family 80, 177

Echenique, F. 21
Echenique, J. J. 133, 134, 177
Echezuría, J. B. de 90, 92, 110, 130–1
Echezuría, J. E. 64, 110, 131, 177
Echezuría, J. M. de 82, 90, 176, 177
Echuzuría family 80, 177
Eckard and Company 131–3
economy: and politics (1783–96) 108–15; *see also* agriculture; commerce; export economy
Ecuador 100
Egaña, A. 92, 177
elites 77–97; *junta* and 151–3, 158–60; and politics 87, 91, 95; see also *hacendados*; merchants; professional class
Emasabel, J. de 92
Emparán (Governor, later Captain-General) 87, 97, 154, 155, 156
entail to prevent land fragmentation 82–3
Escalona, L. 176
Escorihuela, J. V. 64, 67, 81, 82, 90, 92, 110, 176; and *junta* 152
Escoriheula family 80
España, J. M. *see* Gual
Espejo, Dr F. 128, 166
Espinosa, J. T. 176
export economy (1777–1810) 35–45; changing markets, role of 39–45; diversification of production 35–9
export merchants 63–70

Ferdinand VII of Spain 2, 145, 147, 148, 150, 156, 158–9
Fernández de León, A. (Marqués de Casa León): in *junta* 151; and Ruy Blas conspiracy 137; as wealthy merchant 26, 68, 69, 81, 127–8, 154
Fernández de León, E. (Intendant) 16, 87, 97, 138; and currency drain 110; and

French prisoners 137; and *junta* 152; and trade 109, 127, 128, 130–4
Fernández de Léon, L. 97
Fernández de Léon family 84, 166
fianzas system and power 86, 92
Figueroa, F. B. 176
Filipinas Company 63–4, 65, 114–15, 133
flour monopoly 141, 143
France: Caribbean possessions 39; prisoners from 129–30, 136–7; revolution 125, 128, 137; war *see* Spain, wars with France
Francia *see* Clemente y Francia
Francia, F. de 52
Franco, D. 16
Franco, J. M. 92
Franco, M. 72
free trade 103, 130–5, 141, 174
free-coloured population *see pardos*
freed slaves 23–4
Fuentes, A. 71

Galguera, J. V. 91, 152, 177
Garate, D. de 16
Garay family 89
Gédler family 86, 177
Godoy, M. 148, 150
Gonzales, J. de E. 90, 176
González, J. C. 125
González (Captain-General) 97
Granja *see* La Granja
Gual, M. and Gual-España conspiracy (1797) 128, 130, 135–8, 145
Guanare (town) 12, 175
Guapo valley 47
Guarenas district 49, 175
Guaruto area 58, 59
Guatemala 39
Guayana 4, 29, 106
Guayaquil 109–10
Guillelmi (Captain-General) 97, 109, 127, 139
Guipuzcoana *see* Caracas Company

hacendados 17, 20, 28, 78–88; and merchants, disagreements between 111–13, 132–4; merchants classed as 90, 91; as traders 67–8, 69; *see also* elites
haciendas: geographical distribution 175; *see also* agriculture; *hacendados*
Haiti: agriculture 38, 43, 55; attacked by Spain and Britain 129; refugees from 14, 24, 135; slave revolt 124, 125

hatos 47; geographical distribution 175; *see also* livestock
Havana 4, 22, 24, 55
Heredia, J. F. 172, 173
Hernández Quintero, J. 54
Hernández Sanabria, Dr J. 51, 53, 176
Hernández Sanabria family 80, 82
Herrera family 79, 84, 86
Herrera y Rada, M. E. 81
hides, exports of 36, 108
Hispaniola 14; *see also* Haiti
Holland, Caribbean possessions *see* Curaçao
Humboldt, A. von 13, 47, 48, 81

Ibarra, A. 152
Ibarra, F. 17
Ibarra, J. de 68
Ibarra, V. 82, 176
Ibarra family 69, 79, 84, 177
immigrants: as *hacendados* 17–18, 80; as merchants 88–9; *see also under* Canary Islands; Spain
Imperial Appellate Court *see* Audiencia
imports 70, 71–2, 109; decline 130, 143; *see also* contraband; trade
independence: declared (1811) 167; wars of 170–3, *see also* massacres
Indians 9–10, 25
indigo 10, 46–8, 51–3; crisis 111, 113–14, 139–40; exports 36–7, 39, 42, 43, 45, 108
Intendancy 93, 96–7, 126, 174; *see also* Abalos; Alcalde; Arce; Fernández de León, E.; Saavedra
intermarriage 15, 89
internal market 70–3
investment: agricultural 50, 53, 55, 111; merchants' 89; retail trade 72–3
Iriarte, J. C. de 106, 177
Iriarte, P. M. de 92
Iriarte family 64, 67, 80, 107, 133, 176
isleños see Canary Islands, immigrants from
Isnardi F. 161, 167

Jamaica 55
jornaleros 19, 47–8; see also *pardos*
Joseph I, King of Spain 150
junta, emergence of 151–8, 162–4, 166
Justices of Peace 86, 126–7; *see also* lawyers

Key Munôz, F. 92, 133, 152, 159, 166

La Granja, Condes de 53, 54, 81, 84, 152, 176
La Guaira (port) 10, 11; agriculture

and 49, 175; commerce in 72, 89; politics in 135–6; population in 12; prisoners in 136–7; trade, foreign 4, 14, 36–7, 44, 64–7, 70, 130, 142
La Victoria (town) 12, 171; agriculture 51–2, 175; commerce 71–2; population 21
land: fragmentation prevented 82–3; ownership 17, 20, 46–7, see also *hacendados*; rented 46–8, 52, 57; sale policy 101–2; *see also* agriculture; haciendas
Lander, J. T. 90, 177
Larrain, B. 131, 134
latifundia 47; *see also* livestock
lawyers 93–5; *see also* Audiencia; Justices of Peace
Leal, I. 176
Lecuña, V. 219
legal system *see* lawyers
León *see* Fernández de León
León, N. C. de 47
Limonta, G. de 16
Linares, V. 44, 177
livestock 11, 12, 47, 48, 59–61; internal market 71; *see also* hides; meat
Llamosas, J. de las 131, 134, 159
Llanos (interior plains): agriculture 48, 60, 175; invasions from 169, 171–2; population 11–12, 20, 29, 101–2, 119–22
local politics (1783–96) 125–8
Lombardi, J. 9, 10, 12
Longa, F. X. de 90
López Méndez, I. 53–5, 110, 160, 166, 177
López Méndez, L. A. 82, 90, 91, 131, 176, 177
López Méndez family 70, 71, 80, 91, 152, 159
López Quintana, A. 127–8, 135–9, 152
L'Ouverture, Toussaint 14, 135

Machado family 80, 82, 177
Machillanda family 53, 82, 176
Madariaga, J. C. 161
Madrid, P. de la 20
Madriz (de la) family 69, 79
Malpica family 86
manumission 23–4
Maracaibo 4; rebels in 105, 106; Regency and 162
Maracay (town) 12, 171; agriculture 48, 52; commerce 72; politics 126; population 17

Margarita 4, 86, 106
markets *see* trade
Marti, Bishop M. 17
Martínez de Porras family 79, 177
Martinique 14
massacres (in independence wars) 170–3
Mayora, S. 133, 177
meat 60, 71; *see also* livestock
Méndez *see* López Méndez
Mendoza, C. 160, 170
Merchant and Planter Guild *see* Consulado
merchants 16–17, 21, 88–93;
    export 63–70; and *hacendados*,
    disagreements between 111–13, 132–4;
    see also commerce; trade
Merida, R. D. 161
Mexías, J. J. 21
Mier y Teran, S. V. 81, 176
Mijares (de Solórzano) family 79, 82, 84,
    176; Marqueses de 67, 84, 152
militias: *hacendados* in 84–5, 86; merchants
    in 92; *pardos* in 116–17
Mintegui, J. J. 110, 132, 133, 134
Miranda, F. de 138, 144, 145, 161,
    164–6
Mixares family 69; *see also* Blanco y Mixares
Miyares, F. (Captain-General) 163
Monasterios, M. 176
monoculture 35
monopoly: flour 141, 143; *see also* Caracas
    Company *and under* tobacco
Monteverde, D. 169, 170, 171
Mora, J. J. 94–5, 176
Mora family 80
Moreno, A. 54
Moreno, D. 67, 82, 109, 176
Moreno, Dr J. I. 81, 83, 128, 176
Moreno family 53, 80, 84
Morillo, P. 169, 173, 174
Mosquera, J. de 152–3, 155, 172
Munõz *see* Key Munõz
Munõz Tebar, A. 164
Muro, J. M. 176
Muro family 80

Napoleon: invasion of Spain (1808) 2, 77,
    139, 147–50, 153, 154, 157
New Granada 4, 101; Communero
    revolt 105, 106, 115;
    independence 165; invasion from 169,
    171
New Spain: Church in 30; famine 60;
    militias in 85; population 26, 28; riots
    in 115; trade with 38–9, 41–2, 45, 63,
    66–9, 99–100, 109–10

newspapers 164–5
Nueva Barcelona 87
Nuñez, D. R. 91

Obelmexías family 79, 86
occupations and caste society 15–17, 19, 26
Ocumare del Tuy (town) 72, 175
Olavarriaga, population estimated by 124
old families *see* whites
Orituco area 58
Oruesagasti, J. B. 64
Otamendi, E. 92
Ovalle, M. 52

Pacheco family 79, 176
Pacheco y Toro, J. A. (third Conde de San
    Xavier) 81
Paine, T. 137
Palacios family 53, 69, 86, 89, 91, 159,
    176, 177
Palacios y Sojo family 79, 81, 176
pardos (free-coloured) 9, 10, 11, 18–22; in
    agriculture 19, 47–9, 52; intractable
    mass 119–21; and whites, relationship
    between 116–22, 125; wills of 235–6
Patrullo, G. 160
Paul, F. 164, 166
Paz del Castillo family 80, 82, 86, 177
Peña, M. 164
Peñalver, F. 161
peninsulares see Spain, immigrants from
peónes libres 19; see also *pardos*
Pérez, D. A. 90, 91
Peru, revolts in 105, 106, 115; at
    Quito 163
Philippines 114
Picornell, J. 136
Picton, T. 135, 136
Piñango, J. 20
plantations *see* agriculture
Plaza family 79; *see also* Blanco y Plaza
Plaza y Liendo, J. I. 176
Poder Ejecutivo 166
politics 98–168; *1777–83* 99–107;
    1783–96 107–28; *1797–1802* 128–38;
    1802–8 139–45; *1808–10* 146–68;
    1811–21 169–74; *see also* elites
Ponte, G. de 20, 61, 219
Ponte, P. D. de 61
Ponte family 79, 82, 84, 176, 177; *see also*
    Blanco y Ponte; Tovar y Ponte
population distribution and growth 9–13;
    see also caste society
poverty 17, 22, 26
Prat *see* Coll y Prat

professional class 87, 93–7; *see also*
 Captaincy-General; Church; Indendancy;
 lawyers
profits: agricultural 51, 52–3, 54–5, 56–7,
 58–9, 61, 62; overseas trading 69–70;
 retail trade 73; *see also* wealth
promissory notes 69, 110–11, 114; *see also*
 credit
Puerto Cabello (port) 10, 11;
 agriculture 175; Church in 30; elites
 in 92; fleet at 129; population 12;
 trade in 44, 67

Quintana *see* López Quintana
Quintero, J. Hernández 54

race question: and politics
 (1783–96) 115–25; *see also* caste
 society
Rada family 79, 81, 177
radicalization of conflict (1810–11) 156–68,
 169, 171, 173
religion *see* Church
Rengifo family 79
rented agricultural land 46–8, 52, 57
republicans *see* radicalization of conflict
retail trade 65–6, 71–3
Revenga, J. R. 161
Reverón family 80
Ribas, J. F. 160, 161, 165, 177
Ribas, M. 81, 82, 100, 176
Ribas family 53, 57, 68, 69, 80, 86, 152,
 159, 166, 176–7
Roscio, J. G. 161, 165, 166, 167
royal officials 15–16, 87, 93, 95–7; *see also*
 Captaincy-General; Intendancy
royalists and partial colonial restoration
 169–70, 172–4
Rueda, F. de 127
ruling class *see* elites
Ruy Blas complot 136–7

Saavedra, F. de (Intendant) 79, 97, 127,
 139, 176; on Abalos 104; on
 currency 68; on economy and
 trade 63–4, 107–9, 113; on wealth 26
Sabana de Ocumare district 49
Sabas Berdú, J. R. 177
St Thomas (island) 131
Salias, V. 152, 164
San Carlos (town) 11, 12, 13, 175
San Fernando de Apure (town) 13, 29
San Mateo (town) 87, 171
San Sebastián (town) 11, 175

San Xavier, Condes de 53–5, 81, 84, 86,
 132, 152, 176
Sanabria *see* Hernández Sanabria
Santander, F. 170
Santo Domingo 4; lost 147; military
 base 129; refugees from 14, 135; trade
 with 68
Sanz, M. J. 94–5, 152, 161, 166, 177
Sanz family 51, 80
Segovia Highlands: agriculture 55, 175;
 population 12–13, 23, 25
Segura y Grasi, J. 67
ships: ownership of 66; shortage of 108
Sierra, P. de 92
slaves 9–10, 11, 22–4; in agriculture 22,
 47–9, 51, 54, 56; fugitive 120–1,
 122–4; rebellions of 124–5, 136, 145,
 172; trade in 24, 36, 39–40, 45, 100,
 108, 123
social characteristics, general 25–8
social institutions, role of 28–31
Sociedad Patriotica de Agricultores y
 Economia 164
society *see* caste society
Spain: American War of Independence
 and 38; Haiti attacked by
 129; immigrants from 13–17, 80, 89,
 136, 230–1; Regency period and collapse
 of authority 146–68 *passim*; trade
 with 5, 36–45, 64–71, 109–11, 129,
 130, 139–40, 155, 165; wars with
 Britain 24, 37, 102, 107, 128, 130,
 135, 140–4, 147, 154; wars with
 France 2, 77, 128–9, 131, 139, 147–50,
 153–4, 157
status symbols, *hacendados'* obsession
 with 84–5
sugar 12, 46, 55–7; exports 36; internal
 market 71

tax 114, 125; abolished 159;
 crisis 129–32; right to collect 86, 92;
 on trade 105, 109; for war 139, 141–4
tenants, agricultural 46–8, 52, 57
'Tierra Firme' 4
titles, nobles, *hacendados'* obsession with 84
tobacco 10, 47, 48, 57–9; exports 36, 37,
 39, 108–9, 140, 143, 144; internal
 market 71; monopoly 57–8, 101, 110,
 113, 115; sales for munitions etc 131–3
Tocuyo (town) 12, 23, 175
Toro, F. (fourth Marqués) 110, 177; in
 junta 152, 164; in opposition to
 León 128; as radical 160, 166; as
 royalist 137

Toro, J. M. de 53, 67
Toro, S. (third Marqués) 176; as *hacendado* 57, 81–3, 87–8; as merchant 67–8, 105–6
Toro family 69, 79, 84, 86, 165
Torrecasa, Marqués de 84
Tovar family 61, 69, 79, 82, 84, 159
Tovar y Blanco, D. 177
Tovar Y Blanco, Manuel F. de 67, 68, 133, 176
Tovar y Blanco, Martín (first Conde de) 26, 81–3, 137, 152, 176; *see also* Blanco family
Tovar y Ponte, M. de 53, 67, 152, 159, 177; *see also* Ponte family
Tovar y Tovar, F. 177
Town Council *see* Cabildo
trade *see* commerce; export economy; merchants *and under individual countries*
Trinidad 4; British conquest of 130, 135, 147; rebels in 136
Tupac Amaru revolt in Peru 105, 106, 115
Tuy valleys 10; agriculture 49, 55; exports from 66; population in 120, 123, 173

Ucelay, J. 173
Ugarte, S. 160
United States: trade with 40, 44–5, 141–3, 147; War of Independence 38, 106, 137–8
Unzaga y Amezaga (Captain-General) 97, 104, 105, 107

urbanization 12, 20–2, 23
Urbina family 89, 177

Valencia (town) 12, 72, 171, 175
Valle, J. T. de 20
Valle, Marques del 84
Vargas Machuca family 86
Vasconceles, G. (Captain-General) 97, 134, 138–9, 142, 145
Vega family 80, 176, 177
Velez Mier y Teran family 80
Veriois, V. 176
Victoria (town) 87
Villalonga, S. 68

wars: economy and trade affected by 40, 43, 102–3, 129–31, 139–43; independence wars 170–3; *see also under individual countries*
wealth: of *hacendados* 80–3; of merchants 88, 90; *see also* profits
whites 9–10, 13–18, 89; and *pardos*, relationship between 116–22, 125; and slaves, relationship between 122; wills of 219–35
wholesalers 71–2; *see also* export merchants
wills 219–37

Zea, L. 170
Zulueta, D. F. 70, 90, 132, 177

CAMBRIDGE LATIN AMERICAN STUDIES

1 Simon Collier. *Ideas and Politics of Chilean Independence 1808–1833*

3 Peter Calvert. *The Mexican Revolution 1910–1914: The Diplomacy of Anglo-American Conflict*

7 David Barkin and Timothy King. *Regional Economic Development: The River Basin Approach in Mexico*

8 Celso Furtado. *Economic Development of Latin America: Historical Background and Contemporary Problems* (second edition)

10 D. A. Brading. *Miners and Merchants in Bourbon Mexico, 1763–1810*

15 P. J. Bakewell. *Silver Mining and Society in Colonial Mexico, Zacatecas 1564–1700*

16 Kenneth R. Maxwell. *Conflicts and Conspiracies: Brazil and Portugal, 1750–1808*

22 James Lockhart and Enrique Otte. *Letters and People of the Spanish Indies: The Sixteenth Century*

23 Leslie B. Rout, Jr. *The African Experience in Spanish America: 1502 to the Present Day*

24 Jean A. Meyer. *The Cristero Rebellion: The Mexican People between Church and State 1926–1929*

25 Stefan de Vylder. *Allende's Chile: The Political Economy of the Rise and Fall of the Unidad Popular*

29 Anthony Hall. *Drought and Irrigation in North-east Brazil*

30 S. M. Socolow. *The Merchants of Buenos Aires 1778–1810: Family and Commerce*

31 Charles F. Nunn. *Foreign Immigrants in Early Bourbon Mexico, 1700–1760*

32 D. A. Brading. *Haciendas and Ranchos in the Mexican Bajio*

33 Billie R. DeWalt. *Modernization in a Mexican Ejido: A Study in Economic Adaptation*

34 David Nicholls. *From Dessalines to Duvalier: Race, Colour and National Independence in Haiti*

35 Jonathan C. Brown. *A Socioeconomic History of Argentina, 1776–1860*

36 Marco Palacios. *Coffee in Colombia 1850–1970: An Economic, Social and Political History*

37 David Murray. *Odious Commerce: Britain, Spain and the Abolition of the Cuban Slave Trade*

38 D. A. Brading. *Caudillo and Peasant in the Mexican Revolution*

39 Joe Foweraker. *The Struggle for Land: A Political Economy of the Pioneer Frontier in Brazil from 1930 to the Present Day*

40 George Philip. *Oil and Politics in Latin America: Nationalist Movements and State Companies*

41 Noble David Cook. *Demographic Collapse: Indian Peru, 1520–1620*

42 Gilbert Joseph. *Revolution from Without: Yucatan, and the United States, 1880–1924*

43 B. S. McBeth. *Juan Vicente Gomez and the Oil Companies in Venezuela, 1908–1935*

44 J. A. Offner. *Law and Politics in Aztec Texoco*

45 Thomas J. Trebat. *Brazil's State-owned Enterprises: A Case Study of the State as Entrepreneur*

46 James Lockhart and Stuart B. Schwartz. *Early Latin America: A History of Colonial Spanish America and Brazil*

47 Adolfo Figueroa. *Capitalist Development and the Peasant Economy in Peru*

48 Norman Long and Bryan Roberts. *Miners, Peasants and Entrepreneurs: Regional Development in the Central Highlands of Peru*

49 Ian Roxborough. *Unions and Politics in Mexico: The Case of the Automobile Industry*

50 Alan Gilbert and Peter Ward. *Housing, the State and the Poor: Policy and Practice in Three Latin American Cities*

51 Jean Stubbs. *Tobacco on the Periphery: A Case Study in Cuban Labour History, 1860–1958*

52 Stuart B. Schwartz. *Sugar Plantations in the Formation of Brazilian Society: Bahia, 1550–1835*

53 Richard J. Walter. *The Province of Buenos Aires and Argentine Politics, 1912–1945*

54 Alan Knight. *The Mexican Revolution*, vol. 1: 'Porfirians, Liberals and Peasants'

55 Alan Knight. *The Mexican Revolution*, vol. 2: 'Counter-revolution and Reconstruction'